The Digital Revolution in Banking, Insurance and Capital Markets

The digital transformation of finance and banking enables traditional services to be delivered in a more effective and efficient way but, at the same time, presents crucial issues such as fast-growing new asset classes, new currencies, datafication and data privacy, algorithmization of law and regulation and, last but not least, new models of financial crime. This book approaches the evolution of digital finance from a business perspective and in a holistic way, providing cutting-edge knowledge of how the digital financial system works in its three main domains: banking, insurance and capital markets.

It offers a bird's-eye view of the major issues and developments in these individual sectors. The book begins by examining the wider framework of the subsequent analysis and over the next three parts, discusses the opportunities, risks and challenges facing the digitalization of these individual financial subsectors, highlighting the similarities and differences in their digitalization agenda, as well as the existing linkages and dependencies among them. The book clarifies the strategic issues facing the development of digital finance in these major subsectors over the coming years. The book has three key messages: that digital transformation changes fundamentally the way financial businesses operate; that individual trades have their own digitalization agenda; and that the state with its regulatory power and central banking and money has a particularly important role to play.

It will be of interest to scholars, students and researchers of finance and banking, as well as policymakers wishing to understand the values and limitations of new forms of digital money.

Lech Gąsiorkiewicz is a Professor of Finance at the Warsaw University of Technology, Poland.

Jan Monkiewicz is a Professor of Financial Management at the Warsaw University of Technology, Poland.

Routledge International Studies in Money and Banking

Responsible Finance and Digitalization
Implications and Developments
Edited by Panu Kalmi, Tommi Auvinen and Marko Järvenpää

Digital Currencies and the New Global Financial System
Edited by Ranjan Aneja and Robert Dygas

Negative Interest Rates and Financial Stability
Lessons in Systemic Risk
Karol Rogowicz and Małgorzata Iwanicz-Drozdowska

Digital Finance and the Future of the Global Financial System
Disruption and Innovation in Financial Services
Edited by Lech Gąsiorkiewicz and Jan Monkiewicz

Sovereign Debt Sustainability
Multilateral Debt Treatment and the Credit Rating Impasse
Daniel Cash

Environmental Risk Modelling in Banking
Edited by Magdalena Zioło

Money, Debt and Politics
The Bank of Lisbon and the Portuguese Liberal Revolution of 1820
José Luís Cardoso

The Digital Revolution in Banking, Insurance and Capital Markets
Edited by Lech Gąsiorkiewicz and Jan Monkiewicz

For more information about this series, please visit: www.routledge.com/Routledge-International-Studies-in-Money-and-Banking/book-series/SE0403

The Digital Revolution in Banking, Insurance and Capital Markets

Edited by
Lech Gąsiorkiewicz and
Jan Monkiewicz

Routledge
Taylor & Francis Group
LONDON AND NEW YORK

First published 2023
by Routledge
4 Park Square, Milton Park, Abingdon, Oxon OX14 4RN

and by Routledge
605 Third Avenue, New York, NY 10158

Routledge is an imprint of the Taylor & Francis Group, an informa business

British Library Cataloguing-in-Publication Data
A catalogue record for this book is available from the British Library

ISBN: 978-1-032-31507-2 (hbk)
ISBN: 978-1-032-31509-6 (pbk)
ISBN: 978-1-003-31008-2 (ebk)

DOI: 10.4324/9781003310082

Typeset in Bembo
by codeMantra

Contents

Figures

Tables

Contributors

Katarzyna Ciupa PhD hails from the SGH Warsaw School of Economics, Warsaw. Her research interests include financial technology (FinTech) with a strong focus on digital assets, blockchain incl. blockchain-enabled financing schemes, financial innovations and financial intelligence. Consultant and strategist with international experience across global financial players incl. HSBC Consulting Services, Société Générale Securities Services, Raiffeisen Centrobank and Simon Kucher & Partners among others.

Magdalena Dziedzic, PhD, specializes in the subject of new technologies in law, in particular the application of artificial intelligence and smart contracts in the provision of financial services. Her area of interest is also the subject of consumer protection of financial services, especially as it relates to information obligations of financial institutions. She also publishes on the subject of tourism consumer protection. She is an Assistant Professor at the European University of Law and Administration, where she teaches classes on broadly defined private law.

Lech Gąsiorkiewicz, PhD, is an Associate Professor in the Chair of Finance and Financial Systems of the Faculty of Management at the Warsaw University of Technology. Previously he was a member of the supervisory boards of PZU Życie S.A., counselor of the Chairman of the Insurance and Pension Funds Supervisory Commission, vice-president for financial affairs of the Polish Insurance Association S. A. Author and academic editor of numerous academic publications and textbooks in the field of financial management of enterprises and financial institutions. His latest book is Innovation in financial services, Routledge 2021, edited jointly with Jan Monkiewicz. His research interests include company finance, financial institutions and insurance undertakings.

Leszek Jasiński, full professor at the Warsaw University of Technology. In 2005-2013, he was the director of the Institute of Economics of the Polish Academy of Sciences. He conducts research in the field of international economics, European integration, finance, economic fundamentals and regional analysis. In 2011, he won the "Historical Book of the Year" Oskar Halecki Award for the book (in Polish) "Closer to the Center or on the

Peripheries? Polish economic relations with foreign countries in the 20th century" in Polish.

Stanisław Kasiewicz, PhD, is an Emeritus Professor at the Warsaw School of Economics. He was an employee of the Warsaw School of Economics in the years 1971–2019. He was a member of the supervisory boards of three open pension funds and the Bank Guarantee Fund. He participated in research on competitiveness, globalization, business value management, insolvency, risk and regulations. He was a long-term member of the team headed by Professor Leszek Balcerowicz, which prepared the reform of the Polish economy. Author of more than 300 scientific publications, member of the Program Councils of four financial quarterlies. Currently Research Director at the Center for Research and Analysis of Financial Systems ALTERUM in Warsaw.

Marcin Kotarba is a researcher in the Management Faculty of the Warsaw University of Technology (WUT), specializing in the digital transformation of the financial sector, with a focus on banking institutions and their business model. Very closely linked to the business community of multinational banking and to the advisory in the areas of information technology implementation. Trusts in the leading role of technology in financial services, however, recognizes human resources as the most important organizational assets and a key enabler of the client-centered digital transformation which brings benefits for all stakeholders.

Marta Kruk, PhD, holds a PhD in Economics in the discipline of management science at the Warsaw University of Technology, Assistant Professor at the Department of Finance of the Faculty of Management at the Warsaw University of Technology. Author of publications in the field of cost accounting, financial management and process management. She focuses her academic interest on company finance, management accounting and process management.

Lech Kurkliński, PhD, is a Professor at the Warsaw School of Economics (WSE), a specialist in banking, risk management, regulatory impact assessment, and cross-cultural management, head of Digital Finance FINTECH Department at WSE, director of the ALTERUM Center for Research and Analysis of Financial System, studied at WSE, University of Virginia, University of Oklahoma City; since 1991 in banking: CEO of Craftsmanship Bank in Warsaw, CEO of Polski Bank Inwestycyjny, management board member of the BIG Bank Gdanski, Managing Director of Household International in Poland, deputy CEO of HSBC in Poland, member of supervisory boards a.o. Warsaw Stock Exchange, Toyota Bank Polska.

Jan Monkiewicz, PhD, is a Professor of Financial Management at Warsaw University of Technology. His research interests include risk and insurance, the economics of financial markets and their regulation as well as financial consumer protection issues and the digitalization of financial systems. He is a member of the Editorial Board of the Geneva Papers on Risk and Insurance Issues and Practices. From 1994 to 1996 and from 2002 to 2006 he held a senior position in the Polish government. Between 2007 and 2014 he served as Vice Secretary General of the Geneva Association for the Study of Insurance Economics, the think tank of the top 100 global insurers. He is a founding member of the International Centre for Digital Finance in Warsaw. He edited recently, together with Lech Gąsiorkiewicz, "Innovation in financial services. Balancing public and private interests", Routledge 2021 and "Finanse cyfrowe. Informatyzacja, cyfryzacja i danetyzacja", OW PW, Warszawa 2021.

Marek Monkiewicz, is a graduate at the International Relations Institute at Warsaw University (ISM UW). Since 2020, he has been a Professor at the Warsaw School of Economics (SGH) in Warsaw as well as Director of International Cooperation within the Polish Insurance Guarantee Fund (UFG). His scientific interests include a number of issues: compulsory MTPL insurance in Poland and the EU, insurance sector safety (with particular attention to victim protection funds as well as policyholders protection funds in connection with insurers' insolvencies), consumers' protection in the financial sector, including insurance (trends, regulations and institutions), financial innovations in digital finance, including digital insurance.

Adam Śliwiński, PhD, is a Professor at the Warsaw School of Economics, Institute of Risk and Financial Markets. Since 2015, he has been a university professor. Before joining the Warsaw School of Economics he was a postdoctoral fellow at University College London and visiting researcher at Cass Business School City University, focusing on risk and insurance development in Europe, especially Central and Eastern Europe Countries. He has been a visiting lecturer at the Edinburgh Napier University, Cass School of Business, City University and the University of California Berkeley, Hass School of Business. He taught courses in corporate finance, risk management and development economics. He is an alumnus of Ignite 2012 Programme, organized by Judge Business School, Cambridge University. In his research, he focuses on risk management and empirical aspects of finance and insurance. The business experience he gained was a result of his collaborative work with many international insurers and financial companies

Lidia Sobczak, holds a PhD in Economics and is an Academic Teacher and Assistant Professor in the Department of Finance at the Faculty of Management, Warsaw University of Technology. Conducts research in management science and quality studies, specializes in financial management, management accounting, and cost accounting, and is also interested in corporate social responsibility and its reporting.

Daniel Szaniewski, is an Assistant in the Finance Department of the Management Faculty at the Warsaw University of Technology. His research interests include valuation of business entities and researching the reasons for their bankruptcy. He graduated from the Faculty of Mechatronics at the Warsaw University of Technology, majoring in automation and robotics. He graduated from the Faculty of Management in 2016 in the field of management, focusing on finance and risk management. He obtained his master's degree in 2018 at the same Faculty, majoring in management, specializing in markets and financial institutions.

Piotr J. Szpunar, PhD, is the Director of the Economic Analysis and Research Department at the National Bank of Poland. He has worked at NBP in the area of monetary policy and financial stability as an expert and manager since 1995. He is an author of numerous publications in the field of economics and the financial system.

Arkadiusz Szymanek, holds a PhD in Finance from the Warsaw School of Economics. For 20 years he worked at the Warsaw Stock Exchange, commercial banks and other financial institutions. At present, he is employed at the Management Faculty, Warsaw University of Technology. He focuses on capital market issues, in particular in the field of portfolio investment, stock indices and core sectoral analyses.

Tomasz Wiśniewski, PhD, is a Manger on the Warsaw Stock Exchange with over 20 years of experience. He holds MSc in IT and a PhD in Finance. He is a member of Polish economics, statistics and XBRL associations. He is also a Lecturer and speaker at numerous courses and conferences, including postgraduate studies at Polish universities. He is the author and co-author of reports, articles and academic research, and focused on capital markets and sustainable finance.

Piotr Żuk, PhD, is the Head of the Global Economy Division at the Economic Analysis and Research Department of the National Bank of Poland. He previously worked at the Ministry of Economy, the Chancellery of the Prime Minister and the European Central Bank. He earned his PhD degree at the Warsaw School of Economics in 2015. He is an author and co-author of articles and research papers on monetary policy and financial stability, capital flows, pension economics and convergence.

Introduction

Jan Monkiewicz and Lech Gąsiorkiewicz

1 Initial remarks

The future of finance is undoubtfully digital. We are quickly departing from the dominance of analog model toward a digital one. Social and economic life becomes increasingly impacted by digitalization and virtualization. Additionally, it is affected by a rapidly growing transmission, processing and application of data in different public and private contexts. Digitalization is an era of data as a crucial new economic resource. It generates new opportunities, risks and challenges.

The book we propose concentrates on a specific part of the digital economy which is digital finance. It allows natural persons and legal entities to be active on the financial market via the Internet, without having physical contact with the financial institution. It also enables a different set up of back-end and front-end activities of the financial institutions, platformization of business organizations and processes and the growth of specific ecosystems around them.

Digital finance owns particular characteristics in the digital context as financial transactions are largely an exchange of pure data with no material base behind it. Therefore they can become virtualized to an exceptional degree. The end result is that the financial sector belongs to the largest users of information and communication technology, accounting for about 20% of all IT expenditures worldwide (Digital Economy Report, 2019). It has also become a major area of cyber-related risks. The future of financial services is increasingly weightless requiring few physical assets to establish or maintain a business.

Digitalization of finance changes entirely the way financial businesses operate, the balance of their strengths and weaknesses. In its futuristic study released in 2018 by Gartner, the company claims that by 2030 that 80% of all existing financial companies will cease to exist or achieve a zombie status unless they accelerate their digitalization transformation (Gartner, 2018).

The book undertakes an analysis of the most salient features of the trends in contemporary financial businesses. Digitalization disrupts existing analog reality and introduces numerous changes to the financial systems. It changes their products and services. At the same time, it enables delivering both new and traditional services in a more effective and efficient way. It reshapes their

DOI: 10.4324/9781003310082-1

profiles and balances their strengths and weaknesses. The discussion aims at the clarification of strategic issues facing the development of digital finance in its major subsectors in the coming years.

2 Our approach

We approach the problem from the business perspective in a holistic way, providing cutting-edge knowledge of how the digital finance system works in its three main domains: banking, insurance and capital markets. We offer a bird's eye horizontal view of major issues and developments in individual sectors of digital finance, avoiding detailed technical discussions.

The book looks at the problem in four steps. For the start, it offers a wider framework for the subsequent analysis. In the next three steps, it discusses opportunities, risks and challenges facing the digitalization of individual financial subsectors: banking industry, insurance sector and capital market. Using this approach we are able to see similarities and differences in the digitalization agenda in the subsectors discussed. We are also able to indicate existing linkages and dependencies among them.

The digital agenda of individual subsectors differs depending foremostly on the specificity of the trade and its propensity to the application of enabling technologies. Thus for example the issue of open finance is high on the agenda in banking while practically non-existent in insurance and capital markets. Techfins seem to make a difference in banking but have no real reflection in the other subsectors. The Internet of things seems to bring revolutionary changes to insurance, whereas it is largely absent in the banking trade. The same is true with the application of telematics in different financial subsectors. It is widely used in insurance, whereas it is largely absent elsewhere. Cryptoassets set the program for capital markets and to less extent in banking but are quite absent in insurance reality so far.

We bring with the book three key messages: that digital transformation changes fundamentally the way financial businesses operate, that individual trades have their own digitalization agenda and that the State with its regulatory power and central banking and money has a particularly important role to play.

The book should be of interest to all people applying digital finance in their everyday life, including journalists, students and researchers. In this sense, it is a trade book. It should be also useful for business people and representatives of the public sector to understand its values and limits. It is written by academics and practitioners in a friendly manner, avoiding unnecessary technical jargon.

3 Organization of the discussion

The book is split into four parts. In the first part, which is composed of three chapters, we draft the framework for the understanding of subsequent analysis. We present here some cross-sectoral issues which shape the fate of individual trades. We begin with the exploration of regulatory developments and challenges facing digital finance. As indicated by Jan Monkiewicz in his chapter focusing on regulatory agenda, digital transformation of finance requires in addition to the situation existing in the past identification and resolution of numerous new regulatory issues and challenges. Some of them are more finance-specific, some others are cyber-specific, and still others are technology-specific. The current regulatory landscape in finance is obviously heterogeneous with old analog and new digital elements intersecting, colluding and collaborating. Digital transformation in finance raises inter alia the crucial issues of fast-growing new asset classes, new currency in use, datafication and data privacy and finally algorithmization of law and regulation. This chapter provides a synthetic review of principal digitalization-related developments in the regulatory area and discusses responses offered by the EU, confronting them with the US approach.

Thereafter in Chapter 2, Leszek Jasiński explores the issue of the digital money of the central bank. Money is the monopoly of the sovereign state, still delivered by central banks in a paper form. This chapter focuses on the issue of digital money of the central bank, its challenges and opportunities. These days we are facing an economic transformation which by the dissemination of digital technologies squeezes cash payments by non-cash ones. In this chapter, we analyze the progress of this process and try to find answers to the following questions: will paper money cease to exist in the nearest future? what are the economic results of changing forms of payments? does the digital transition contribute positively to the effectiveness and dynamics of economic systems?

In Chapter 3, on the other hand, Marcin Kotarba is jumping into the review of issues facing the digital transformation of financial institutions. He observes that the financial sector is continuously seen as a leader of the digital transformation in the economy, actively adopting new technologies and business models, and following the overall macroeconomic and social developments. Financial institutions dynamically transform themselves in search of profitability, but also venture into new relationships that increase sector connectivity and resistance to new competitive models brought about by pure technology companies. This chapter provides analysis of various changes introduced in financial intermediation due to digital transformation. It aims at the identification of changes in the operation of financial corporations resulting from their digitalization. To assess the changes a standard Business Model Canvas (BMC) is applied. It helps identify major operating elements of financial corporations including customer segments, relationship models and distribution channels. For the specific models of financial corporations, more changes are needed. The description of the current state of digital transformation is followed by a perspective on its future direction.

The second part of the book concentrates on banking issues. It is composed of four chapters. It begins with this chapter by Piotr Szpunar and Piotr Żuk on the central banking in the era of digital finance. In their text, they stress that central banks are remaining an important part of current financial structures. This chapter elaborates on new roles, tasks, tools and instruments of central banking in the digital era. This is presented in the context of the historical evolution of central banking and the key functions that central banks currently play in a market economy and in the two-tier banking system.

Digitalization makes it possible to increase the efficiency of many processes carried out by central banks. This applies in particular to the conduct and organization of payments. Digitalization also enables central banks to conduct increasingly advanced economic analyses. However, the essence of central banking remains broadly unchanged. Central banks still perform the functions of the bank of issue, bank of banks and the state bank.

The second chapter in this part by Stanisław Kasiewicz and Lech Kurkliński is focusing on the drivers of accelerated digitalization in commercial banking. This chapter identifies the principal characteristics of digital banking and discusses its accelerated transformation induced by the pandemic combined with the economic crisis. The aim of this chapter is to present an assessment of the state of digital banking development in the current world, especially in Europe. It also discusses what changes have taken place in the functioning of banks as a result of the COVID-19 pandemic and economic crisis. Special attention is paid to the analysis of the maturity of the digital transformation processes carried out for various bank categories and the identification of the forecasted trends in the development of the banking sector.

The third chapter in this part by Marcin Kotarba focuses on the open banking issue. It stresses that banking is one of the most dynamically changing elements of the financial system. The pace and size of changes are driven not only by new technologies but also by market conditions and customer behaviors. All dimensions of the banking business model are subject to digital transformation – either directly or via the necessity to adapt to changes taking place in other areas. The adaptation contains a strong regulatory component which is no longer oriented mainly toward maintaining system stability but also looking into building more sector competitiveness, resilience, innovation and proximity to the client or third-party business needs. The concept of "open banking" represents one of the current strong change trends, allowing for the banks to move into a new territory where potential opportunities are accompanied by a series of threats. This chapter explains the concept of open banking, focusing on its core concept of open/third-party interfaces, operations and security dilemmas, and business case challenges, including a commentary on its common misconceptions and its potentially inflated value expectations. It then explores possible open banking development scenarios, from the perspective of clients, banks and the ecosystem, including FinTech service providers. This chapter concentrates on the possible impact of the open banking concept on the banking industry and its future developments as well as attempts to assess its effects achieved so far

The second part of the book is terminated with a discussion of the complex relationship between bigtechs-techfins and the banking system. The focus of this chapter is a discussion on the impact of bigtechs on the financial system and banking institutions in particular and the changing market competition resulting from their expansion to banking activities. Its purpose is to identify the advantages and weaknesses of the main market players and tools used to compete (strategies and business models) in digital competition in financial markets. The main conclusion of this chapter is that the final result of the ongoing competition between banking institutions and FinTech companies cannot be predicted precisely, as it depends on banks' future active actions, and also on the unpredictable behavior of regulators and politicians.

The third part of the book concentrates on the digitalization of insurance. It is composed of four chapters. It begins with an overview by Jan Monkiewicz and Marek Monkiewicz of the impact of digital technologies on the various aspects of the insurance value chain.

They stress in their text that digitalization of insurance activities brings numerous changes to the organization and value proposition of insurance companies. It changes their product offer, applied processes and used tools. Additionally, the population of the market players undergoes far-reaching changes. The purpose of this chapter is the assessment of these changes and their implications for the insurance market operation. Particular attention in this assessment is given to data collected, processed, applied and stored and the technologies which make it possible. This chapter reviews principal changes introduced into the insurance value chain due to its digitalization and their impact on business development and applied business models.

The second chapter in this part by Marta Kruk and Lech Gąsiorkiewicz concentrates its attention on the Internet of things which is now one of the key technologies impacting the functioning and development of insurance businesses. According to them, it represents the mainstream of digital transformation of businesses, which is the essence of the fourth industrial revolution. This chapter explores the application of the Internet of things in insurance and discusses its impacts and challenges. In this context, attention is drawn to the changes in the whole system of the insurance value chain covering three areas: solution providers, insurance companies and customers.

The third chapter of this part by Marek Monkiewicz and Adam Śliwiński is devoted to different aspects of telematics application in motor insurance. It discusses the challenges and opportunities of its development with a particular focus on the European market.

In the beginning, the authors underline that though most commonly telematics associated with motor insurance it can be applicable to other kinds of insurance and other areas of the economy. Therefore practical and potential applications of telematics are presented in selected spheres of economic life (such as transport/logistics, medicine, agriculture, etc.).

In the second part of this chapter, the authors focus on different aspects of telematic development in the motor insurance in general. Particularly they draw their attention to the specificity of different models of personalized motor insurance, i.e. Usage Based Insurance – UBI). Using field data the authors try to predict further development trends. The last part of this chapter is focusing on the development of telematics applications in motor insurance of selected EU countries.

The last chapter in this part by Daniel Szaniewski discusses the use of big data analytics in property and life insurance and its impact on the insurance value chain. In the era of globalization and computerization, obtaining, storing, processing and analyzing information has become a particularly important aspect of business operations. The dissemination of digital technologies contributed to the exponential growth of the amount of generated data, which is distinguished by high diversity, complexity and poor structuring. This data is called Big Data, and managing it is one of the biggest challenges that the insurance industry has to face today. Big Data has contributed to the transformation of processes, organizations and many aspects of the insurance sector.

The last part of the book concentrates on the digitalization of capital markets. It is composed of four chapters. It begins with a discussion by Magdalena Dziedzic on the use of smart contracts and artificial intelligence.

A smart contract is defined as an agreement whose terms are written in a computer language, not a legal one. There are views that smart (technologized) contracts in the undefined future might be able to replace lawyers due to the fact that they are self-executing and allow for the reduction of the overall transaction costs. Artificial intelligence, on the other hand, is a machine or information system that has been programmed to act like a human. This chapter focuses on the discussion of the use of blockchain and artificial intelligence in the context of smart contract development. Both smart contracts and artificial intelligence, are used in many areas of the economy, more and more recently also in the capital market, causing a number of discussions concerning, in particular, their legal aspects.

The next chapter by Krystyna Ciupa focuses its attention on cryptoassets market and its development trends. The cryptoassets' market since the publication of Bitcoin's whitepaper, which described the concept of the first decentralized cryptocurrency, has undergone dynamic development. Both individual and institutional players were entering the market introducing new propositions of concepts based on distributed ledger technology. As a result, the cryptomarket has become highly diversified, filled with new versions of already existing cryptocurrencies as well as completely new concepts of other cryptoassets. The whole movement has been highly unstructured, leading to various misunderstandings and often prohibiting the sustainable development of blockchain-based innovations.

The aim of this chapter is to discuss the development of the cryptoassets' market, paying particular attention to emerging trends, ongoing changes and possible prospects for further development. This chapter provides a review of the cryptoassets development and discusses future scenarios in this area

The next chapter in this part by Arkadiusz Szymanek and Tomasz Wiśniewski addresses the issue of the reporting processes on the capital market. They underline that the reporting process around the world is still characterized by different models of data flow. Despite the decreasing use of paper forms, the digitalization of reporting leads to a large variety and difficulties in achieving consistency of the data. There are text formats, spreadsheets, PDF documents, XML and XSD files. Electronic formats usually do not provide the required data quality. Precise numerical information is essential in financial statements, tax returns or reports for banks. This chapter focuses on the developments of new business reporting standards born by digitalization and its new areas of applications. It particularly looks at its challenges and promises. The last chapter of Part 4 is by Lidia Sobczak which raises the issue of the growing role of non-financial reporting. She traces this phenomenon back to the end of the 1990s when enterprises have begun publishing non-financial data in addition to financial information. Initially, the communication of non-financial data was arbitrary and entirely voluntary. Today it is standardized and essentially in many jurisdictions mandatory. The obligation to disclose non-financial information in a specific scope is imposed on all enterprises or only large and listed on the stock exchange, public organizations and agencies, sector organizations, small and medium-sized enterprises, or state-owned companies.

Why do enterprises communicate non-financial data? What data and through what channels do they communicate? Has the shift from voluntary to mandatory disclosure of non-financial information affected their practices? What effects are generated by financial digitalization? Answering these questions is the purpose of this chapter. The objective will be achieved based on a literature review and a case study of a financial institution operating in the European Union.

4 Closing remarks

The book is prepared by a team of contributors coming from various institutions and with different backgrounds. We have among us economists, engineers, management science experts, financial system specialists and lawyers. We have people from academia, concentrating on research and teaching, and from the business community as well as from public institutions. There are young generation representatives and old established senior workers. This rich composition of contributors helped us in putting together an adequate level of diversity in the final text. The book we propose has been written during a time of pandemia. It could reach its timing and goals as digitalization helped us tremendously technical-wise. While preparing the book we used actively online digital finance seminars. Most of the papers were presented in draft form to the participants of the seminar and profited from the internal discussions. A good part of our contributors are employees of the Warsaw University of Technology, School of Management. Their research of the topic was profiting in a natural way from the regular interactions with our undergraduate as well as graduates and Ph.D. students. The future of digital finance is decidedly in their hands.

References

Digital Economy Report (2019), NASK, Cyber Policy.
Gartner (2018), Digitalization will make most heritage financial firms irrelevant, 29 January.

Digital finance

Basic terminology

Jan Monkiewicz and Marek Monkiewicz

1 Introductory remarks

The definitions provided in this glossary are on purpose very synthetic, using plain language and therefore sometimes not very accurate in reflecting inherent complexity. They are intended to convene in a friendly manner a non-technical description of the underlying terminology. We believe this is helpful in view of the relative novelty of the digital finance area and may help the readers in understanding further analysis and discussion contained in the book. The basis for the selection were the recommendations of contributors. For ease of use of terminology, it is presented in alphabetical order. We deliberately avoid structuring our glossary according to some predefined criteria, which may make it untransparent for potential users. Most of the terms included in this review will be further developed in the core text.

2 Glossary

Advanced analytics – tools and models for studying data sets of any size and structure, ready not only to provide information but also to create complete decision-support solutions

Aggregator – digital platform providing some valuable services to their users, in addition to their interaction with external producers that they facilitate. It is a business organization that combines data from various sources, standardizes it, and prepares data sets for sale

Algorithms – a sequence of instructions telling a computer what to do. Any kind of software consists of algorithms

Algorithmic trading – trading in financial instruments where a computer algorithm automatically determines individual parameters of orders, with limited or no human intervention

Altcoin – abbreviation of "Bitcoin alternative"; alternative cryptocurrencies launched after the success of bitcoin

Anti-money laundering (AML) – laws, rules, and systems aimed at detecting and detaining the use of financial systems for disguising utilization of funds criminally obtained

DOI: 10.4324/9781003310082-2

Artificial intelligence (AI) – simulation of human intelligence in machines that are programmed to think like humans and mimic their actions

Application Programming Interface (API) – a software program which allows different application programs to interact with each other and share data

Authentification – a system of ensuring that a person or a transaction is valid for the process being performed

Authorization – the procedure of checking whether a customer has the right to accomplish a specific action

Balance sheet consumer lending – provision of a loan directly from the platform entity to a consumer borrower

Big data – large data sets that may be analyzed computationally to discover patterns and trends relating to human behaviour. Often come from multiple sources

Big data analytics – a set of automatic and semi-automatic computational techniques for processing large data sets, including machine learning and artificial intelligence

Big tech – major information technology companies operating in a form of platforms such as for example Google, Apple, Amazon, Facebook, Tencent, and Baidu, having currently a capitalization ranging from $1 trillion up to $2 trillion each

Biometric identification – a technology facilitating the identification of a person through biometric verification by evaluating biological traits such as fingerprints, hand geometry, earlobe geometry, retina, iris patterns, and voice waves

Bitcoin – digital currency or cryptocurrency created in 2009. Bitcoins are not issued or backed by any central bank or government so far with the exception of Salvador

Blockchain – the technology of a shared digital ledger. Underlies bitcoin and other cryptocurrencies

B2B – Business to business payment

B2G – Business to government payment, including paying taxes

B2P – Business to person payment, including salary payment

Chatbot – virtual assistance programmes that interact with users in natural language, enabling automated capture, and interpretation of qualitative data

Cloud computing – delivery of different IT services on external data centers without direct management by the user

Cognitive systems – systems that use intelligent data processing and artificial intelligence to imitate Cognitive systems human thinking, e.g. computer learning, natural language processing, speech recognition, image processing

Collaborative finance – a category of financial transaction occurring between individuals without the intermediation of a traditional financial institution

Crowdfunding – collection via online internet platforms of small amounts of funds to finance a new business venture

Cryptoassets – digital assets which utilize cryptography, peer-to-peer networking, and a public ledger to regulate the generation of new units, verify and secure the transactions without the intervention of any middleman

Cryptocurrency – a digital/virtual/currency that uses cryptography for security and hence is difficult to counterfeit

Cyber – relating to, within, or through the medium of interconnected information infrastructure of interactions among persons, processes, data, and information systems

Cyber event – any observable occurrence in an information system

Cyber incident – a cyber event which jeopardizes the cyber security of an information system or violates the security policies or security procedures

Cyber resilience – the ability of an organization to carry out its activities withstanding cyber incidents and anticipating and adapting to cyber threats

Cyber risk – the combination of the probability of cyber incidence occurring and their impact

Cybersecurity – protection of internet-connected systems, including hardware, software, and data from cyberattacks

Dashboards – customizable, dynamic reporting tools that automatically fetch and render data in meaningful visualization

Data anonymization – removal of personal information from a data set while maintaining information about transactions involving the same user

Data breach – a cybersecurity mishap when data falls into the wrong hands without the knowledge of the owner or user

Data broker – a business organization that facilitates trading in data

Data enrichment – combining data sets generated internally in a business organization with additional data procured from external providers, which contains required features that are lacking in the original data set

Data lake – scalable storage solution for diverse structured, semi-structured, and unstructured data

Data quality – the fit between data characteristics and user needs including data accuracy, completeness, consistency, reliability, and recency

Data standardization – preparation of data sets in accordance with accepted technical standards to facilitate further processing and use

Data storytelling – a method of communicating information, tailored to a specific audience, using three major components: data, narrative, and visuals

Data visualization – using images and interactive technologies to analyze data sets in a user-friendly graphic environment

Digital ecosystems – denotes, by drawing an analogy to natural ecosystems, an interdependent group of actors, sharing standardized digital platforms to achieve the mutually beneficial purpose

Digital finance platforms – multilateral IT systems that connect a network of participating institutions to one another and to the operator of each system for the purpose of conducting financial transactions

Digital financial services (DFS) – a range of financial services accessed and delivered through digital channels. It includes payments, savings, credit, remittances, and insurance

Digital financial service provider – entity which provides a digital financial service to consumers, businesses, or government

Datafication – the creation of a new economic resource from data

Digital fraud – criminal use of digital finance to take funds from another business or individual

Digital payment – any payment which is executed electronically

Digital platform – a group of technologies used as a base for other applications and processes to be implemented

Distributed ledger technology – a digital system for recording the transaction of assets in which the transactions and their details are recorded in multiple places at the same time

Donations-based crowdfunding – donors provide funding to individuals or companies on philanthropic or civic motivations

Electronic banking – Provision of banking products and services through electronic channels

Electronic payment (E-payment) – Any payment made through an electronic funds transfer

Electronic money (E-money) – a type of monetary value electronically stored on payment devices like chips, prepaid cards, mobile phones, or on computer systems

Electronic wallet – a place to store electronic money to allow rapid and secure electronic transactions. It could take the form of a smart card or a mobile phone

Equity based crowdfunding – individuals or institutional funders purchase equity issued by a company via a digital platform

Financial inclusion – sustainable provision of affordable digital financial services that bring the poor into the formal economy

Financial regulator – governmental organization empowered to set up and enforce standards and practices referring to the financial system

Financial services comparison platforms – provide the users a possibility of comparing the conditions of diverse financial products offered by different companies

Fintech – new technologies used in financial applications. It is also used to refer to businesses providing software services and products for digital financial services

GDPR – The General Data Protection Regulation, EU law on data protection and privacy for all individuals within the EU and EEA (European Economic Area)

Hybrid cloud – services combining public and private cloud resources, with technology allowing data and applications to be shared between them

Initial coin offering (ICO) – a type of fundraising primarily done by crowdfunding

In-memory databases – data repositories enabling the collection of unstructured data in non-relational structures and processing of data resources in the operational memory of a computer system. Their growing popularity is conditioned in particular by the need to access Big Data sets

Insurtech – use of technological innovations to improve the performance of the insurance sector

Internet of things (IoT) – a system of interrelated computing devices, mechanical and digital machines, objects, animals, or people equipped with unique identifiers and the ability to transfer data over a network without requiring human-to-human or human-to-computer interaction

Interoperability (interconnectivity) – the ability of the payment system to allow different digital platforms to interact seamlessly. The end result provides an ability to exchange payments transactions among providers

Know Your Customer (KYC) – the process of identification of a new customer at the time of the start of commercial relations. It is also an international regulatory standard which requires all financial institutions to ensure that they validate the identity of all their clients

Machine learning (ML) – entails computers learning from data without human intervention. It is a method of designing problem-solving rules that improve automatically through experience. Machine-learning algorithms give computers the ability to learn without specifying all the knowledge a computer would need to perform the desired task

Marketplaces – digital platforms that have as the primary objective creation of efficient matches between consumers and suppliers of goods (examples: eBay, Uber and Booking.com)

Mining – verifying transactions and securing the public ledger

Mobile banking (M-banking) – The use of a mobile phone to access banking services and execute financial transactions

Natural language processing (NLP) – the capacity of computer programs to process human language. As a component of artificial intelligence, NLP is an interdisciplinary field comprising computer science, AI, and computational linguistics. NLP applications are designed to understand natural human communication, either written or spoken and to respond using natural language

Near-field Communication (NFC) – a short-range high-frequency wireless communication technology enabling the exchange of data between devices

Network effects – arise when the value a user derives from a product or service increases with the number of other users

P2P – Peer-to-peer lending, called alternatively social lending. It enables individuals to obtain loans directly from other individuals using internet platforms

Predictive analytics – combines data, algorithms, and machine learning to identify future outcomes based on historical data

Prepaid card – e-money product where the record of funds is stored on the payment card or a central computer system

Private cloud – services in which computer resources are used exclusively by one single organization and are not accessible by others

Public cloud – services, including general computing and software resources offered by a third-party provider over the public internet

Real-time payments – payments incurred instantaneously

Regtech – the management of regulatory processes within the financial sector through technological innovations

Reward-based crowdfunding – financing is provided to individuals or companies in exchange for non monetary rewards

Robotic process automation – a software technology that makes it easy to build, deploy, and manage software robots that emulate human actions interacting with digital systems and software. The main goal is minimizing the risk of error, optimizing process efficiency, and guaranteeing the stable quality of its implementation

Scalability – the measure of a service's capacity to increase or decrease in performance in response to changes in volumes, or general computing needs

Smart contracts – self-executing contracts with the terms of the agreement between buyer and seller being directly written into lines of code

Sup tech – application of financial technology to supervisory purposes

Software as a service – a model of cloud service allowing customers to connect to use the cloud-based applications over the internet on a subscription basis

Systemic risk – the risk of collapse of an entire financial system or entire market as opposed to risk of collapse of individual provider or end user

Text mining – the process of exploring and analysing large amounts of unstructured text data aided by software that can identify concepts, patterns, keywords, and other attributes of the data

Usage-based insurance – type of vehicle insurance where the premium depends on the distance and the driving style of the policyholder

Wearable technology – a category of electronic devices that can be worn as accessories, embedded in clothing, implanted in the user's body, or tattooed on the skin

Bibliography

AFI, Digital financial services. Basic terminology, August 2016.
Alliance for Financial Inclusion, Basic terminology, 2013.
BIS CPSS-A glossary of terms used in payments and settlement systems, 2003.
CPMI-IOSCO, Guidance on cyber resilience for financial markets, June 2016.
FSB, Cyber lexicon, 12 November 2018.
NIST, Glossary of key information security terms, Rev.2, 2013.

Part I

The framework

1 Digital transformation of finance

Uncharted waters of regulation

Jan Monkiewicz

1.1 Introductory remarks

The regulation of traditional analogue finance is characterised by thesilo approach. The entire financial system is split into semi-autonomous groups of entities –banks, insurance providers, and investment companies – with each one regulated by a different set of laws and rules that reflect their specific nature. The focus of regulation is entity-based and principally covers prudential measures, in terms of capital adequacy and solvency, liquidity and risk mitigation, on the one hand, and market conduct on the other. Prudential measures include control of risk via integrated business processes and the elimination, as far as possible, of the use of external providers of critical services. Value chains are thus entity-centred and aggregated. The overall financial system is highly centralised. Central banks control the money supply and financial trading is carried out by licensed intermediaries. Competition among the entities is limited and the provision of services is highly concentrated. As one leading banking expert claims, "Banking systems in nearly all countries are oligopolistic structures which are dominated by the largest banks. The chances that they will compete among themselves and bring prices down are rather small" (Sławiński, 2019, p. 33). A recent study published by the US Federal Reserve Board (FRB, 2020) confirms this observation, revealing that between 1984 and 2020 the four largest US banks by deposits increased their countrywide share from 15% to 44%.

The digitalisation of finance is transforming regulatory remit due to a number of new processes that are taking place simultaneously. First, it is the result of the arrival of new entrants into the financial systems in the form of technology-based companies – fintechs and bigtechs. Second, it is the effect of the emergence of large digital finance platforms. Third, it is due to the disaggregation of value chains and the emergence of ecosystems interacting via those platforms, and fourth, it is an outcome of the underlying digital technologies and the subsequent need to respond to them. Digital assets are a flagship example of this. Finally, there are also new risks and new risk exposures resulting from the departure from analogue finance to digital. Cybersecurity issues may serve as an example of this. Another example is the new remit for

DOI: 10.4324/9781003310082-4

consumer protection resulting from the increased use of personal data. These new digitally inspired challenges have to be placed within the regulatory architecture, covering both the traditional elements of the financial systems and also the innovative ones, thus creating a complex hybrid structure. In the discussion which follows, we will concentrate our attention on the regulatory aspects of platformisation, bigtechs, the algorithmisation of the law, the digitalisation of assets, and consumer protection.

1.2 Online platforms and bigtechs in finance – regulatory challenges

A characteristic feature of the digitaltransformation with high impact potential is the growth of online platforms that are able to create vast interconnected ecosystems, thus reshaping business models and the way the participants of these platforms interact. According to the predictions of the Digital Transformation Initiative of the World Economic Forum, by 2025 digital platforms will create $100 trillion of value, and half of all large enterprises will have created their own platforms or partnered with industry platforms (WEF, 2017). This will result, among other things, in the departure from a linear value chain to a circular one with shared outcomes.

Platforms may be defined in many different ways to take into account their different models and evolving approaches (Szpringer, 2020). In this chapter, the term will be used simply to refer to technology-enabled business models which create value by facilitating exchanges and interactions among their stakeholders. They are built on a shared and interoperable infrastructure and based on multi-stakeholder interactions which are offered opportunities to collaborate and transact (WEF, 2017). From a purely technical point of view, platforms are equipped with two functional layers: infrastructure and interactions. The infrastructure layer offers the tools for the platform's operation and it covers the underlying technology and architecture, focusing mainly on interoperability, the use of Application Programming Interfaces (APIs), security, and reliability.

A major concern are the issues connected with managing complex sets of collaborating technical elements. The interactional layer, on the other hand, offers the rules of interaction and cooperation of the stakeholders. The platform's stakeholders include, first of all, its producers and suppliers that provide the goods and services for the platform's consumers. They also include infrastructure providers, such as telecommunication networks, IT, software, system integration, etc. They manage, monitor, and deploy the technology applied to the platform. Finally, there is the orchestrator, who owns and manages both the strategic and operational framework.

Each of these stakeholders may simultaneously play different roles across the ecosystems. From the regulatory point of view, the platform ecosystem orchestrators and policymakers play a central role. The orchestrators introduce civil law remedies, while the policymakers rely on ones from public administrative law. Infrastructure suppliers are additional elements of private regulatory

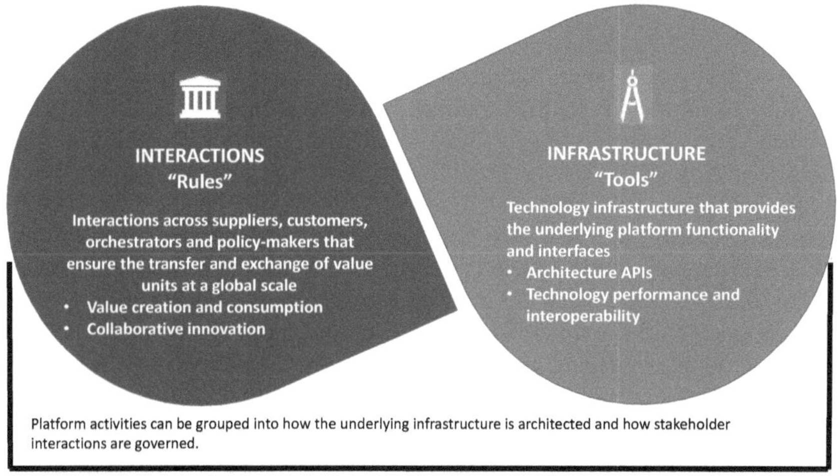

Figure 1.1 Functional layers of a platform
Source: WEF (2017, p. 5)

power. The idealised structure of a platform ecosystem and the role of individual stakeholders is presented in Figure 1.1. It should be noted that platform ecosystems may also interact with a number of other institutions, such as governments and policymakers, consumer agencies, industry associations, etc.

Bigtechs are simply a class of platform characterised by their extremely large size networks. No legal definition of these entities exists and no legally binding criteria have to date been formulated, unlike with systemically important financial institutions, even though they are believed to have similar potential. The Financial Stability Board, a leading global standard-setter in finance, defines bigtechs as large companies with established technology platforms (FSB, 2019), while a recent IMF study defines bigtechs as a platform-based business model focused on maximising interactions between a large number of mainly retail users (IMF, 2022/002). It should be noted perhaps that neither platforms nor bigtechs are finance-related phenomena but, for good reason, they seem to be attracting the growing interest of financial regulators.

Bigtechs are still relatively newcomers to the financial services domain. Their principal area of activity to date has been located outside of finance, mainly in social media, internet search engines, and e-commerce. However, for a few years now, they have been increasingly entering the area of financial services and supplying such services as part of their wider offer. They offer these services either on an independent basis, competing with traditional financial institutions, or in partnership with them, offering intermediating layers. They also invest in other financial institutions outside their own groups (FSI, 2021). To date, they have been largely concentrated in the banking area and on capital markets.

Financial services are generally still a secondary source of income for bigtechs. In 2018, for example, bigtechs' core businesses accounted for about half of their revenues (BIS, 2019). However, their internal potential, in spite of the resultant risk, has already made them a target for different regulatory initiatives.

Regulatory-wise, biotechs are "mixed activity groups" (MAGs) which are governed by a combination of finance-specific regulations and non-financial or cross-industry regulations (FSI, 2021). As far as finance-focused regulations are concerned, there has been no specific regulatory treatment of bigtechs operating in finance to date. By and large, they are subject to the same requirements as other participants, including ones that are too big to fail. To run their business, they are expected to receive the appropriate licences and cooperate with the supervisory authorities in their daily operations. With regard to the non-financial regulatory agenda for bigtechs, there are a number of issues which principally represent wide horizontal cross-industry considerations, spanning from data protection and data sharing, the application of artificial intelligence, cyber risk, the operational resilience and conduct of the business towards competition, and market contestability. This last issue evidently seems to be at the top of the agenda for current global regulatory debates and actions with a major focus on bigtechs. The business model of bigtechs enabled them to quickly create opportunities to achieve a dominant position in their selected market segments. This, in turn, could lead to various market abuses and anti-competitive actions, as documented, for example, in the report of the US House of Representatives (US House of Representatives, 2020). In response to these documented dangers, competition authorities in key jurisdictions – the US, EU, and China – have begun both to strengthen traditional ex-post competitive measures against bigtechs and also discuss introducing ex-ante competitive measures, which have been largely absent until now in the new toolkit of competition authorities (FSI, 2021a). Of the ex-post actions taken, the most widely publicised case was the refusal of the Chinese authorities in 2021 to accept a proposal for the public listing of Ant Group, the biggest-ever proposed IPO in China, for not complying with the listing criteria and disclosure requirements (Figure 1.2). The group was forced by the public authorities to restructure, and it was additionally fined the amount of $2.8 billion (FSI, 2021a).

In the US, the competition authorities initiated action in 2020 against Google and Facebook for anti-competitive behaviour, although with mixed results. The EU authorities have also imposed high fines and initiated court proceedings against the anti-competitive behaviour of Google, Amazon, and Apple, among others.

A completely new development in this respect are the actions taken to develop ex-ante entity-based competition rules which would prohibit certain actions for bigtechs, including the interoperability of online platforms with third parties, among others, and also mandate equal treatment for all potential business users (FSI, 2021a). An interesting new development is the recent legislative proposal of the EU Commission for a Digital Services Act, tabled

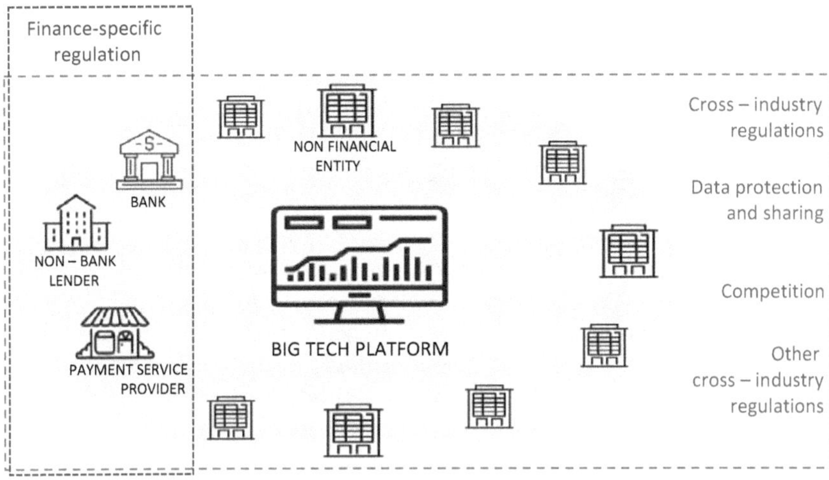

Figure 1.2 The regulatory environment for bigtech groups
Source: FSI (2021, p. 5)

in 2020, which intends to address the issue of the challenges posed to the EU by large online platforms. It is focused on the prevention of possible risks that they would pose to their users, in particular their fundamental rights and competition protection. This initiative is being coordinated in parallel with the Digital Markets Act, which focuses on the gatekeeper role and the unfair business practices of some classes of online platforms.

1.3 Data and the financial sector – regulatory responses

Data today represents a core input into the digital provision of financial services. The digital transformation of finance is also responsible for the observable explosion in the amount of data used in economic and social life. Technological innovations feeding the digital transformation, such as the internet of things (IoT), robotics, biometrics, and advanced computing, have dramatically improved the ability of businesses and states to capture and use consumer data. The use of consumer data is central to the business model of financial sector institutions. This is even more true for the bigtechs, which possess a large number of customers interacting in their digital ecosystems and are therefore fed new customer data continuously. Using this data potential efficiently, however, requires the global community to develop international regulatory standards to accommodate the global nature of the digitalisation processes. This entails the possession of a minimum set of principles for data protection and data sharing across borders, covering principles on data portability and interoperability, and also principles of data sharing for regulatory purposes (IMF, 2021). A number of regulatory initiatives have already been registered in this area. In its paper, the World Economic Forum estimated that by 2018 more than 120 countries had enacted some form of data protection legislation (WEF, 2018). It is possible to discern some quite different approaches that have been taken in this regard, however. Europe was the pacesetter for the comprehensive approach with its General Data Protection Regulation, adopted in 2016 and put into practice in 2018 (Regulation, 2016). This is based on the application of seven high-level principles to safeguard the said area, which apparently have wide global acceptance. The first principle states that the Regulation requires the users of the data to respect the principle of lawfulness, fairness, and transparency towards data subjects when processing the data of EU residents. Processing should be based on the clear consent of the data subject, which may be withdrawn by them at any moment. The second principle introduces a purpose limitation, which specifies that the data should be collected only for specified, explicit, and legitimate purposes. The third principle introduces the data minimisation rule, which means that the data processing should be adequate for the purpose, relevant and limited. The fourth principle calls for steps to be taken to ensure the data being processed is accurate and kept up-to-date. The regulation also guarantees the right of data subjects to have their data erased or rectified. The fifth principle provides for the storage limitation of the data, which should be kept for no longer than necessary and in a form permitting identification of the data subjects. The sixth principle is concerned with the integrity and confidentiality of the data processing and requires that it be processed in a manner that ensures the appropriate level of security of personal information, with protection against unlawful or unauthorised processing. Finally, the seventh principle introduces the rule of accountability, which lays the burden of administering the system in the hands of the data controller, who should be responsible for demonstrating compliance with the appropriate data processing rules.

The whole chapter, which deals with Regulation, focuses on the rights of the data subjects. The first one is the right to receive information from the data controller (Articles 13 and 14). In principle, this right refers to the right of the data subject to be informed about what data is being processed and why. This covers both situations where the data is collected directly from the data subject, and also indirectly. The second right of the data subject is the right of access (Article 15), which basically says that the data subject is allowed to access the personal data belonging to them and receive from the data controller information regarding, among other things, what data is being processed, the purpose of the processing, and the recipients of the results, etc. Another right of the data subject is the right to rectification (Article 16). This gives the data subject the right to change or modify data which they believe to be inaccurate or out-of-date. The data subject also has the right to erasure, also known as the right to be forgotten (Article 17). This could happen, for instance, if the purpose of the processing has already been accomplished, if the consent has been withdrawn, or if certain other conditions are met. Article 18 provides the data subject with the right to restriction of processing. This could be justified, for example, if the data used is inaccurate or the processing is unlawful. Another important right contained in the regulation is the right to data portability (Article 20). This is defined as the right of the data subject to receive his/her personal data held by the data controller in a commonly used format and for it to be sent to anotherdata controller. The right to data portability is instrumental for the concept of open finance which is currently under global development. Article 21 addresses the right to object. This right is related to specific situations defined in the text of the Regulation and covers, among other things, use of the data for direct marketing objectives or some other purposes indicated in the law. Finally, the Regulation gives the data subject the right to avoid automated individual decision-making, with some exceptions (Article 22).

The approaches to data protection and data sharing adopted in both the USA and China have largely followed the European approach explained above (FSI, 2021). They also share the main features connected with the rights of the data subject. The underlying common principle is that individuals have distinct rights with regard to their personal data (Table 1.1).

Table 1.1 Data protection and data-sharing approaches in the EU, US and China

	EU	*US*	*China*
Data protection			
Collection and use of personal data			
Of which: Lawfulness, fairness and transparency	□	□	□
Purpose specification	□	★	□
Security	□	□	□
Users' data rights			
Of which: Consent and access	□	★	□
Rectification and deletion	□	★	□
Data portability	□	★	□
Data-sharing			
Open banking			
Approach: prescriptive, facilitative★★, market-driven★★★	Prescriptive	Market	Market

Legend: Comprehensive | Partial | Early stages

★ While there is no federal law addressing these elements at present, they are subject to ongoing debate.

★★ Under a facilitative approach, jurisdictions issue guidance and recommended standards, and release open API standards and technical specifications.

★★★ No explicit rules or guidance that either require banks or prohibit them to share customer-permissioned data with third parties.

Source: FSI (2021a, p. 10)

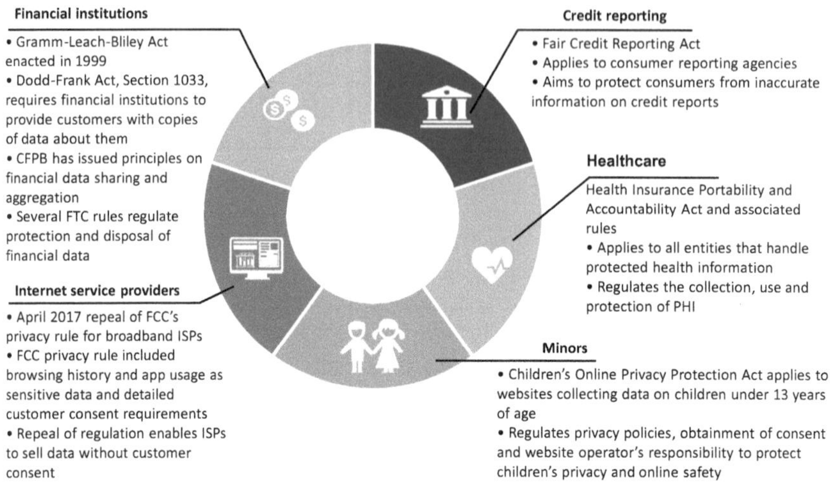

Figure 1.3 US federal legislation on customer data
Source: WEF (2017, p. 12)

Of course, there are also some important differences in the approach of the EU on the one side, and China and the US on the other. A characteristic feature of the US approach is the scattered regulatory framework at the federal level, which allows for a narrow sectoral approach compared to the EU's trans-sectoral solution (Figure 1.3). As of today, there are some rules and regulations concerning financial institutions, with separate rules for credit reporting, healthcare, internet service providers, and minors (CRS, 2019).

At the same time, data privacy issues are generally regulated at the state level. The best-known example is the California Consumer Privacy Act (CCPA), which resembles the solutions adopted in the EU, while other states concerned include Colorado (Colorado Privacy Act), Virginia (Consumer Data Protection Act), and New York (NY Privacy Act). In 2018, China decided to provide a holistic framework for personal data protection but left the issues of interoperability out of its scope (WEF, 2017).

1.4 Digital assets, cryptoassets, digital tokens

Digital assets are a natural product of the digital transformation of finance. To date, there has been no universally accepted definition of digital assets since they can take different forms and have different characteristics. In principle, they can simply be defined as assets which are issued and transferred using distributed ledger or blockchain technology. One of the key differences between traditional assets and this new asset class is the way their ownership, and changes to it, is recorded. For traditional assets, there are central intermediaries, such as banks, whereas for digital ones there are decentralised digital ledgers (CRS, 2021).

From a bird's eye view, digital assets can be broken down into two main categories – cryptocurrencies and tokens. Cryptocurrencies can be further classified into traditional non-backed cryptocurrencies on the one hand and stablecoins on the other. Cryptocurrencies are cryptoassets which are intended to perform the role of a medium of exchange, store of value, and unit of account. By their very nature, they are an alternative to government-issued legal tender. Since they are not backed by any underlying asset, their value is extremely volatile. This problem is resolved by a sub-category of crypto-currencies – stablecoins. Stable coins are a variant of cryptocurrency that are pegged to another asset, or pool of assets, in order to maintain a stable value. Tokens, on the other hand, are cryptoassets that offer their holders certain economic rights. Simply speaking, they are the digital representation of the rights to certain assets, products, or services (European Parliament, 2020). They are frequently split into investment tokens and utility tokens, both of which are used to raise funds on the financial market but also offer their holders different rights. Cryptocurrencies were historically the first type of cryptoasset to arrive in late 2008 when Bitcoin was introduced. Even today, it is still a major global cryptocurrency in use. Tokens, on the other hand, have only become popular since 2017.

The overall market size of cryptoassets is still limited. In May 2021, the value of the global market for cryptocurrencies reached the level of $2 trillion, compared to $20 billion in 2017, representing a 100-fold increase. However, it is still relatively small compared to the size of the traditional assets market. At that same time, for example, just the US fixed-income market alone was worth ca. $50 trillion, with the value of publicly traded shares represented in the S&P 500 index amounting to $35 trillion (CRS, 2021).

Investors, users and cryptoasset service providers are exposed to high risks, resulting, among other things, from the high volatility of certain cryptoassets, the features of the underlying technology, or the transactional anonymity. Some risks stem from exposure to operational and cyber risk, while there are also traditional financial risks, such as market risk, credit risk, and default or market integrity risk, though additionally mixed in the digital environment. For these reasons, many national authorities have issued warnings regarding their use, while some have even banned them altogether (Figure 1.4).

Cryptoassets also potentially create risks connected with money laundering and terrorist financing. The anonymity-related features of the crypto market make it difficult for the authorities to track the criminal use of cryptoassets. As was reported to the G20 leaders in 2019, "Cryptocurrencies pose serious money laundering and terrorist financing risks that criminals, money launderers, terrorists and other illicit actors could exploit" (FATF, 2019). The serious threat that cryptoassets could be used for money laundering led to the concentration of regulatory initiatives around these issues, which then became more balanced with the growth of other cryptoassets such as stablecoins and

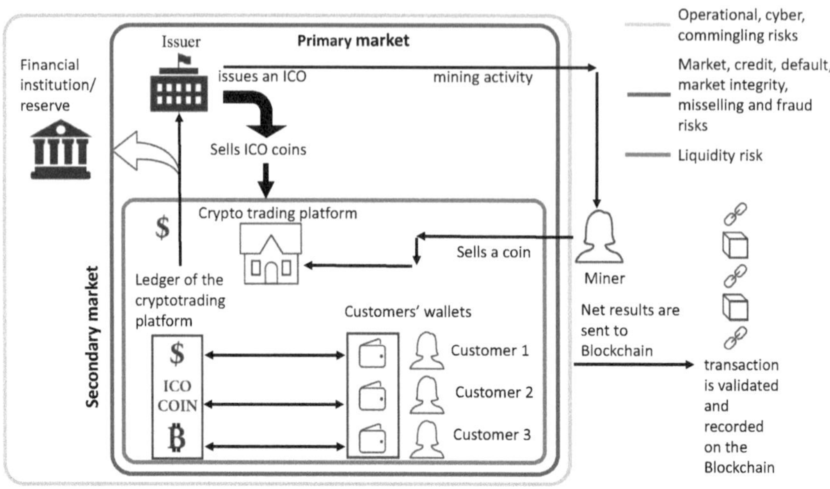

Figure 1.4 Market structure of cryptoassets
Source: Based on IMF (2019, p. 3)

tokens. Attention was then switched from the anti-money laundering regulators to prudential and security regulators. As a result, many relevant initiatives were launched in individual jurisdictions. In Europe, for example, Switzerland introduced a new DLT and blockchain law for the financial sector in 2020, Liechtenstein passed its Tokens and Trusted Technology Service Providers Act in January 2020, and France introduced an amendment to its Code Monétaire et Financier in 2019 to include tokens.

The most far-reaching regulatory project in this domain was tabled recently by the EU Commission on 24 September 2020 with its draft Regulation on Markets in Crypto-assets (MiCA), which is intended to provide the first comprehensive regulatory framework for digital assets worldwide. The proposal, which is part of the EU's Digital Finance Strategy, covers all cryptoassets from outside the existing EU financial services regulation, as well as e-money tokens. It has four general objectives: to provide legal certainty and clarity for the stakeholders; support innovation by providing a safe and proportionate framework; support consumer and investor protection, and finally; secure the protection of market integrity. The proposed regulation will replace existing national solutions. The Regulation is divided into 9 Titles and 126 Articles (EU Commission, 2020).

Title I sets out the subject matter, scope, and definitions. Article 1 on the subject matter declares that the Regulation provides uniform rules for:

a the transparency and disclosure requirements for the issuance and trading of cryptocurrencies

b the authorisation and supervision of cryptoasset service providers and issuers of asset-referenced tokens and electronic money tokens
c the operation, organisation, and governance of issues of cryptoassets and service providers
d consumer protection rules for the issuance, trading, exchange and custody of cryptoassets
e measures to prevent market abuse and ensure the integrity of the markets

Title II regulates the offerings and marketing to the public of cryptoassets other than asset-referenced tokens or e-money tokens. It envisages, among other things, that such an offering may only take place if certain conditions are met, in particular the obligation of the issuer to be established as a legal person or the obligation to draw up a white paper on the relevant cryptoasset.

Title III regulates the issues related to asset-referenced tokens, while Title IV regulates e-money tokens. TitleV regulates the authorisation and operating conditions of cryptoasset service providers. Among other things, it specifies the content of the application and its assessment, and the requirement on all cryptoasset providers to act honestly, fairly, and professionally.

Title VI specifies the prohibitions and requirements to prevent market abuse involving cryptoassets. It defines the scope of market abuse rules and the notion of inside information and also bans insider dealing. Title VII is concerned with the powers of national supervisory authorities and also defines the role of the European Banking Authority (EBA) in relation to the issuers of significant asset-referenced tokens and significant e-money tokens. Title VIII regulates the issue of delegated measures, and Title IX contains the transitional and final provisions, including the obligation for the Commission to produce an evaluation report on the impact of the Regulation. As we can see, the MiCA Regulation is an ambitious European project, but it remains to be seen how far it can drive the digital finance market in Europe and worldwide.

1.5 Algorithmisation of the law: the issue of governing machines

The digitalisation of economic and social life opens up increased possibilities for a new form of regulation by private actors, who may impose their own values by implanting them into the software algorithms. This is sometimes called algorithmic regulation, which refers to standard-setting and modifying behaviour by means of computational algorithms. As the extent of our digital activity increases, we rely more and more on the regulatory role of algorithms.

As opposed to the "old" type of regulation, which determined what should be done rather than what should not be done, algorithmic regulation has a much stronger impact as it decides what can and cannot be done in a specific online setting (Hassan and De Filippi, 2017).

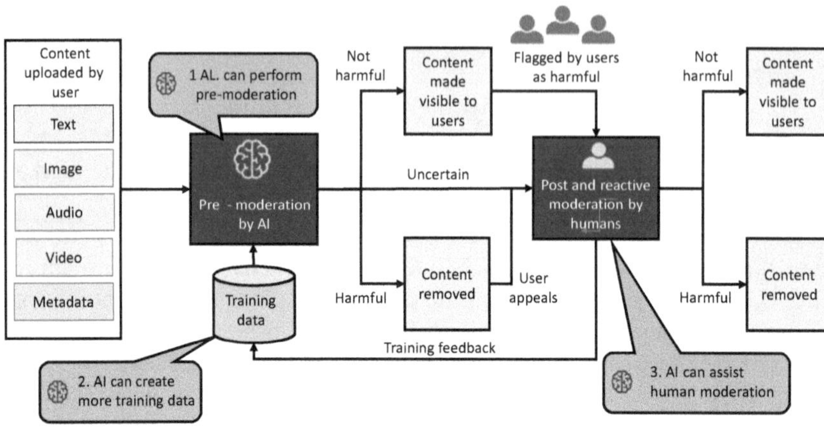

Figure 1.5 AI in the online content moderation workflow
Source: European Parliament (2020a, p. 33)

This can be well illustrated by an analysis of the possible role of artificial intelligence in online content moderation (Figure 1.5). As the diagram shows, AI is engaged in the moderation of content at various stages. It can be driven by positive factors to eliminate harmful content, such as hate speech or child abuse, or by different considerations representing the views of the software engineer, or even representing views self-developed by the AI itself using the training data. This is, of course, a good argument in favour of involving humans at the final stage.

Applying code-based regulation brings a number of benefits but also creates risks. The first one to mention is the fact that in contrast to classic traditional rules that have to be assessed by a judge who makes the final decision, code-based rules do not offer such flexibility. They are written in a rigid, formal form. Additionally, the choice is made by the software provider, which means it is not neutral but reflects their own values and approaches.

Generally speaking, an algorithm may be described as a sequence of well-defined operations that should be performed in an exact order to carry out certain tasks or solve certain problems. Algorithms could be usefully classified by the task they perform, the input parameters, and also their method of learning. In the last case, there are two distinct classes of algorithms –there are fixed algorithms, with human-chosen parameters that do not change over time in response to new information provided, and also self-learning or machine-learning algorithms. These are algorithms that derive their conduct parameters from a set of training data, and they are capable of improving their performance in an automated way with increasing experience (Bundeskartellamt, 2019). This is where the issue of artificial intelligence comes to the fore. Given the potential impact of artificial intelligence, it has become an important policy priority for the international community over the last few years. In May 2019, the OECD adopted its high-level Principles on Artificial Intelligence. This was the first international standard agreed upon by member governments for managing responsible and trustworthy AI. The five recommendations laid out in the Principles formulate a value-based approach which defines the way governments should promote responsible AI. According to them, the trustworthy application of AI should (OECD, 2021, p. 53):

- benefit people and the planet by driving inclusive growth, sustainable development, and well-being
- be designed in a way that respects the rule of law, human rights, and democratic values
- include transparency and responsible disclosure around AI systems
- ensure that AI systems function in a robust, secure, and safe way
- involve all producers and providers of AI being held accountable for their proper functioning

In 2021, the European Commission, after several years of discussions, decided to table a comprehensive proposal for a Regulation on Artificial Intelligence (EU Commission, 2021), drawing on the European Parliament's Resolution on a Framework of Ethical Aspects of Artificial Intelligence, Robotics and Related Technologies. This proposal, which sets out harmonised rules for the development, placement and use of AI systems in the EU, declared four main objectives:

- to ensure that AI systems on the EU market are safe and respect laws on fundamental rights and EU values
- to ensure legal certainty to facilitate investment and innovation
- to enhance governance and effective enforcement applicable to AI systems
- to facilitate the development of a single market for trustworthy AI

The proposal was technically divided into 12 Titles and 85 Articles. Title I defines the scope and provides the definitions. It defines the subject matter and scope of application, covering the placing of AI systems on the market and putting them into service and use. Title II establishes a list of prohibited AI practices, comprising all AI systems which are considered unacceptable as contravening Union values. Title III refers to high-risk AI systems and contains specific rules for AI systems that create a high risk to the health and safety or fundamental rights of natural persons. They are permitted on the EU market subject to mandatory requirements. Title IV deals with transparency obligations for certain AI systems and requires them to take account of the specific risks of manipulation they pose. Transparency obligations apply to those systems which interact with humans, are used to detect emotions, or generate or manipulate content. Title V elaborates on the measures supporting innovation in AI. It encourages the setting up of regulatory sandboxes and sets a framework in terms of governance, supervision, and liability. Title VI sets up the governance systems on AI at Union and national levels. At the Union level, it establishes, among other things, a European Artificial Intelligence Board to coordinate national supervisory authorities and advise the Commission. Title VII establishes an EU-wide database for stand-alone high-risk AI systems with mainly fundamental rights implications. Title VIII sets out the monitoring and reporting obligations for providers of AI systems with respect to post-market monitoring, reporting, and investigating of AI-related incidents and malfunctioning. Title IX formulates a framework for the creation of codes of conduct, which should be applied voluntarily by the providers of non-high-risk AI systems, but are mandatory for high-risk AI systems providers. Titles X, XI, and XII contain the final provisions. As we can see, therefore, the overall approach is a cross-sectoral one, where the issues of the algorithmisation of finance have not been given a sectoral treatment.

The European regulatory approach to algorithmic tools, and AI, in particular, differs substantially from the approach taken by the US. The US approach is based on a reliance on soft standards and certifications rather than unified rules or sector-specific regulation. There is a plethora of fragmentary regulations at the federal and state level (Yoo and Lai, 2020). In February 2019, President Trump signed Executive Order 13859 on Maintaining American Leadership in Artificial Intelligence. This document represented the first step towards a coordinated federal strategy – the American AI Initiative. It is basically focused on the R&D aspects of AI and the need for the US to maintain a key role in this regard. The Biden administration has not yet presented its plans with respect to AI. Apart from the general federal initiatives mentioned above, we should perhaps also mention the regulatory initiatives in certain sectors, namely those of the Food and Drug Administration (FDA) and the Department of Transportation (DOT). In 2019, the FDA released its regulatory proposal on software as a medical device, while in 2020 the DOT published its framework for autonomous vehicles. Additionally, state-level regulations, particularly on consumer-related issues and data protection, are also taking place.

1.6 Concluding remarks

As evidenced from our analysis, regulatory issues in the area of digital finance are gathering momentum. However, it is clear they are still only at the initial stages. This is a result of their complexity, the lack of empirical evidence, and their relative novelty. There is also an understanding that proper coordination with the old analogue financial regulation is necessary to avoid inconsistencies and regulatory arbitrage. As we have indicated, the approaches to the regulation of digital finance are very diversified among the major jurisdictions, not so much with regard to the content but more in connection with the frameworks and processes. The EU favours big-ticket hard regulatory solutions, whereas the US and some other jurisdictions prefer the piecemeal and soft approach. In any case, due to the global nature of digitalisation, a strong demand for global regulatory standards is present.

References

BIS (2019), *Annual Economic Report*, Chapter III, June.

Bundeskartellamt (2019), *Algorithms and Competition*, Bundeskartellamt and Autorité de la concurrence, November.

CRS (2019), *Data Protection Law: An Overview*, Congressional Research Service, 25 March.

CRS (2021), *Digital Assets and SEC Regulation*, 23 June.

EU Commission (2020), Proposal for a Regulation of the European Parliament and of the Council on Markets in Crypto-assets, and amending Directive (EU) 2019/1937.

EU Commission (2021), Proposal for a Regulation of the European Parliament and of the Council laying down harmonised rules on artificial intelligence (Artificial Intelligence Act), COM (2021) 206 final.

European Parliament (2020), Crypto-assets: Key developments, regulatory concerns and responses, Study requested by the ECON committee, April.

European Parliament (2020a), New aspects and challenges in consumer protection: Digital services and artificial intelligence, Study by the IMCO committee, April.

FATF (2019), FATF Report to G20 Leaders' Summit, June.

Federal Reserve Board (2020), Corbae, D. and D'Erasmo, P., *Rising Bank Concentration*, Staff Paper 594, FRB of Minneapolis.

FSB (2019), *Bigtech in Finance: Market Developments and Potential Financial Stability Implications*, Basel.

FSI (2021), Crisanto, J.C. et al., *Big Techs in Finance: Regulatory Approaches and Policy Options*, FSI Briefs, No. 12, March.

FSI (2021a), Crisanto, J.C. et al., *Big Tech Regulation: What Is Going On?*, FSI Insights, No. 36, September.

Hassan, S. and De Filippi, P. (2017), *The Expansion of Algorithmic Governance: From Code Is Law to Law Is Code*, Field Actions Science Reports, Special Issue 17.

IMF (2022), Bains, P. et al., *Bigtech in Financial Services: Regulatory Approaches and Architecture*, Fintech Notes, 2022/002.

IMF (2021), Haksar, V. et al., *Toward a Global Approach to Data in the Digital Age*, Staff Discussion Note (SDN), October.

IMF (2019), Cuervo, C. et al., *Regulation of Crypto Assets*, Fintech Notes, 2019/003.

OECD (2021), *Artificial Intelligence, Machine Learning and Big Data in Finance*, Paris.

Regulation EU (2016), Regulation (EU) 2016/679 of the European Parliament and of the Council of 27 April 2016 on the protection of natural persons with regard to the processing of personal data and on the free movement of such data, and repealing Directive 95/46/EC.

Sławiński, A. (2019), "Czy i na ile można liczyć na zmiany w systemach bankowych?", in: Hausner, J. and Paprocki, W. (eds), *Dewiacje Finansjalizacji*, CeDeWu, Warsaw.

Szpringer, W. (2020), *Platformy cyfrowe i gospodarka współdzielenia*, Poltext, Warsaw.

US House of Representatives (2020), Investigation of Competition in Digital Markets, Subcommittee on Antitrust, Commercial and Administrative Law of the Committee on the Judiciary.
WEF (2018), *The Appropriate Use of Customer Data in Financial Services.*
WEF (2017), *Digital Transformation Initiative: Unlocking B2B Platform Value*, March.
Yoo, C.S. and Lai, A. (2020), *Regulation of Algorithmic Tools in the United States*, University of Pennsylvania Carey Law School.

2 The digital finance in central banking

Leszek Jerzy Jasiński

2.1 The electronic money

Generally, digital money can be defined in three ways. First, this is the time when payment has only an electronic record; second, the digital money leads to conducting all financial operations with computer technologies; and third this becomes common that decisions in financial institutions are automated and for this purpose, the artificial intelligence is widely implemented (Jürgens, Hoffmann, Schildmann 2018). We are interested in the economic aspects of the transition of finance toward the electronic, non-cash forms of money, which has a big impact on many areas of social life (Baader 2020).

Electronic or digital money (*e-money*) is a monetary stock or a stock similar to the money in computer, Internet, or card files (Gąsiorkiewicz, Monkiewicz 2020). It has no physical form which is typical of other kinds of money (Focardi 2018). Because of this any money or medium of exchange of goods, similar to money, other than banknotes or coins is electronic money. If we accept this definition, a big range of resources, including cryptocurrencies and virtual currencies, will be embraced in this concept (Gąsiorkiewicz, Monkiewicz 2020).

One can argue if the two last-mentioned mediums are typical of money. Generally, virtual currencies, with some exceptions, are not a legal medium of payment. But it is not very important in our analysis if they are really mediums of money from the point of view of the financial law.

Electronic money can be understood in a narrow sense. It means this is a purchasing power on pre-paid cards which makes it possible for users to pay without making any banking operation at this very moment. An example of this kind of electronic money is an electronic purse for fares in the public transport system. Another understanding of electronic money will arrive later when we will interpret the statistical data.

The classification can be studied by introducing various criteria, not restricted only to the electronic form of money. In Table 2.1, four criteria are established to distinguish between currencies: who is an emitter? what is a form of money? are means of payment easily available and do they operate on a face-to-face basis? In Table 2.1, cryptocurrencies and virtual currencies,

DOI: 10.4324/9781003310082-5

Table 2.1 The taxonomy of money from the point of view of four criteria: money emission by the central bank, electronic form of money, its common availability, face-to-face operations

Kind of money	*Central bank*	*Electronics*	*Availability*	*Face-to-face*
Reserves at centarl bank	X	X	–	–
Digital currency of central bank	X	X	X	–
Bank deposits	–	X	X	–
Cash	X	–	X	–
Commodity money	–	–	X	X
Local money	–	–	–	X
Virtual money	–	X	X	–
Cryptocurrencies (retail)	–	X	–	X
Cryptocurrencies (wholesale)	–	X	–	X
Cryptocurrencies of central bank (retail)	X	X	–	X
Cryptocurrencies of central bank (wholesale)	X	X	X	X

Source: Bech, Garratt (2017).

even though they do not fulfill all functions of money, were included. These two should be rather called investment assets (Gilder 2015).

In Poland, electronic money is the subject of regulation by the act on payment services since 2011. To settle this kind of transaction, it is necessary to have the permission of the Financial Supervision Authority. In the European Union, these money operations are regulated by the directive of the Parlament and the Council on electronic money institutions from 2009.

2.2 Digital technologies and the essence of money

Any money must fulfill properly its functions. A well-graded unit of payment must be satisfactory in view of universally accepted criteria. If the position of a given money from these two points of view is satisfactory, we have a good currency. How these properties will eventually change when money becomes a digital currency?

Money fulfills three functions (Handa 2007). It is a medium of exchange, that is when traded it is an equivalent of all wares. It serves also as a measure of value, which means it makes it possible to determine prices. Money is also a store of purchasing power. If this did not happen, no savings could occur in the economy and no part of the current income could be pooled for future payments.

It should also be effective in a given sense. The transfer of purchasing power must take place in a safe way. The inflation rate must be low and predictable. The currency must be legally exchanged for other currencies and the exchange rate should not be a subject of volatility: sharp rises and drops are inadvisable. In other words, fulfilling basic functions must be accompanied by keeping high internal and external values, necessary for domestic and foreign settlements. There is always one more desired characteristic of money: confidence. Economic agents must trust that in the long run they will make business with the money they just use.

Do digital technologies reshape the essence of money? Do contemporary legal tenders, both cash and electronic ones, fulfill the functions of money well? Are they equally efficient, as some time ago in economic history, records in paper books typical of the banking sector?

Generally, we can say that there is no big difference between these two financial manners. The best evidence that all goes well in the world economy is the expansion of both kinds of money. If the non-cash and electronic money were seen as something worse than cash, the first two would become a margin of economic activities. The new financial technologies do not change the essence of money. Even if there is some change, we do not face a completely new situation.

The transformation of the financial system starts with the velocity of money. Consequently, this changes at least partly the way money fulfills its function of a medium of exchange and to some extent other functions too.

How the velocity of money can be altered? We must recall the quantity theory of money (Barro, Grilli 1994). It is one of the oldest economic theories and describes how the internal value of money is determined. The modern version of the theory is: we have the following so-called equation of exchange (Fisher equation, Froyen 1990):

$$MV = PT,$$

where M stands for the money supply, V for the velocity of money, P for the price level and T for the supply of products on the market (Pietras 2013). The quantity theory of money states the equality of two flows: the available supply of money, which is the left-hand side of the dependency, and of the money just spent, which can be found on the right-hand side of the equality.

The Irving Fisher theory was commented on in many ways. In the short run, the velocity V is stable. So is the supply of products T. These two developments are caused by consumer preferences and the lack of quick reactions of the firms to changes in their environment. The volatility is the case of money supply M and price level P too, which makes us conclude that the increase of money supply brings the drop in the value of money. This is how the problem was analyzed by neoclassical economists.

Keynesians were of the opinion that the increase in money supply can lead to a lowering of the velocity V and, partly, a change of the bulk of products T. For them in the Fisher equation all parameters were not fixed. Monetarists declared that the parameter M did influence the parameter V. As regards the relation between M and T they were of a different opinion: the change of money supply M has no impact on production T. Some exceptions are possible but for the short run.

We assume in our analysis, which is not exploring the future very far from the point we are now, that the product *PT*, the real value of available goods and services, and money supply *M* are exogenous. They influence what is happening in the market as an effect of the action of suppliers and of the monetary policy. These parameters are mutually adjusted by the money velocity *V*.

If the Fisher equation describes the long-term trends, its understanding needs to assume that the creation of real value *PT* and of money supply *M* are all the time stable. This does not have to happen in the real life. The way the central bank of a country performs its policy can change. The GDP, and also the product *PT*, are cyclical values. The parameter *V* is a resultant force of many determinants, and the velocity of money is only one of them.

2.3 Cash or electronic money?

The convenience of using cash can be easily assessed when comparing it to cashless payment systems. Cash is heavy, and has a large capacity and it is necessary to count the amount before making a payment. It can be lost, stolen or faked. Very often it is not in line with the hygiene requirements. Expenditures to produce and distribute cash are substantial. Simultaneously cash makes payments anonymous, but sometimes this can lead to suspicion of spending dirty money. Today using cash can manifest to many people as a sign of a lack of prosperity. One cannot leave tips with digital money, which in some countries are the main source of income for employees in the catering business. Cash is also convenient when enforcing charity and during all kinds of public collections.

The non-cash money is inconvenient in many ways too. It is hard to lose it, but it also can be stolen or faked. It also needs money to make and have such new money. Cash-free settlements are operational, provided necessary computer and security systems are implemented. If interest rates are negative, as it was in 2018 in Denmark and Switzerland, the cost of non-cash operations increases. This would not happen if coins and notes were circulated.

The economic analysis states what should be preferential for all kinds of money. The key concept is an alternative cost. In the case of finance, this will be the cost of depositing money at a bank instead of using notes and coins.

Cash money is especially well seen by a number of small retail traders. For these economic agents, the cost of installing electronic devices can be a barrier. So is also, naturally, the position of illegal traffic: attempts to avoid paying taxes and running illegal economic activities.

It is worth noticing that in 1994 in Los Angeles around three-quarters of notes were contaminated with cocaine or other drugs. In the United Kingdom at the same time, similar research gave evidence that the contamination ratio was 80%. In 1999 in London, totally cocaine-free were just 0.8% of notes. In 2003, during the SARS epidemic, the 24-hours quarantine of notes was introduced. This time it was a necessity to get viruses disintegrated. In Germany, many euro notes crumbled when withdrawing from ATMs. The reason for this was the contamination by a substance which included a sulfate. The heat of hands activated the sulfur acid which did devastate fibers from which notes were made.

Many countries worldwide have entered the era of polymeric notes. The material used in the production process is usually biaxial-orientated polypropylene taken together with the segmented ink. This makes the time of using notes longer. It is a better solution for environmental protection which reduces the cost of production and distribution. When first such notes started to circulate, it was a common opinion that forgers will have to face much more difficulties to do their job than it was earlier.

The list of countries, where polymer notes were emitted, is quite long. We shall mention some of them, including these, where new notes were issued occasionally: Albania, Angola, Botswana, Canada, Chile, Gambia, Guatemala, Haiti, Hong Kong, Israel, Kuwait, Lebanon, Lybia, Mauretania, Meksyk, Mozambique, Morocco, New Zealand, Nicaragua, North Macedonia, Papua New Guinea, Poland, Russia, Romania, Saudi Arabia, Singapore, United Kingdom and Vietnam. The first country to move in this direction was Australia, where the change took place in 1996. This list includes countries differentiated from the point of view of economic development. The number of advanced countries is rather small.

The new form of cash points that the non-digital arrangement will still be used for many years. Making cash more convenient and safer will prolong the time of paper money.

There are also hybrid notes which could be called paper-polymer ones. Again the list of countries where they are available is long and they are not on the same level of growth and development. The first such note was issued in Bulgaria.

2.4 Faltering position of cash

The first virtual bank branch was opened in 1995 by the Nationwide Building Society (Dobosiewicz 2003). In 2003, in the United Kingdom, the value of sales using credit and debit cards was larger than that using cash. In 2015, sales of all consumer goods by means of credit and debit cards was thrice bigger.

In March 2015, the number of cash transactions in Britain was for the first time lower than the number of non-cash transactions. In 2014 the value of cash transactions, between big firms and banks, was only close to 3% of "automatic" transactions. From 2014, cash transactions ceased to exist in London buses.

In 2008 in Sweden, the country leading in cashless sales, 110 bank robberies were reported. In 2011, the number of these crimes was 11. The decrease in such criminal assaults appeared to be a permanent trend (Rooney 2019).

The symbol of the new position of cash was the lack of glasses which for a great many years used to separate customers from employees in the operating rooms of banks. Today dealing with cash needs a small part of existing banking facilities and is a sign of a special treatment given to a customer.

South Korea is moving step by step to eliminate cash or at least to make it a rare instrument of commercial operations. The progress is not very quick, but in the last few years, the supply of coins is going down and down. They do not come in handy. It is customary to make a change, received when shopping, for a bigger amount on the customer's card. The Korean coin od the highest face value is equivalent of US 45 cents. This is not something new in the world of today. China made huge progress when they decided to switch over to digital. (Turrin 2021).

The inauguration of state money in digital form is a subject of analysis by the Swedish central bank. The arrangement to come was already called e-krona. What makes it different from non-cash money, being a record on bank accounts, is that its securement will come from the central bank, not from a capacity to go bankrupt financial institution. This plan looks realististic. Two developments speak for this: the rapid increase of mobile payments in the country and the dismantlement of many ATMs, also in small towns and villages.

In the middle of 2022, no final decision regarding e-krona was made. If this happens, cash will not stop immediately its circulation. There is no announcement that such a withdrawal will for sure take place sometime later. The Swedish central bank has already declared that notes and coins will be emitted as long as demand for them remains in the economy and society. It was decided in December 2020 that in November 2022 a comprehensive study on the e-krona will be published.

In Poland, it is not compulsory for entrepreneurs to have a bank account, but starting from 2018, there is a legal limit on the value of transactions settled in cash. Any payment when running a business must be done with a bank account or with cash, in the second case provided its value does not exceed 15,000 zlotys, no matter how many payment operations are performed. In payments done in foreign money, the value of transactions is to be converted into zlotys using current exchange rates.

It is a common expectation that the total withdrawal from cash will happen in many countries approximately in 2030. There is no formal declaration in this point and what will really take place is an open question.

2.5 Withdrawal from cash and the GDP growth

The analysis made in 2015 demonstrates that the elimination of cash in the USA will increase the GDP by 0.47% (Rooney 2019). This means that the long-term growth rate in this country can be significantly larger. This kind of economic estimate is usually debatable, mainly because of assumptions which are fundamentals of analysis. Nevertheless, this specific thesis looks convincing. Why is it so?

We should go back to the definition of the gross domestic product (Jasiński 2021). This aggregate usually does not include non-registered economic activity (Kwiatkowski, Milewski 2007). Consequently, the GDP does not show the Do It Yourself (DIY), that is the production on the basis *do it yourself*, which includes the casual, paid help for neighbors and the large informal sector of the economy.

The second element of the DIY is of big importance for the analysis of the results of the cash withdrawal. We must distinguish between casual and permanent DIY. If it is permanent, we have a case of informal economic activity. This can be easily changed when non-cash payments become a standard. If so there will be hardly any ground for calling this a transfer payment. Under new circumstances, it will become clear this is a normal payment with some contribution to the GDP. This way the formal growth rate will be bigger, which will not happen if many activities stay informal.

Consequently, the budget receipts will also grow. The income and indirect taxes will get larger. This, once again, will work positively for the GDP growth. The development we describe would not be caused by the growth of number of products but by the new systemic arrangement.

The quantitative easing has grown as a vital instrument of today's monetary policy (Jasiński 2021). For the first time, it was implemented in Japan in the last decade of the twentieth century. Later this was repeated in the USA, the UK and the euro area. The quantitative easing consists in a one-time substantial increase of the monetary base M0, which is followed by the increase of the money supply M1. The first monetary aggregate consists of all cash money and balances on accounts at the central bank. If the monetary base M0 is attached by current accounts at commercial banks, we receive the second aggregate: the money at any moment ready to finance economic transactions. This is the supply of transaction money M1 (Jasiński 2017).

To make the base M0 bigger the central bank buys large quantities of securities, usually treasury bonds. This way it makes it possible to enlarge crediting economic agents and also to lower interest rates and indirectly expand general prosperity (Choudhry 2012). This is one of the methods the government can influence the GDP, especially in times of recession, the threat of recession or stagnation.

The effect of the quantitative easing is that all money added to the amount already operating is non-cash. This action increases electronic balances of bank accounts. This is sufficient to achieve accepted objectives and to buy back securities. Quantitative easing is a non-conventional instrument of monetary policy. Its effectiveness gives rise to controversy. The set of methods in the monetary policy, which has to stabilize the level of the GDP, was enriched by the new remedy which needs no cash. To make the economy more active one does not have to drop cash to financially idle areas from helicopters.

2.6 The statistical picture of all kinds of money

In 1987 Robert Solow (Solow 1987) mentioned: "You can see the computer era everywhere but the productivity statistics". Significance of this observation is crucial to make any general judgment of the economic state of the art.

Nonetheless, the effects of transforming technology should not be reduced to productivity: new devices change the technology and economy in many ways. In economic analysis, productivity will always take the first place.

Will a novelty, that is non-cash money, dynamize the economy? Will the economic effectiveness grow? Will prosperity grow? Explicit conclusions in these points are difficult to find.

In the late 2020s world leaders in cash-free operations were considered to be Sweden and Somaliland, two countries of quite different economic advancement. The latter one is not worldwide recognized diplomatically, despite being a democratic country, a successor of the failed state: Somalia. The economy of Somaliland, which does not belong to the advanced systems, is built to much extent on money transfers from abroad. There is a general agreement that this is a stable system.

The following tables present the relative position of cash in the United States and the euro area. We trace two aggregates: the monetary base M0 and the money supply M1. The M0 has two components: cash and reserve balances. We shall monitor the relations between these two macroeconomic variables. We start with the USA, later we shall describe the euro area (Table 2.2).

In the USA in the second part of 2019 and 2020, which is rather a short period of time, the relations between cash, reserve money, monetary base and money supply M1 have changed significantly. Generally, the share of cash became evidently smaller.

Table 2.3 illustrates the relation of cash to money supply M1.

If we consider the period 2001–2019, the share of cash in the money M1 has lowered. This was happening slowly, but systematically. In the second part of 2019 and 2020 this transformation speeded up.

The data in Table 2.4 give evidence that from 2001 to 2019 the relation of cash to the GDP did not change much in the USA. At the end of the period, it was bigger than at the beginning. This happened for a number of reasons. Probably the main reason was the asymetric dynamics of monetary

Table 2.2 The relation of cash to reserve balances (C/R), cash to monetary base (C/MB) and cash to money supply M1 (C/M1) in the USA, August 2019–December 2020

Time	*C/R*	*C/MB*	*C/M1*	*Time*	*C/R*	*C/MB*	*C/M1*
VIII 2019	1.151	0.535	0.455	V 2020	0.600	0.375	0.385
IX 2019	1.224	0.550	0.455	VI 2020	0.643	0.392	0.375
X 2019	1.196	0.545	0.452	VII 2020	0.729	0.422	0.372
XI 2019	1.168	0.539	0.455	VIII 2020	0.717	0.418	0.374
XII 2019	1.102	0.524	0.445	IX 2020	0.711	0.415	0.371
I 2020	1.092	0.522	0.452	X 2020	0.709	0.415	0.366
II 2020	1.085	0.520	0.456	XI 2020	0.679	0.404	0.343
III 2020	0.899	0.473	0.429	XII 2020	0.661	0.398	0.306
IV 2020	0.640	0.390	0.390				

Source: Author's calculations using www.federalreseve.gov

aggregates and the GDP, caused by the active, counter-cyclical monetary policy of that time.

The relation shown in Table 2.4 can be understood as the velocity of money we have defined and discussed earlier. Our calculations point to a limited, but noticeable, increase in the velocity. One should not be surprised by this: non-cash money, recorded and electronically transferred, is circulating in the economy quicker than cash (Table 2.5).

Table 2.3 The relation of cash to money supply M1 in the USA in 2001–2019, percentage, the situation at the end of year

Year	*Relation*	*Year*	*Relation*	*Year*	*Relation*
2001	51.6	2008	53.7	2014	44.3
2002	53.0	2009	52.6	2015	44.7
2003	52.8	2010	50.8	2016	43.9
2004	52.8	2011	48.0	2017	43.5
2005	55.5	2012	45.8	2018	44.6
2006	56.8	2013	45.4	2019	44.2
2007	57.5				

Source: Author's calculations using www./fred.stlouisfed.org and www.fedralreserve.gov

Table 2.4 The relation of money supply M1 to GDP (nominal) in the USA in 2001–2019, percentage.

Year	*M1/GDP*	*Year*	*M1/GDP*	*Year*	*M1/GDP*
2001	10.8	2008	9.7	2014	16.1
2002	10.9	2009	11.3	2015	16.6
2003	11.1	2010	11.6	2016	17.4
2004	11.0	2011	12.9	2017	18.0
2005	10.5	2012	14.3	2018	17.9
2006	9.9	2013	15.2	2019	17.9
2007	9.5				

Source: Author's calculations using www.federalreseve.gov

Table 2.5 The relation of cash to money supply M1 in euro area in 2001–2017, percentage, the situation at the end of year

Year	*Relation*	*Year*	*Relation*	*Year*	*Relation*
2001	12.9	2007	16.0	2013	16.9
2002	13.6	2008	17.8	2014	16.4
2003	14.4	2009	16.9	2015	15.7
2004	15.6	2010	17.0	2016	14.2
2005	15.4	2011	17.7	2017	14.2
2006	15.9	2012	17.0		

Source: The author's calculations using www.ebc.europa.eu

In the case of the euro area, the relation of cash to the GDP was in 2001–2017 more stable than in the United States. For the two areas, the trend was the same: going down the relation of cash to money supply M1.

It is estimated that around 20% of the total value of emitted euro notes circulates outside the euro area countries and about half of American notes have left for good in the USA. This indicates that the importance of cash in both monetary areas is in fact much smaller than one can think after examining the statistics.

The main argument which illustrates the purchasing power of economic agents is the money supply M1. The monetary aggregate called the monetary base M0 is only a part of the supply M1. In turn, cash is a part of the monetary base M0. This means that cash is a minor component of resources located in the economy which determine the total purchasing power. The lion's share of the supply M1 is money recorded and transferred electronically, and it is electronic money in a wide sense. Let us make the long story short: digital money dominates the financial system.

2.7 The position of electronic money in Poland

What is the share of cash in financial operations in Poland? It the position of Poland different from that in the euro area and the USA? Table 2.6 gives some idea about cash and money supply in this country in the last few years.

It follows from Table 2.6 that the changes in both aggregates have reached a similar pace. Table 2.7 informs about the share of cash in supply.

Table 2.6 The dynamics of cash and money supply M1 in Poland in 2008–2020, end of the year, the previous year = 100

Years	*Cash*	*M1*	*Years*	*Cash*	*M1*
2008	118.79	104.38	2015	114.22	114.16
2009	98.21	110.97	2016	114.94	117.80
2020	102.71	115.67	2017	105.94	111.17
2011	108.94	104.20	2018	110.47	111.69
2012	101.40	103.58	2019	108.80	114.08
2013	110.99	114.65	2020	134.81	132.62
2014	113.33	109.08			

Source: Author's calculation using .nbp.pl

Table 2.7 The relation of cash to money supply M1 in Poland in 2007–2020, end of the year, percentage

Years	*Relation*	*Years*	*Relations*	*Years*	*Relation*
2007	25.5	2012	23.4	2017	21.9
2008	29.1	2013	22.6	2018	21.7
2009	25.7	2014	23.5	2019	20.6
2020	22.9	2015	23.5	2020	21.0
2011	23.9	2016	23.0		

Source: Author's calculation using .nbp.pl

Table 2.8 The relation of cash to GDP in Poland in 2010–2019

Lata	*Relacja*	*Lata*	*Relacja*	*Lata*	*Relacja*
2010	7.10	2014	8.30	2017	9.97
2011	7.14	2015	9.11	2018	10.34
2012	6.96	2016	10.08	2019	10.49
2013	7.60				

Source: Author's calculation using .nbp.pl and www.stat.gov.pl

In Poland, the share of cash is high but step by step goes down (Table 2.8). From 2010 to 2019, paradoxically, the relation of cash to the GDP has grown. This development should be seen from the point of view of the combination of monetary resources of all kinds and the general level of economic activity.

2.8 The expansion of electronic money in the narrower sense of the word

We have already mentioned that electronic money can be understood in two ways. First, this will be any stock of money or something close to money provided it is included in computer, Internet and card bases. Second, this will be any stock of pre-paid cards which make it possible to pay without using bank accounts. At this very moment, we are interested in the second arrangement.

The Directive of the European Parlament and of the Council of 16 September 2009 on the taking up, pursuit and prudential supervision of the business of electronic money institutions uses two concepts and definitions:

- the institution of electronic money: a legal person which is entitled to issue electronic money,
- electronic money: the value which can be obtained electronically, including magnetically, giving ground for claims toward the emitter, and emitted in return for purchasing power to make payments, accepted by natural and legal persons other than the emitter of the electronic money.

How strong is the position of electronic money defined in the above way? The statistical presentation is limited to the euro area and the EU member states.

Data in Table 2.9 show that the electronic money supply grew quickly. It did not take a lot of time for them to increase by 40%.

The number of transactions with electronic money was differentiated in 2018 in the EU countries (Table 2.10). It is hardly difficult to explain this phenomenon while it is an effect of dissimilar economic development in all dimensions.

The structure of cashless payments in euro area countries in 2008 and 2018 is shown in Tables 2.11 and 2.12. The frequency of using e-money has changed in that time. For example in Germany at the beginning, it was already low and at the very end of the period, it became even lower.

Table 2.9 The dynamics of electronic money in euros, the position in the previous year = 100

Year	*Dynamics*	*Year*	*Dynamics*	*Year*	*Dynamics*
2013	117.5	2016	119.7	2018	111.2
2014	117.0	2017	112.7	2019	140.4
2015	120.0				

Source: Author's calculations using www.statista.com

Table 2.10 The number of transactions when electronic money was used in some EU countries in 2018, was millions of transactions

Countries	*Transactions*	*Countries*	*Transactions*
Luxembourg	2993.8	Germany	33.5
Italy	739.0	Croatia	5.5
Portugal	72.3	Austria	4.4
France	61.5	Sweden	4.4
Belgium	48.7	Netherlands	0.6
Greece	36.1		

Source: www.statista.com

Table 2.11 The structure of non-cash payments in some euro area countries in 2008 number of payments, %

Forms of payment	*Countries*
E-money	Luxembourg 70.8%, Germany 0.3%, Portugal 0.1
Payments with cards	Portugal 64.3%, Malta 36.1%, Slovakia 24.3%, Germany 14.4%, Luxembourg 11.5%
Cheques	Malta 42.6%, Portugal 10.7%, Luxembourg 0.0%, Germany 0.4%, Slovakia 0.0%
Direct debits	Germany 49.5%, Slovakia 17.0%, Portugal 14.3%, Malta 3.8%, Luxembourg 3.2%
Credit transfer	Slovakia 58.7%, Germany 35.4%, Malta 17.6%, Luxembourg 14.4%, Portugal 10.5%
Other payments	Portugal 0.1%

Source: www.euro-area-statistics.org

Table 2.13 shows the structure of payments in the euro area. Between 2008 and 2018 the position of e-money grew substantially. Still, this is a marginal part of all payments.

Table 2.12 The structure of non-cash payments in some euro area countries in 2018, number of payments, %

Forms of payments	*Countries*
E-money	Luxembourg 91.8%, Malta 4.5%, Portugal 2.9%, Slovakia 0.2%, Germany 0.1%
Payments with cards	Portugal 70.5%, Germany 23.4%, Luxembourg 5.3%
Cheques	Portugal 1.9%, Luxembourg 0.0%, Germany 0.0%, Slovakia 0.0%
Direct debits	Germany 46.9%, Portugal 9.7%, Luxembourg 0.6%
Credit transfer	Slovakia 43.6%, Germany 28.5%, Malta 24.0%, Luxembourg 21.4%, Portugal 11.9%
Other payments	Portugal 3.0%, Germany 1.1%, Malta 0.8%, Luxembourg 0.0%

Source: www.euro-area-statistics.org

Table 2.13 The structure of non-cash payments in the euro area in 2008 and 2018, number of payments %

Form of payments	*2008*	*2018*
E-money	1.4	4.4
Payments with cards	32.6	45.6
Cheques	8.0	2.3
Direct debits	30.0	22.7
Credit transfer	27.1	23.2
Other payments	0.9	1.8

Source: www.euro-area-statistics.org

2.9 What is to happen in the future

The new information and communication technologies do not and will not omit the financial sector. Today electronically stored money dominates, which does not mean that the era of coins and banknotes is over. All we know about financial operations points that the cash will still circulate but its role will be smaller. There is some evidence that cash withdrawal works positively for economic growth, nevertheless only to some extent. The expansion of many forms of electronic money is moving ahead mainly due to the common desire to get payments easier and quicker.

References

R. Baader, *Koniec Pieniądza Papierowego*, DeReggio, Warszawa 2020.

R. Barro, V. Grilli, *European Macroeconomics*, Macmillan, London 1994.

M.L. Bech, R. Garratt, *Central Bank Cryptocurrencies*, BIS Quarterly Review, September 2017.

M. Choudhry, *The Principles of Banking*, Wiley, New York 2012.
Z. Dobosiewicz, *Bankowość*, PWE, Warszawa 2003.
S.M. Focardi, *Money*, Routledge, London 2018.
R.T. Froyen, *Macroeconomics: Theories and Policies*, Macmillan Publishing Company, New York 1990.
G. Gilder, *Standard złota w epoce pieniądza cyfrowego. Informacyjna teoria pieniądza*, Fijor, Warszawa 2015.
J. Handa, *Monetary Economics*, Routledge, Milton Park 2007.
Innowacje na rynkach finansowych, L.Gąsiorkiewicz, J.Monkiewicz (red.), OWPW, Warszawa 2020.
L.J. Jasiński, *System Finansowy*, OWPW, Warszawa 2017.
L.J. Jasiński, *Finanse współczesne. Wybrane zagadnienia*, OWPW, Warszawa 2021.
K. Jürgens, R. Hoffmann, C. Schildmann, *Let's Transform Work! Recommendations and Proposals from the Commission on the Work of the Future*, Hans Böckler Stiftung, Düsseldorf 2018.
E. Kwiatkowski, R. Milewski, *Podstawy ekonomii*, PWN, Warszawa 2007.
C. Pietras, *System pieniężno-kredytowy*, w; *Makro- i mikroekonomia*, S.Marciniak (red.), PWN, Warszawa 2013.
A. Rooney, *Think Like an Economist. Get to Grips with Money and Markets*, Arcturus, London 2019.
R. Solow, *We'd Better Watch Out*, "The New York Times Books Review", July 12, 1987.
R. Turrin, *Cashless: China's Digital Currency Revolution*, Authority Publishing, Village Marketplace 2021.

3 Digital transformation of financial institutions

Marcin Kotarba

3.1 Introduction

Both academic and industrial discussions of the digital transformation of financial institutions are filled with visible excitement over the unavoidability and impact of the digital revolution. They are filled with impressive research results, where percentage points easily activate the appetite for delivering beneficial changes in our own (as employees or clients) institutions. Leading research and consulting companies provide claims on the widespread visibility and importance of digital transformation, e.g. 69% of institutions declare that digitalization is accelerating (Gartner, 2022), 74% of chief information officers (CIOs) increase the pace of digitalization and create the next generation operating model (KPMG, 2022), 68% of financial services companies have developed a digital transformation strategy (BDO, 2022), 75% of Accenture focus groups claim to be excited about the future of digital experiences (Fjord, 2022), 70% of banks are reviewing their core banking platforms to make room for more digitalization (Lhuer et al., 2019), 80% managers said digital is helping to survive the pandemic (BCG, 2022) and 88% of 60 leading European banks have already started or plan the end-to-end process digitalization (Roland Berger, 2021). With these few examples and the results around the impressive 70% or more, there are no doubts that financial institutions are subject to strong strategic change pressure and the need to rethink the ways financial services are offered. At the same time on the opposite side of the excitement we can place a number of doubts and essential questions, for example: what does the digitalization of finance mean in practical terms and how does it differ from the past decades of technological advancement in financial services? Is it a new phenomenon or a well-established pattern that is simply experiencing new waves of evolution thanks to overall technological progress? In this chapter we take a look at digitalization from a pragmatic perspective, aiming to describe the essence of the concept and to provide a view of its future development. The study is focused on the observations from the European Union economic ecosystem and its regulatory framework for financial services.

DOI: 10.4324/9781003310082-6

3.2 The substance of digitalization

Before we start the analysis in the context of financial services, we need to take a brief look at the definition of digitalization itself. The role of the great ancestor of digitalization needs to be attributed to "digitization", understood as the conversion of the analog form of various artifacts into a digital form that allows arithmetical machine processing. The word "digit" refers to the binary notation invented by the great G. Leibniz[1] who laid the foundation for modern, transistor-based computing. The heritage of the 1980s and 1990s gave digitization a powerful momentum, mainly with digital photography, scanning and optical character recognition (OCR) as well as compressed sound (e.g. the mp3 format). While extremely expensive at the beginning, high levels of competition and technological advancement, especially in microprocessor speeds, volume and performance of storage, connectivity (including mobile), operating systems (e.g. Windows and UNIX/Linux) as well as battery life extension, brought a true smart-device revolution. Forty years later, we are living in the reality of "digital first" where omnipresent digital sensors not only capture the content in a digital form but are also storing it in cloud-based solutions. The 1980s and 1990s created new generations of "digital immigrants" and "digital natives"[2] who over their lifetime respectively either migrated fully to the digital reality or simply have not even had a chance to enjoy the analog world of books, 35 mm camera film or sound played from the records. Naturally, these rising generations speak loudly in their digital-only voice, demanding further advancement of digital solutions offered by product and service providers. The analog and digital worlds still coexist quite well, with certain activities making it even back into the analog cradle. A perfect case study of such a situation can be seen in the development of lego blocks. Before the time of game devices and personal computers, youth would spend endless hours playing legos, enjoying a platform of creativity and expandability. Computer games have massively captured the time of the youth, resulting in the creation of one of the most successful game ventures in the world – the Minecraft (number one with respect to the number of licenses sold – 238 million, since its launch in 2009[3]). The game became a digital version of lego blocks, offering practically the infinite ability of construction of places and interactions, wrapped into a very lively biome, with seasons, days, fauna and flora (including creative monsters/organisms) and natural resources, all working based on impressive reflection of physics, chemistry and biology to simulate a real world, shareable with other users. Observing the competition from computer games, lego ventured into the digital world, launching a number of very successful lego block games, and partnering with powerful brands such as Star Wars, Harry Potter or the Pirates of the Caribbean. Turning the attention back to lego blocks via digital experiences brought a positive result on the sales of the analog version of the blocks, including successful new sets of Minecraft, with typical game scenes and heroes in their iconic cubicle form. This case study can be used to show that agile traditional (or analog) players, with strong strategic thinking, are capable of finding business and profitability in both the worlds of analog and digital.

In the discussion of popular digital case studies, it is easy to maneuver toward digital media, such as pictures, movies or sounds, however, the essence of the digital revolution for financial institutions was related to the digitization of customer, product and transaction data, which allowed the creation of elaborated databases and processing systems, including front ends and interfaces. With this in mind, we need to understand the advantages of the digital paradigm that stand behind its rapid and mass adoption. The following characteristics of digital reality are prominent:

1. **portability** – digital data can be stored and moved without the constraints of the physical form (e.g. a paper book needs to be delivered to a client via a logistical chain, an eBook can be downloaded from an Internet web site),
2. **replicability** – the potential to copy the digital data is practically limited only to the number and size of locations transmitting and storing it,
3. **redundancy** – provision of backup solutions to support the disaster recovery process,
4. **security/safety** – can be encrypted or managed with user rights to allow authorized access only,
5. **searchability** – by means of indexing digital data can be browsed for specific keywords and sorted according to user criteria,
6. **transformability** – once digitized the data can be processed to create another form, e.g. by SQL (Structured Query Language) operations on the database, image processing, pattern recognition,
7. **accessibility** – shorter time to access the data and to process it into the required form, for use in decision-making and communication,
8. **sustainability** – less natural resources are needed to create and store the digital assets, mainly referring to the cost of paper logistics,[4]
9. **interoperability and standardization** – simplifying and securing the data exchange internally and with the external world,
10. **cancellability** – digital assets which are no longer needed, can be easily disposed of or archived for future purposes, without significant environmental cost (e.g. landfill or recycling).

All of the above have the potential to improve the bottom line of any type of business, bringing in more efficiency and effectiveness of the processes and decision-making. We do have to mention that digitization also brings certain challenges, for example:

1. portability and replicability support piracy/illegal copying and distribution,
2. having multiple copies increases the risk of desynchronization of information,
3. certain standardization may lead to counterproductive effects (e.g. the case of Adobe Flash, the technology used by many organizations failed in the ability to keep up with the overall development),
4. ease of potential undetected manipulation may compromise the original (rightful) content of the form.

Naturally, with the benefits significantly outweighing the issues – the focus is to mitigate such risks, depending on their significance in the organization.

With clarity on the concept of "digitization" – we may now enter a discourse on the substance of its descendant, "digitalization". At first sight, both terms are very close, containing the same "digit" core and representing an activity – either undertaken or induced. In order to provide an unbiased interpretation of digitalization, let us take a look at definitions selected from a wide range of sophisticated perspectives and interests. Digitalization, among others, is described by research companies, scientists, commercial businesses and linguists as:

1 **business model change** – the use of digital technologies to change a business model and provide new revenue and value-producing opportunities; it is the process of moving to a digital business (Gartner[5]).
2 **social change** – the way in which many domains of social life are restructured around digital communication and media infrastructures (Brennen, J. and Kreis, D. in Bloomberg (2019)).
3 **data management activity** – data from throughout the organization and its assets is processed through advanced digital technologies, which leads to fundamental changes in business processes that can result in new business models and social change, that is, Systems, Applications and Products (SAP[6]),
4 **process of converting something to digital form**, the definition is the same as of digitization (Merriam-Webster Dictionary[7]),
5 **process of changing data into a digital form** that can be easily read and processed by a computer (Oxford Learner's Dictionary[8]),
6 **change of something such as a document to a digital form**, understood as a form that can be stored and read by computers (Cambridge Dictionary[9]),
7 **starting to use digital technology such as computers and the Internet to do something** (Cambridge Dictionary),
8 **using digital data** to simplify how you work (Salesforce.com[10]),
9 **ongoing integration of digital technologies and digitized data** across the economy and society (Eurofounds[11]),
10 **strategic implementation of digital technologies** (Citrix[12]),
11 **processes that change the way work is performed** (Vereinte Dienstleistungsgewerkschaft – Verdi, labor union[13]).

While looking at the above definitions of digitalization we may conclude that they are characterized by high variety, not leading to a conclusive mainstream view. Naturally, the definitions are subject to relevant contextualization, e.g. the labor union Verdi emphasizes the impact of digital technology on the humans-workers, their motivation and well-being while the technology giant SAP underlines the aspect of data management. Some definitions seem to be similar to digitization, while others move toward a higher level of abstraction, speaking about strategic or business model changes. This brings us to the point of placing "digital transformation" in the taxonomy of "all things digital". A common conception is that digital transformation reflects the highest level of dealing with digitization and digitalization, being its strategic planning and steering layer. This digital flow (frequently presented also as a pyramid) was presented by Kiron and Unruh (2017), aligning the digital terminology in the following way:

1 digitization is the conversion of products to the digital format (followed by resulting innovations),
2 digitalization is the innovation in business models and processes, aimed at benefiting from digitization,
3 digital transformation is the system-level restructuring of economies, institutions and societies that takes place due to the digitalization and widespread diffusion of digital technology.

This hierarchical flow shows how the base technology is impacting single elements of the ecosystem (e.g. companies, organizations and humans) leading to paradigm changes affecting entire populations and systems. At the same time a Harvard-based group of researchers suggests that digital transformation is not about technology, but rather about the adaptation of organizational behavior (Tabrizi et al., 2019). The authors point out the significance of strategic planning that should precede any technological investment and the necessity to drive the transformation based on a deep internal understanding of the business model rather than using external "one size fits all" logic. They also emphasize the need to properly address the human aspects of "being replaced by automation" as well as the necessity to modify the organizational culture to gain agility and the start-up mentality with rapid, prototype-oriented development and limited initial budgets. In the author's opinion, both views are complementary by providing the perspectives of "what" (the MIT Sloan publication) and "how" (Harvard), in the same spirit of taking proper decisions on the opportunities and risks offered by the implementation of digital technologies.

The above-presented flow: from digitization, through digitalization to digital transformation can be extended by a notion of the target form to be achieved from traveling along this digital path. The target shape may be represented by "digital reality", where digital entities (e.g. technology-equipped humans, artificial intelligence, "smart" devices[14]) interact with and within digital organizations, in the digital economy run by digital states. Naturally, a part of this new reality is "digital finance". The European Commission defines it as the "impact of new technologies on the financial services industry", including "a variety of products, applications, processes and business models that have transformed the traditional way of providing banking and financial services".[15] The World Bank uses a term "digital financial services" that rely on digital technologies for their delivery and use by consumers.[16] The emphasis of the financial "services" aspect is important to separate the ontology of the financial ecosystem from the internal finance and accounting function present in every organization that requires financial management. Naturally, for financial and insurance institutions both meanings are applicable and their digital transformation covers not only the business model (including products, channels and client segments) but also all support and control functions such as finance, procurement or human capital management. The coverage of both perspectives (sectoral and internal/organizational) should provide additional leverage in the benefits of digitalization for the operators of the financial ecosystems. Simply saying, the digital front office combined with digital partnerships and the digital back office opens up new possibilities for better information flow and usage in the decision processes.

Digital finance has a prominent place within the digital economy, not only being the natural front-runner of technological progress but also serving as the cradle of technology-driven innovation. In addition to incumbent financial institutions undergoing their digital transformation, a space on the market is being made for non-licensed ventures that build on technological superiority. This includes the "big tech" companies (e.g. Google or Apple) and "X-tech", e.g. fin(ancial)-tech, insur(ance)-tech or reg(ulatory)-tech. Such players focus on providing solutions that build on the available value chains by improving or extending them with new customer experiences, networking or powerful processing capabilities. The expansion of the financial ecosystem leads to higher competitiveness, market liberalization, increased coverage of the non-banked population and tighter integration of various financial services within the economy. The development of digital finance is actively moderated by financial services regulators, which recognize the inevitability of technological progress as a powerful source of new opportunities and threats for the financial ecosystem. Common practices of the regulators include:

1 establishing "digital finance" or "x-tech" departments which group experts including technology and data engineers, as well as legal experts in technology,
2 creation of catalytic regulations, e.g. the 2nd Payment Services Directive of the European Commission (PSD2[17]) which partially forces and partially encourages the development of open banking,
3 development of "regulatory sandboxes" where innovative companies can proof-run their prototypes against their future regulatory approval for usage on the market,
4 driving the setup of industry-wide technological standards for a more integrated financial sector with minimized waste of standards bridging,
5 acceleration of adopting base solutions needed to achieve the efficiency of the ecosystem (e.g. digital identity and signatures, digital rights and principles).

The positive involvement of the regulators in achieving the benefits of digitalization on a global scale is a part of a larger trend of digital interests and investments undertaken by public institutions such as governments or cross-country alliances like the EU. Digitalization is seen as a way to foster societal and economical progress while simplifying public administration. An excellent example of public policy and steering is seen in the digital strategy of the European Union, code-named "The Digital Decade" and introduced in March of 2021.[18] The aim of the EU is "to empower businesses and people in a human-centered, sustainable and more prosperous digital future". The following goals are envisioned by Europe by the end of the year 2030:

1 **Human capital and digital skills**: 20 million information and communications technology experts, convergence/balancing of the gender mix and basic digital skills to be displayed by a min 80% of the population.
2 **Secure and sustainable digital infrastructure**: 5G and Gigabit fixed connections everywhere, doubling the EU share in global production of advanced semiconductors, 10,000 climate-neutral highly secure edge/cloud data nodes and the first computer with quantum acceleration.
3 **Digital transformation of businesses**: tech up-take with 75% of EU companies using Cloud/AI/Big Data, grow scale-ups & finance innovators to double EU Unicorns, more than 90% of SMEs to reach at least a basic level of digital intensity.
4 **Digitalization of public services**: 100% of key public services are available online, 100% of citizens have access to medical records (e-Health) and 80% of citizens use a digital ID.

The digital ambitions set by the EU require a significant amount of investments and coordination, which is expected to be covered by a joint governance framework, multi-country projects with public and private contributions and a system of targets, projected trajectories and progress monitoring. What must be emphasized is that the EU considered a number of social guidelines for the execution of the digital strategy, containing among others:

1 **people at the center** – EU and global protection of rights, democracy and assuring all digital solutions are safe and used responsibly,
2 **solidarity and inclusion** – using the digitalization to unite people and provide equal access to the internet, digital skills, e-Government,
3 **freedom of choice** – fair and safe online environment, free from illegal and harmful practices and content, empowerment in the interactions with new technologies, especially artificial intelligence, as well as full control of personal data and its usage by various parties,
4 **safety and security** - assuring all user segments (across demographic and behavioral criteria continuums) are able to use digital services with the right level of protection from undesired events and influences,
5 **sustainability** – digital solutions, platforms and the infrastructure should operate in a sustainable way, respecting environmental and social impacts as well as energy consumption.

These rights and principles for Europeans address many of the challenges of digitalization, which carries new risks, frequently not yet visible, understood and mitigated. The promise of digitalization has extreme positive potential, however, it must be emphasized that crime and illegal activity are using digital technologies to explore vulnerabilities in the new solutions. An invisible and silent war of "firewalls" and "hackers" is taking place in the background, with unmatched intensity and unpredictability. Financial institutions, being members of the "publicly trusted organizations" play an instrumental role in setting standards for protecting the clients and markets against attacks or negative market development.

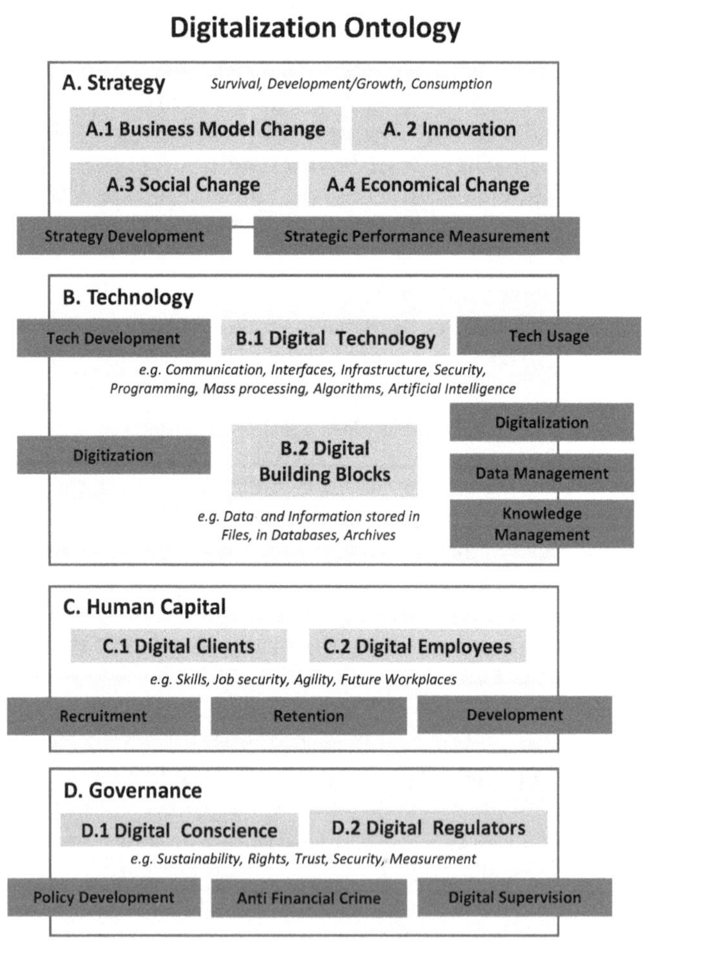

Figure 3.1 Digitalization ontology
Source: Author

Bringing all of the above perspectives into a single ontology allows to create a reference model for use in the study of what is the impact of digitalization on financial institutions. A proposal of a unified model is shown in Figure 3.1.

The ontology consists of four areas: (A) strategy, (B) technology, (C) human capital and (D) governance. Each area is split into core-sub elements (e.g. B.1 Technology and B.2 Building blocks) including samples to visualize their content. Key processes are listed for every group, forming a list of activities that can be analyzed and discussed in the context of the financial institutions participating in the digital transformation. The process dimension of the model is used to conduct the discussion on a practical level, showing what impacts on the actual actions of the financial sector are present or expected, referring to activities ("what and how and when should we stop or start doing"). As shown in the chapter the ontology is based on current paradigms and sectoral discussions, providing a comprehensive view of the topic, across several domains and perspectives.

3.3 Evaluation of digitalization of financial institutions

The digitalization ontology introduced in the previous chapter is well suited for the evaluation of the digitalization of financial institutions. In the next sub-chapters, the four ontological areas are described in the context of the financial sector's current state and the development trends at play, using the main ontological objects as a structuring backbone.

3.3.1 Digitalization strategy

In recent decades the world economy undergoes wave after wave of crisis and stress conditions, e.g. the financial crisis of 2008 and resulting fiscal engineering with low-interest rate conditions, the Covid pandemic or the war in the East of Europe resulting in an energy market collapse and record inflationary pressure. All of these events significantly impact financial institutions and force them to continually review and redesign their strategies. The long-term planning horizon is extremely shortened (or its sense practically denied, but that is hard to explain to shareholders of publicly traded companies), plans are built with additional contingencies and fashioned to include several scenarios that are dynamically triggered. The following can be observed with respect to digitalization:

1 strategy development:
   a technology is migrating from previous "operations" or "support": areas of strategy into prime spots of key strategic drivers,
   b dedicated digitalization strategies are being developed as a part of strategic planning, covering every dimension of the business model (especially products, channels and client segment approaches) and every organizational function,

- c traditional strategic advisors develop digital capabilities to match the strategy development expectations of their clients, where digitalization plays a key role,[19]
- d selected financial institutions declare themselves "technology companies"[20] showing the increased importance of information technology,
- e internal organization and culture are being adjusted to the benefits (but also demands) of fast digitalization – moving stronger toward agile working methods and design thinking where quick idea generation and prototyping is taking place of previous waterfall approaches,
- f the structure of investment budgets is being digitized in a sense that previous investments in physical assets (e.g. branches, agent networks) are shifted to digital change initiatives,

2 strategic performance measurement:
- a digital key performance indicators (KPI) are being added to the traditionally standard business and finance-centered measurement criteria,
- b IT organizations are being monitored via scorecards with the KPI availability of digital solutions for business (both the delivery of new initiatives and the stable running of the existing ones),
- c key business indicators, such as the net promoter score (NPS) are being enhanced to cover all digital channels and customer touch points.

The role of digitalization in strategic activities is increasing and it is expected that the trend will remain strong, moving financial institutions even closer toward technological superiority, including the ability to compete with the neo-banks and X-tech ventures.

3.3.2 Digital technology in financial institutions

The technological aspect of digitalization is only seemingly the most obvious and clear. The discourse on digital technology – both in the industry and academia - resembles a bee hive: it is filled with buzzwords, swarming with three-letter acronyms and claims of being the "milk and honey" of digital finance. This feeling is further amplified by the branding of X-tech ventures and startups in the world of finance – the names of products and companies are creative, revolutionary and surrounded by the hipster aura of individuality and exquisiteness. Finding a way through this diversity, heated up by marketing budgets of technology vendors and consulting companies may not be straightforward for IT leaders in financial institutions. First reactions to this information overload may be a strain of questions: "what should we invest in?", "when should we start and with what?", "what if we miss the train of a given technology"? A good example of such a situation may be given with respect to distributed ledger technology (a.k.a. "blockchain"). The popularization efforts behind this technology were immense and led to very wide coverage in conferences, keystone projects or visionary CIO speeches. After several years of talking about potential uses (naturally leveraging on the technological success of cryptocurrencies) at present, we can risk a statement that the "hype" period of this technology is over and the excitement about widespread conversion to the blockchain can be retired or significantly reduced. As much as this is true we have to remember that thanks to a wide discussion and many implementation projects the initial blockchain concepts were significantly improved and tested against business uses. The resulting mature technology still offers its benefits stemming from the distributed and non-repudiated nature,[21] which definitely will continue to be used, however possibly with far less reach than originally anticipated.

The question to answer in this chapter is what are the mainstream technologies that find their use in digital finance? The starting point for a common view was a list assembled by the LBBW Bank,[22] extended with items found in the bibliography of this chapter and partially grouped to reflect similarities. Technologies that can be already considered a market standard, such as the Internet/portals, application stores, location and map services (e.g. GPS, Google Maps, what3words), streaming, 24×7 operations, always on/always mobile, omnichannel or open source were not included in the list, due to their already established position at the foundation of digitalization. At the same time, the list contains items which are not purely new software/hardware solutions but represent the ways to use and manage the technology, For example, the SaaS/BaaS solutions may offer a similar function and business coverage as standard software, but it is delivered in an innovative way where the product is melted together with the service. These items were added due to their transformative nature and importance for the overall impacts of digitalization. The following technologies are commonly discussed:

1 Application Programming Interface (API) Ecosystems, API-based integration,
2 Artificial Intelligence (AI), Machine learning, Autonomous/Autonomic systems, Expert and Decision systems, Cognitive Computing,
3 Augmented Reality (AR), Virtual Reality (VR).
4 Beacons and Near Field Communication (NFC),
5 Big Data, Data Lakes, Data Fabric,
6 Biometrics,
7 Blockchain/Distributed Ledger Technology (DLT),
8 Business Intelligence/Data Analytics,
9 Cloud/Cloud-computing, Edge Computing,
10 Cryptocurrencies,
11 Customer Journey Tracking/Marketing Automation,
12 Cybersecurity Mesh Architecture (CSMA), Privacy Enhanced Computation,
13 Digital assets, Tokenization,

14 Digital Personas, Avatars, Digital Identification,
15 In-Memory Processing and Mass Parallel Processing, Real-Time Data Analytics,
16 Internet of Things (IoT) and Smart Devices, 5G and Mobile as enablers,
17 Micro Services, Software as a Service (SaaS), Banking as a Service (BaaS),
18 Quantum computing,
19 Radio-Frequency Identification (RFID),
20 Robotics, drones (physical devices),
21 Robotic Process Automation (RPA), Digital Workers, Bots,
22 Social networks, Instant Communicators,
23 Three-dimensional (3D) printing and scanning.

The observed number and variety of mainstream digital technologies open up a decision process challenge, in which resources have to be assigned to both the running of the existing technology or to new implementations. In the usage of the technology, the difficulty is to decide whether to maintain the legacy components or to move into time and budget consuming upgrades or replacements. The topic of problematic heritage is expanding due to the shortening of the software (SW) and hardware (HW) lifecycles. The overall technological progress puts the buyers in a situation where the SW/HW being purchased may be already outdated or will become outdated shortly after the implementation is completed. In the time of rapid digital transformation, the paradigm of accelerated obsolescence is amplified and in some cases already agreed upon in maintenance contracts, which may force the user to make an upgrade to the next version in a relatively short time frame.

Technology development is also subject to changes, among which we can point out that:

1 Agile methods are introduced to benefit from rapid prototyping and shorter delivery cycles, assuring a customer journey better fits market expectations.
2 Regardless of the method of software development, financial institutions start to view development projects as test runs, investing small amounts of funding into basic solutions (e.g. without back office automation) and observing the business case performance. In case of positive business verification, the technical solutions receive an additional wave of funding. In the opposite case, the solutions are quickly retired.
3 In previous years business teams were the drivers of IT spending, not bearing consequences in case the business solution was closed (e.g. due to insufficient market response), but the IT solution had to remain due to having some new products or processes, with no sufficient scale. The IT spend is now receiving more scrutiny from the IT, e.g. with respect to maintenance or scrapping costs, where sunk cost may overshadow

any business benefits. Longer business case views are also verified by the finance function, which is considered a guardian of business case verification.

4 The importance of cyber security is continuously growing, financial institutions are expanding not only their individual capacities for defense, but also engaging in market-wide joint initiatives to prevent attacks that explore market vulnerabilities in interfaces or simply join forces (and investments budgets) to develop defensive solutions later to be used by all.

The next area within the technology domain is data management. In the discussions of digitization and digitalization, we are revisiting the dilemma frequently seen at the turn of the century, related to the differences between the terms data and information.Although no longer a key buzzword in the industry - it is necessary to recall the concept of knowledge management (KM), which helps to address the taxonomic discourse on data and information. In its simplest form data, information and knowledge are all encoded observations of the world, reflecting its states at a given time point and represented by various forms of aggregation. The principles of KM not only still hold true, but also gain further significance in the period of increased digitalization. Taking one of the flagship tenets of knowledge management - all knowledge resources have to follow a process of classification into a simple 2×2 matrix, based on the usability and availability:

1 knowledge which we find useful (it is needed for the organization) and which is available is the perfect intangible asset and a source of value generation,
2 useful knowledge which is not available must be acquired and the acquisition cost needs to be taken into account,
3 not useful knowledge that we have might be considered for archiving and future use, however, the cost of storage may be significant enough to justify some disposal or archive optimization,
4 not useful knowledge that we do not have may seem like a pointless quadrant with no importance. We have to remember however that it is common that certain parts of the organization lobby for the acquisition of large data sets which in the end are not useful so such situations must be avoided.

Digitalization will continue to digitize reality by expanding the already ever-growing databases of facts and observations. Financial institutions need to be very mindful of their knowledge management, as digitalization brings a risk of information overflow, where multiple digitized processes will be feeding uncounted repositories which without supervision may end up being costly archives of unused content.

3.3.3 Human capital in times of digitalization

All three aspects of human capital management – from recruitment, to development and retention are under significant stress due to digitalization:

1. The hunt for talent is heating up the market – there are not enough specialists to run digitalization projects and maintain new technology components. Financial institutions not only compete with each other, but also lose valuable employees to X-tech companies, other industries or digital technology giants such as Google.
2. The increasing share of engineers in the staff requires adopting the human capital management models, for example, the career development paths, which have a significantly different shape for high-tech experts (e.g. interested in ongoing participation in certified training programs).
3. New working methods (e.g. agile) require very strong change management investments in order not to bury the concept in misinformation or improper organizational arrangements.
4. Young engineers and technology experts joining traditional financial institutions represent a different culture of work that demands high flexibility of time (e.g. work not constrained to fixed hours, shorter workdays, skip days) of space (e.g. working from home, office like a coffee shop) and quality (e.g. better work-life balance, diversity).
5. Outsourcing is under stress, especially if benefits are achieved via the building of technology centers in offshore locations. As digitalization is draining the market, including students a few years before graduation, the labor arbitrage advantages are diminishing and recruitment is becoming a constant game of candidates switching jobs to obtain better conditions.

3.3.4 Governance of digitalization

A good way to describe the governance aspect of digitalization in financial services is to quote a Member of the Supervisory Board of the European Central Bank, Pentti Hakkarainen, who in his speech made a fine statement on the role of supervisory institutions (Hakkarainen, 2022):

> Digitalisation is a key element in creating a future-proof business model. Banks that are not following this development or lagging behind may struggle to succeed in this competitive environment. As supervisors, our main challenge is to ensure that financial stability and prudential soundness are preserved, while at the same time allowing for technological innovation.

This perspective reflects the role of the regulators as curators of the digital market through:

1. policy development, while the directive approach is still applied, forming a legal base for required practices – regulators increase their industry

dialog activities, placing themselves in the moderator role or simply using the market communication channels to collect the pulse of the sector and prioritize their work,

2. tight control of financial crime practices and conditions, by implementing industry-wide protection mechanisms and enforcing zero tolerance for cyber crime offenses (e.g. two-factor authentication and authorization as seen in the PSD2 regulation),
3. market stability supervision of new, technology-driven solutions, especially those that are not fully regulated, while allowing a lot of freedom to technological entrants, the borders of operation are clear and do not allow for regulations related to capital and risk to be circumvented.
4. pro-market development activities based on digital tools, offering products to the previously unbanked population, reduction of cash circulation by conversion to electronic payment or increasing customer protection via transparency of information provided (e.g. on fees or conditions),
5. ordering mass processing of government related to administration to be facilitated by the commercial banks, a prominent example of that is seen in Poland where banks serve as trusted authentication gateways, giving access to e-Government services based on online banking interfaces (assumption of banks properly conducting the identification of the client),
6. accelerating the adoption of cashless standards for further virtualization of the transactions, this was especially seen during the most difficult times of the COVID pandemic (2019–2021), where regulators and government agencies facilitated the usage of cashless payment terminals or increase of the limits for transactions that do not require a physical entry of the PIN code on the terminal.

We may attempt a conclusion that digitalization has a positive effect on the cooperation between regulated financial institutions and regulators. Both sides of the policy frontier are working on implementing beneficial and market making digital solutions, yet no compromises are made regarding the safety and protection of the customers. On the contrary, the cyber security area enjoys impressive growth aimed at always being a few steps ahead of the dangerously agile and efficient cyber crime scene. This digital partnership between supervisors and market entities is one of the best examples of achieving the common good thanks to a well designed implementation of digital technologies.

3.4 Conclusion

Looking at the substance of digitalization, financial institutions are in the pioneer and leader position in the digital transformation arena, making a foundational contribution to the digital platforms and ecosystems. In the last decades of the 20th century, intensive implementation of information technologies was considered the "computerization" of business, where machines were placed inside the core processes with high demand for calculations and data processing. This computerized core served as a seed for the outward-progressing digitalization of all processes in the financial institutions and the interfaces linking them to the world of clients, partners and vendors. The introduction of computers evolved from a special investment category toward a new normal, dynamically transforming financial institutions into technology leaders. B.Gates once said that "banking is essential, banks are not"[23] claiming that financial services face extinction and replacement by technology companies. Several decades later, financial institutions remain established as the strong base of economical systems around the globe, but that can be attributed to the proper interpretation of Microsoft's founder's thought: survival and growth are won by active engagement in the development of the digital reality. Financial institutions have done their homework and through IT investments transformed themselves toward highly digitalized market players, capable of competing with X-tech, neobanks or other ecosystem participants.

The high diversity and variegated maturity of digital technologies entering the market may serve as a source of anxiety for the CIOs of financial institutions, posing a question of where to direct the IT investment budgets. The response to this feeling is built by developing strong business case capabilities, where the digital, business and finance leaders work together to strategically select the technologies with the most positive impact on the business model, both for the clients and the financials of the institutions. Not all new technologies have to be implemented and there will be new ones coming around in the near future. Certainly, however, financial institutions need to care about the human capital with even higher intensity than about technology. Top talent is needed to manage the new technological solutions and the retention of the best engineering skills is a true condition to achieve success in the digital revolution. In addition to technical work capacities, financial institutions are a true test field for new organizational concepts that leverage the agility, design-oriented thinking and customer centricity – all with built in data management and analytics. Organizational behaviors are strongly subject to digitalization impacts, but not all units and employees are able to quickly shift to new ways of working. Digital change management will remain a key priority for the CEOs.

With a lot of self-confidence, we can also conclude that although we are very proud of humanity's digital achievements – this is still a mere beginning of what is coming in the next years. The author sincerely hopes that future generations will classify our work today as the period of technological renaissance, with the human in the middle, surrounded by at-that-time impressive technical wonders, being the equivalent of aqueducts or roads of ancient Rome. However, there is also a good chance that we will end up with machines at the center of our reality, with humans serving them in the eternal cycle of development, not limited as much as our human potential. Setting the futuristic visions aside, our immediate future is readying a number of further waves of the technological revolution – mainly related to the joint resolution of world's problems such as climate change, the need for more sustainability and awareness of resource usage, health hazards or social changes and conflicts. It is certain that financial institutions will be one of the key architects of this positive change, driven by digitalization and networking, which facilitates cooperation and collaborative problem resolution.

Notes

1 https://www.uni-hannover.de/en/universitaet/profil/geschichte/logo/.
2 https://www.wirtschaftswiki.fh-aachen.de/index.php?title=Digital-Natives.
3 https://www.hp.com/us-en/shop/tech-takes/top-50-best-selling-video-games-all-time.
4 This statement does not fully resonate with the current dilemma of crypto currencies, for which the mining process is an extremely energy intensive operation. This HBR article mentions that 0.55% of worlds energy consumption is used for mining: https://hbr.org/2021/05/how-much-energy-does-bitcoin-actually-consume.
5 https://www.gartner.com/en/information-technology/glossary/digitalization.
6 https://www.sap.com/insights/digitization-vs-digitalization.html.
7 https://www.merriam-webster.com/dictionary/digitalization.
8 https://www.oxfordlearnersdictionaries.com/definition/english/digitalization.
9 https://dictionary.cambridge.org/de/worterbuch/englisch/digitalize?q=digitalization.
10 https://www.salesforce.com/products/platform/what-is-digital-transformation/.
11 https://www.eurofound.europa.eu/topic/digitalisation.
12 https://www.citrix.com/de-de/solutions/digital-workspace/what-is-digital-transformation.html.
13 https://www.verdi.de/themen/digitalisierung/++co++abf19972-cac5-11ec-b8ec-001a4a160129.
14 Understood as any artefact that is equipped with sensors that collect and process data and are able to communicate with other devices.
15 https://ec.europa.eu/info/business-economy-euro/banking-and-finance/digital-finance_en.
16 https://pubdocs.worldbank.org/en/230281588169110691/Digital-Financial-Services.pdf.
17 https://ec.europa.eu/info/law/payment-services-psd-2-directive-eu-2015-2366_en.
18 https://ec.europa.eu/info/strategy/priorities-2019-2024/europe-fit-digital-age/europes-digital-decade-digital-targets-2030_en.
19 Examples: McKinsey Digital (https://www.mckinsey.de/funktionen/mckinsey-digital) or BCG Platinion (https://bcgplatinion.com/).
20 Statements made by managers of leading banks, including Bank of America, Deutsche Bank or ING.
21 More on the topic in the podcast from Accenture's B. Obermeier. https://www.computerwoche.de/a/geht-dem-blockchain-hype-schon-die-luft-aus,3550914.
22 Landesbank Baden-Württemberg (LBBW), Kernbegriffe der Digitalisierung und Industrie 4.0: https://www.lbbw.de/artikelseite/maerkte-verstehen/kernbegriffe-digitalisierung-industrie-4-0_6vip5a4gw_d.html.
23 As quoted in: https://www.handelsblatt.com/meinung/kommentare/kommentar-die-fintechs-ruetteln-am-monopol-der-banken/25641246.html.

Bibliography

Andrus, G., Kejriwal, S., Wadhwani, R., *Digital Transformation in Financial Services*, Deloitte University Press, 2016, https://www2.deloitte.com/content/dam/Deloitte/tr/Documents/financial-services/DUP_Digital-transformation-in-financial-services.pdf

BCG, *Digital Transformation*, 2022, https://www.bcg.com/capabilities/digital-technology-data/digital-transformation/overview?utm_source=search&utm_medium=cpc&utm_campaign=digital&utm_description=none&utm_topic=digital_transformation&utm_geo=global&utm_content=digital_transformation_general&gclid=CjwKCAjws8yUBhA1EiwAi_tpEbwIGVmwy-gqBTbAeSMxc8t-FYgp2T_lydk6EtR4EMiW4V1_ChnqrQxoCKfMQAvD_BwE

BDO, *Digital Transformation in Financial Services*, 2022, https://www.bdo.com/insights/industries/financial-services/digital-transformation-in-financial-services

Bloomberg, J., *Digitization, Digitalization, and Digital Transformation: Confuse them at Your Peril*, Forbes, 2019, https://www.forbes.com/sites/jasonbloomberg/2018/04/29/digitization-digitalization-and-digital-transformation-confuse-them-at-your-peril/?sh=10e0d0902f2c

Fjord, *Fjord Trends 2022, Accenture Interactive*, 2022, https://www.accenture.com/_acnmedia/PDF-169/Accenture-Fjord-Trends-2022-Full-Report.pdf#zoom=40

Gartner, *The Digital Future of Finance*, 2022, https://www.gartner.com/en/finance/trends/the-digital-future-of-finance?utm_source=google&utm_medium=cpc&utm_campaign=RM_EMEA_2022_FINL_CPC_LG1_FINDIGITALFINANCE&utm_adgroup=128919305502&utm_term=finance%20digital%20transformation&ad=571954705658&matchtype=p&gclid=CjwKCAjws8yUBhA1EiwAi_tpESZ5B3pPjQD5LC_CeEbiPE45ldm_0dcG3okJTg4TRgEIDbqYkUy9HhoCsmEQAvD_BwE

Hakkarainen, P., *Speech by the Member of the Supervisory Board of the ECB at the Institute for Financial Integrity and Sustainability*, 2022, https://www.bankingsupervision.europa.eu/press/speeches/date/2022/html/ssm.sp220113~8101be7500.en.html

Khanna, S., Lhuer, X., Sohoni, V., *Next-gen Technology Transformation in Financial Services, Collection of Articles*, Mckinsey Financial Services Insights, 2017–2020, https://www.mckinsey.com/industries/financial-services/our-insights/next-gen-technology-transformation-in-financial-services

Kiron, D. Unruh, G., *Digital Transformation on Purpose*, MIT Sloan Management Review, 2017, https://sloanreview.mit.edu/article/digital-transformation-on-purpose/

KPMG, *The Future of Finance*, 2022, https://advisory.kpmg.us/insights/future-finance.html

Lhuer, X, Tuddenham, P., Kumar, S., Ledbetter, B., *Next-Generation Core Banking Platforms: A Golden Ticket?*, McKinsey & Company, 2019, https://www.mckinsey.com/industries/financial-services/our-insights/banking-matters/when-the-tide-turns-optimizing-us-commercial-banking-deposits

Roland Berger, *Retail Banking Survey: Not Striving for Any Change of Business Models Despite Digitalization*, 2021, https://www.rolandberger.com/en/Insights/Publications/Retail-Banking-Survey-Not-striving-for-any-change-of-business-models-despite.html

Tabrizi, B., Lam, E., Girard, K., Irvin, V., *Digital Transformation Is not about Technology*, 2019, Harvard Business Review, https://hbr.org/2019/03/digital-transformation-is-not-about-technolog

Part II

Digital banking

4 Central bank in the age of digital finance[1]

Piotr J. Szpunar and Piotr Żuk

4.1 Introduction

Technological progress leads to the digitalization of processes in subsequent economic sectors. In this chapter, we analyze how digitization affects activities performed by central banks.

In order to present this impact, the chapter begins with presenting the key functions of central banks in the two-tier banking system. In the following part of the chapter, we analyze the concept of private virtual currencies and the so-called central bank digital currency (CBDC). In particular, we discuss the impact of a possible propagation of private virtual currencies and the introduction of CBDC on the functions performed by central banks and associated risks for monetary systems.

We also present the experience of central banks that are contemplating the introduction of CBDC and cases of countries that have introduced this form of money or are conducting advanced CBDC pilot programs. This chapter ends with conclusions.

4.2 Functions performed by central banks

The first central banks were established in the second half of the 17th century and today there are around 200 of them in the world. Notwithstanding a long history of central banking, there is still no clear answer to the question of what exactly central banking is, as modern central banks differ significantly from each other. This is why today central banks are often contextually defined through the key functions that they perform in an economy: an issuing bank, a bank of the banks and a central bank of the state (Capie et al. 1994).

As "a bank of the state", the central bank keeps accounts of budgetary units and other state institutions. Most often it also manages the state's foreign exchange reserves. The function of "a bank of banks" means that the central bank organizes and manages the infrastructure of the payment system, maintains commercial bank accounts and acts as a lender of last resort.

When it comes to the function of "an issuing bank", central banks have the exclusive right to issue cash (notes and coins), which is a legal tender that is

DOI: 10.4324/9781003310082-8

widely accepted in economic transactions. Issuing money is also recognized as a function that even defines central banking itself (Bindseil, 2019).

4.3 Money and banking system

Due to the fact that money has taken various forms over the centuries (Aglietta 2018), defining money – as is the case of central banking – faces numerous challenges. Hence, money is also often defined by the functions that it performs ("... Money is what money does"; Hicks (1969)).

Money performs three basic functions in the economy: a medium of exchange, a store of value, and a unit of account. When it comes to the forms of money, today economists usually distinguish between deposit money (on accounts at commercial banks) and cash in circulation (issued by central banks). Both forms of money can perform the above-mentioned three functions and there is usually substitutability and equivalence between central bank money and deposit money.

The modern two-tier banking system includes the central bank and commercial banks. Commercial banks enable payments to non-banking entities thanks to the use of deposit money on their accounts. Commercial banks, on the other hand, settle claims with each other using their liquid reserves held on the accounts at the central bank (Szpunar 2006). Commercial banks also provide cash withdrawals to non-banking entities from funds accumulated in their account. In this way, they allow introduction of cash into circulation.

The central bank remains the key element of the banking system. First, the central bank provides the infrastructure necessary for the smooth execution of payments in the economy. Second, by ensuring a stable value of money (low inflation), the central bank creates the foundations for the efficient functioning of money. Third, the central bank acts as a lender of last resort. As deposits in the banking sector can be withdrawn on demand, the role of the lender of last resort – along with deposit guarantee schemes – remains crucial for enhancing the credibility of the banking sector and the security of deposits (Bank for International Settlements 2020a).

Commercial banks in cooperation with the central bank organize and run payment systems (Bank for International Settlements 2020a) and create deposit money through extending loans (McLeay et al. 2014).

4.4 The impact of digitalization on the key functions of central banks

Notwithstanding numerous innovations in the banking system that have been introduced thanks to digitization, the essence of central banking has remained unchanged. Maintaining monetary stability remains the basic objective of central banks. Central banks still perform the three functions considered essential for central banking.

Nevertheless, digitization allows for streamlining many processes carried out by central banks. This applies, for example, to the acquisition and processing of large databases used to conduct macroeconomic analyses (Macias et al. 2022), digitization of interbank settlements or servicing the accounts of the public sector.

It appears that possible changes resulting from the digitization of finance would primarily concern the issuing function performed by central banks. These changes could result from the popularization of private virtual currencies or from the introduction of digital money by central banks themselves. Although the above changes would directly affect the issuing function of central banks, they could have also wider implications for the function of a bank of banks.

Before discussing the possible implications of the introduction of CBDC, it is worth analyzing the issues related to cash, i.e. money issued by central banks. What appears particularly relevant in this context, is that digitization of finance has not yet led to fundamental changes in the area of issuing cash by central banks. The value of cash in circulation in relation to GDP in most economies, both developed and emerging, has not been falling, but even it has been increasing (Bech et al. 2018). Cash remains an important – and in some countries also dominant – means of payment and store of value. According to the latest available data for 2019, in the euro area, 73% of transactions (by number) and 48% (by value) at retail outlets were paid with cash (European Central Bank 2020).

It seems that despite strong competition from electronic payment methods, cash will remain an important means of payment also in the future, although its share in transactions may decrease. From the users' perspective, cash payments have a number of advantages, related primarily to anonymity, certainty and immediacy of payment. Often cash allows for achieving a lower level of risk and costs than electronic forms of payment (Narodowy Bank Polski 2019). Due to these advantages, especially in times of strong increases in uncertainty, cash also remains an important means of a store of value. In this context, the outbreak of the pandemic in 2020 led to a strong increase in cash in circulation in many countries, despite a decline in its use in transactions (Boar, Wehrli 2021).

A change in the role of central banks as money issuers could take place if private virtual currencies (such as Bitcoin or Diem) became widespread in societies. However, it is doubtful that this would be the case. First, the use of virtual currencies in economic transactions remains marginal. Second, the value of virtual currencies is generally characterized by high volatility and - due to the lack of appropriate regulation – high risk for the users (Lagarde 2017). Third, even if the value of a private virtual currency "imports" stability by pegging to the value of money issued by central banks (the so-called stablecoins) such currencies still remain risky. For example, in May 2022, the value of one of the most popular stablecoins (Terra-USD), which was supposed to be pegged to the US dollar, collapsed. Fourth, even if virtual currencies were properly regulated, and their issuers or other organizations could guarantee the security of conducting payments, a stable value and a certainty of settlement, it is hard to expect that states would allow competition for currencies issued by their central banks to arise. The loss of the monopoly of central banks on the issuance of commonly accepted money would lead to many problems and drawbacks in the conduct of monetary policy, performing the function of a lender of last resort, as well as a loss of seigniorage and overall benefits from issuing of reserve currency. For the above reasons, the Diem stable coin project (previously known as the Libra project) proposed by the Meta Platforms company, which in theory could have been promising due to a large number of potential users and the associated positive network effects, has been abandoned.

In the context of the popularization of private virtual currencies, an interesting example is provided by El Salvador, a country which in September 2021 was the first in the world to adopt Bitcoin as legal tender (in El Salvador this status has also the US dollar). As a result, companies are obliged to accept this cryptocurrency for the goods and services they sell. It is worth noting, however, that when making a payment in Bitcoin, the cryptocurrency received by the seller is by default converted into the US dollar. This reduces the risks for the seller related to high volatility in Bitcoin valuation. The exchange is guaranteed by the special fund established by the government, which has purchased Bitcoin worth approx. 0.2% of El Salvador's GDP. Consequently, the risk related to the volatility of the valuation of this cryptocurrency has been to some extent shifted to the state.

Although the so-called Chivo e-wallet for Bitcoin payments was installed by approximately 60% of Salvadoran citizens (Alvarez et al. 2022), the scale of the use of Bitcoin in transactions remains moderate. Alvarez et al. (2022) estimate that 5% of Chivo users have paid taxes in Bitcoin, and only 20% of companies actually accept Bitcoin as payment for their products or services. International institutions, including the IMF (International Monetary Fund 2022), remain critical as regards the idea of adopting Bitcoin as legal tender, pointing to significant risks to financial stability, consumer protection and public finance.

4.5 The concept of a central bank digital currency

An introduction of CBDC would constitute an important change that digitization of finances could bring to central banking. Nowadays, central banks limit access to money they issue to commercial banks. An introduction of CBDC would involve issuing by central bank money in electronic form, which could also be used by non-banking entities. There are basically two ideas for the form that CBDC could adopt: (1) electronic records on accounts at the central bank and (2) a so-called token (digital representative of value) using distributed ledger technology (DLT).

The discussion on the possibility and legitimacy of launching CBDC has been ongoing for several years and recently it has intensified. Surveys conducted among central banks (Kosse, Mattei 2022) indicate that the potential benefits of CBDC perceived by central banks may include: (1) reducing the costs in the payment system, (2) increasing competition and diversification in the payment system (and as a result reduction of costs and risk in the system), (3) limiting demand for private digital currencies (which may constitute a source of risk for users and competition for currencies issued by central banks), (4) supporting the development of technology in the payment system and (5) increasing the efficiency of conducting monetary policy.

An important premise for the introduction of CBDC in developed countries would be to ensure access to central bank money against the background of the declining share of the use of cash in economic transactions. On the other hand, in developing countries, CBDCs could reduce financial exclusion. CBDCs are also seen as an opportunity to increase the efficiency of payment systems.

However, all of the above potential benefits of CBDCs would depend on the efficiency of the payment systems in individual countries. In those countries where the payment system works efficiently, has low operating costs and provides users with a high level of security and functionality, it is hard to clearly indicate the benefits of the introduction of CBDC.

The effects of a potential introduction of CBDC would depend on the modalities of their implementation. In the literature, many concepts and forms of CBDCs are being discussed. The proposals that are being raised differ in terms of the accessibility of this currency, the limits for CBDC holdings and transactions, CBDC's remuneration, technologies used in the CBDC-based payment system, the degree of anonymity that CBDC would provide, the possibility of making offline payments, etc. (Bank for International Settlements 2018).

4.6 The consequences of a possible introduction of CBDC for central banks

The consequences of launching CBDC for the key areas relevant for the central banks, i.e. monetary and financial stability, would largely depend on its design. In particular, the interest paid on CBDC, limits on its holdings and transactions, as well as its popularity among users appear to be crucial in this context.

If CBDC was introduced on a large scale, the consequences for the central bank could be significant. In such a case, CBDC could potentially lead to a change in the paradigm of the two-tier banking system and an increase in financial stability risks. Changes to the banking system after the introduction of CBDC are worth analyzing through the changes in the balance sheets of individual institutions in the banking sector presented in Figure 4.1.

While it is hard to determine whether CBDC would be a closer substitute for deposits or cash (which would depend on its specific form), it can be assumed that its introduction would limit, at least partially, demand for both "traditional" forms money (i.e. cash and deposits).

Central Bank		**Commercial Banks**	
Assets	Liabilities	Assets	Liabilities
Foreign reserves and gold	**Cash** ↓	**Loans** ↓↑	**Deposits** ↓
	Liquid reserves	Liquid reserves	**Refinancing credit from central bank** ↑
Refinancing credit to commercial banks ↑	**CBDC** ↑		
		Other assets	**Other liabilities** (bonds issued) ↑

Sources: Own. A similar diagram could be found also in Smets [2016].
It was assumed that the introduction of a CBDC would lead to a decline in both cash in circulation and deposits in the banking sector.

Figure 4.1 Possible changes in the balance sheet of a central bank and the banking sector after an introduction of a CBDC (a simplified diagram)
Sources: Own. A similar diagram could be found also in Smets (2016)

It could be thus expected, that after the introduction of CBDC, the value of cash on the liability side of the central bank's balance sheet would fall. Similarly, the value of deposits held by the private sector at commercial banks (i.e. banks' liabilities) would decline. This would have significant consequences for the whole model of the banking system, as commercial banks would need to find other than deposit sources for financing their assets. In practice, the main option for banks would be to issue bonds. The decrease in the role of deposits from the private sector (often perceived as the most stable source of financing for the banks) in commercial banks' liabilities could increase the pro-cyclicality of lending, which would depend on the banks' ability to obtain other, less stable, sources of financing. In the possible event of an outflow of deposits from the banking sector, the probability of a collapse in new lending (the so-called credit crunch) would also increase.

In case of an outflow of deposits from the banks that could not be replaced by market financing, banks would need to reach out for a loan from the central bank. Such loans would need to be collateralized by the assets held by the banks (i.e. mainly by loans). In such a situation, banks' lending would largely depend on whether the central bank would refinance their lending. As a result, the credit risk in the economy would not only be transferred from the commercial banks to the central bank (the risk, if materialized, would ultimately lead to losses for the taxpayers) but also would create a strong incentive for state intervention in the lending process. In an extreme case, the central bank would evolve toward a typical command economy central 'monobank' that would *de facto* decide to what extent banks should be refinanced. Therefore, indirectly the central bank would decide the scale of lending to the private sector and which industries or enterprises should obtain financing from banks.

At the same time, an introduction of CBDC may lead to an increase in interest rates on banks' lending. First, the banks could be forced to raise interest rates on deposits held by households and businesses, as they would need to compete for the funds with the central bank. As a result, in order to keep the net interest rate margin unchanged, the interest rates on loans granted by banks would also need to be raised. If banks fail in doing so, a consequence would be a decline in their profitability. This in turn could reduce opportunities for capital accumulation and, consequently, could lead to a decline in lending.

It should be underlined that the potential outflow of deposits from the banking sector toward CBDC would be largely determined by the interest rate that this form of money would bring. In countries where CBDC has been introduced or where advanced pilot CBDC projects are being carried out, CBDCs remain unremunerated. This is due to the fact, that introducing a positive interest rate on CBDC would not only entail costs for the central banks (and ultimately for taxpayers) but also would increase the risk of an outflow of deposits from the banking sector. Nevertheless, even if the central bank sets an interest rate for CBDC lower than the interest rate on deposits in the banking sector, in case of strong shocks and an increase in risk perception, economic agents may shift their funds to a "safe haven", which the central bank money would constitute. As a result, it would bring about liquidity shock to banks and financial stability risks would arise.

As a way to reduce this risk, Bindseil and Panetta (2020) propose the introduction of the so-called tiering in the remuneration of CBDCs. The authors point out that only a relatively small amount held by households in the form of CBDC should bear a non-negative interest. The remaining part of the household funds (and all corporate funds kept in the form of CBDC) could bear negative interest. This would limit the risk of deposit outflow from the banking sector, especially during crises. Alternatively, introducing a limit for the CBDC holdings could also limit the risks to financial stability related to a possible outflow of deposits from banks. However, restricting access to CBDC would run counter to the very idea of money, as access to the existing forms of money is usually not limited. Even if the limits were very high, functionality for the enterprise sector would in principle be excluded, whereas payments to enterprises constitute a significant part of household expenditures. When discussing the potential impact of an introduction of CBDC on monetary policy, it is often indicated that CBDC – if introduced – would allow central banks to limit or even eliminate challenges resulting from the effective lower bound (ELB) for the nominal interest rates (see for example, Goodfriend (2016) and Dyson and Hodgson (2016)). The ELB manifests itself in the inability of a central bank to cut nominal interest rates considerably below zero in order to stimulate the economy and keep inflation close to the target in the event of a strong negative macroeconomic shock. Since the ELB problem results from the presence of cash which always bring zero interest, the introduction of CBDC – in case it would lead to a decrease in the use of cash – would eliminate the restrictions on the reduction of interest rates below zero. However, it should be underlined that the elimination of the ELB would only be possible if cash was eliminated and CBDC would be remunerated at the same level as the main rate of the central bank. The introduction of CBDC would not affect the ELB if economic agents were still able to convert deposits (in case they bear negative interest) into cash or non-remunerated CBDC. Overall, it is rather doubtful that an introduction of CBDC could really improve the transmission of monetary policy, and not only in case of negative interest rates, especially unless physical cash is fully eliminated. It is also doubtful if such a need for an improvement of monetary transmission exists at all.

Another relevant issue related to the potential introduction of CBDC is payment system security. Currently, a safety net for electronic payment systems (e.g. in the event of a blackout or a cyberattack) is provided by cash that is subject to risks of a different nature (e.g. forgery, theft, etc.). Sometimes it is pointed out that an introduction of CBDC would increase the diversification of risks in the payment system and, as a result, would reduce the total risk in this system (Bank for International Settlements 2020b). However, such argumentation seems questionable. Most of all, it is currently difficult to unequivocally assess whether the proposed and discussed technical solutions that could potentially serve as a basis for the introduction of CBDC, may be more resilient to cyber risks than the existing solutions in the payment systems.

If digital money was introduced in the form of accounts kept by the central bank, it would probably be based on the technologies existing in the payment system so far. At the same time ensuring the security of the system could be more challenging due to a much larger number of accounts and users. Cyber risks (hacking attacks, hijacking passwords and identities, etc.) would potentially also occur if digital money were based on tokens in a distributed ledger system (currently this system seems to be still under development). Certainly, it cannot be ruled out that the technological progress that is currently taking place will in future enable the introduction of CBDC without increasing the risk to the security of the payment system. However, it may turn out – which in fact seems more likely – that the security of the systems will decrease precisely due to technological progress and the increase in computing power.

4.7 Launching CBDC – the current state of play

According to the results of surveys conducted by the Bank for International Settlements, 90% of central banks in the world investigates a possible introduction of CBDC (Kosse, Mattei 2022). However, so far (as of the end of 2021) only two countries (the Bahamas and Nigeria) have decided to fully launch CBDC. At the same time, China and the Eastern Caribbean Union are running advanced CBDC pilots. Sweden is also carrying out intensified activities related to a possible launch of CBDC. The experiences of selected countries related to the work on CBDC or the introduction of this form of money are presented below.

The first central bank that introduced CBDC was the Central Bank of the Bahamas (the introduced currency was called the "sand" dollar). The fact that the Bahamas consist of 700 islands and many of them, especially those less populated, have limited access to banking services and ATMs was an important premise for the introduction of this form of money. At the same time, extreme weather events (such as hurricanes) increase the costs of maintaining the physical banking infrastructure. According to the available information access to the CBDC can be obtained after the registration of the e-wallet in some of the financial institutions operating in the country. Sand dollar payments are possible with a smartphone or a special payment card. So far, the use of the sand dollar has remained modest and the value of the CBDC amounts to only 0.1% of cash in circulation (International Monetary Fund 2022). At the same time, there are limits on CBDC holdings, which reduces the risks to financial stability related to the potential outflow of deposits in the banking system. Limits also apply to the CBDC holdings in Nigeria, which was the second country to introduce central bank digital money (International Monetary Fund 2021).

As regards the People's Bank of China, the plans to introduce CBDC should be analyzed in the context of the high degree of development of electronic payments and the digitization of the payment system in this economy (Auer et al. 2020). At the same time, competition in mobile payment – where two entities play a dominant role – is low. Coupled with the rapid decrease in the use of cash among a large part of society, this increases the concentration of risk in the payment system. Reducing the financial exclusion of residents in remote regions of China with low banking penetration remains another reason indicated by the Chinese authorities for contemplating the introduction of CBDC. Currently, CBDC (e-CNY) pilot is being implemented in China. In the pilot, 10% of the population has already access to this form of digital money. As in the case of countries that have introduced CBDC, e-CNY is interest-free and there are quota limits for its holdings (Soderberg 2022).

In the case of Sweden, a considerable decline in the use of cash remains the main premise for the intensified work on CBDC that is carried out by the Swedish central bank (Riksbank). The decline in the use of cash creates numerous risks, related to among others the formation of private monopolies in the payment system (Ingves 2018, 2022). In this context, an introduction of CBDC by the Riksbank would be therefore a pre-emptive move aimed at safeguarding the access to central bank's money that constitutes an alternative to cash. Currently, the Riksbank conducts subsequent phases of the CBDC pilots. However no decision has yet been made on whether CBDC will be introduced, and if so, what form this money will take and what legal and technological solutions will be adopted (Sveriges Riksbank 2022).

Work on digital money has also been intensified in recent years by the European Central Bank. In October 2021, the ECB started the investigation phase of the CBDC project, where economic implications and legal challenges related to a possible introduction of CBDC will be thoroughly analyzed. This phase will end in October 2023, after which a decision is to be made on whether or not to introduce CBDC. In the case of the US Federal Reserve, the work on CBDC is mainly limited to conducting technological experiments, research and analysis on the economic implications of the introduction of CBDC and consultations with stakeholder groups (Federal Reserve System 2022).

It should be emphasized, however, that despite the ongoing work, the above-mentioned two major central banks have not made a decision on whether CBDC will be introduced in their jurisdictions. However, at the current juncture it seems that the EBC is more likely to introduce CBDC. At the same time, it is worth underscoring, that these two central banks clearly state (as do other central banks from the largest developed economies working on CBDC) that any introduction of CBDC will not be intended to replace cash and other forms of money. Moreover, they indicate that the possible introduction of CBDC should not infringe on monetary and financial stability (Bank for International Settlements 2020b).

4.8 Conclusions

Innovations related to digitization have radically improved the efficiency of many processes performed by central banks. However, the essence of central banking and the basic functions of central banks have remained unchanged so far.

A significant change in central banking could occur if the use of virtual currencies became widespread. However, such development appears unlikely due to the still marginal use of these currencies, the high risk for the users and the lack of consent of the states to the emergence of competition for the currencies issued by the central banks.

A significant change in the role of the central banks could take place if they decided to introduce CBDC. There are numerous different concepts regarding what form such money could take and what exactly would be the modalities of its functioning in the payment system. Although the consequences of introducing CBDC would largely depend on the form this money would adopt, in countries where payment system operates efficiently it is hard to clearly indicate the benefits of its introduction. This applies to the functionality of the payment system, its security, and the effectiveness of monetary policy implementation.

An introduction of CBDC in the economies where development of the payment system is less advanced appears to be more justified. In such economies CBDC can act as a catalyst for changes, could promote the development of new forms of payments, reduce financial exclusion and rein in the costs of the payment system. Due to this reason, emerging economies are on the frontier of the work on central bank digital money, while central banks from developed economies are generally more cautious about the possible introduction of CBDC.

The introduction of CBDC could, however, pose substantial risks to financial stability related to the outflow of deposits from banks. In an extreme case, if the use of CBDC became widespread and outflow of deposits from the banking sector took place, central banks would have to significantly and constantly increase their refinancing of the banking sector, which could infringe the current structure of the two-tier monetary system.

Although many central banks are carrying out analytical work on the new form of digital money, only few of them are running advanced CBDC pilot projects. Even less countries have actually introduced CBDC and so far the use of this form of money has not been widespread in these economies. Therefore, it is difficult to fully assess the impact of the introduction of digital money on economies and monetary- and payment systems. It should be noted, however, that the countries that have introduced CBDCs or conducted advanced CBDC pilot projects decide to introduce limits on the holdings of this form of money. Furthermore, CBDCs holdings remain unremunerated. These two traits limit the risks to financial stability and the construction of monetary systems related to the introduction of CBDCs.

Note

1 The views presented in this chapter are those of the authors and do not necessarily reflect the stance of the institutions with which the authors are affiliated.

References

Alvarez F., Argente D., Van Patten D., (2022), *Are Cryptocurrencies currencies? Bitcoin as Legal Tender in El Salvador*, NBER Working Paper Series 29968.

Auer R., Cornelli G., Frost J, (2020), *Rise of the central bank digital currencies: drivers, approaches and technologies*, BIS Working Papers No 880.

Aglietta M., (2018), *Money. 5000 Years of Debt and Power*, Brooklyn: Verso.

Bank for International Settlements, (2017), *Central bank digital currencies and monetary policy implementation*, Bank for International Settlements 2017.

Bank for International Settlements, (2018), *Central bank digital currencies*, Committee on Payments and Market Infrastructures, March 2018.

Bank for International Settlements, (2020a), *Central banks and payments in the digital era*, BIS Annual Economic Report, Bank for International Settlements 2020.

Bank for International Settlements, (2020b), *Central bank digital currencies: foundational principles and core features*, Report No 1 in a series of collaborations from a group of central banks, Bank for International Settlements 2020.

Bech M.L., Faruqui U., Ougaard F., Picillo C., (2018), *Payments are changing but cash still rules*, BIS Quarterly Review, Bank for International Settlements 2018.

Bindseil U., (2019), *Central Banking before 1800: A Rehabilitation*, Oxford: Oxford University Press.

Bindseil U., Panetta F., (2020), *Central bank digital currency remuneration in a world with low or negative nominal interest rates*, voxeu.org, 5 October 2020.

Boar C., Wehrli A., (2021), *Ready, steady, go? – Results of the third BIS survey on central bank digital currency*, BIS Papers No 114.

Capie F., Goodhart C., Schnadt N., (1994), The development of central banking, in: Capie F., Goodhart C., Fischer S., Schnadt N. (eds.),*The Future of Central Banking: The Tercentenary Symposium of the Bank of England*, Cambridge: Cambridge University Press, pp. 1–231.

Dyson, B., Hodgson G., (2016), *Digital cash: why central banks should start issuing electronic money*, Positive Money.

European Central Bank, (2020), *Study on the payment attitudes of consumers in the euro area (SPACE),* European Central Bank.

Federal Reserve System, (2022), *Money and Payments: The U.S. Dollar in the Age of Digital Transformation*, January.

Goodfriend M., (2016), *The case for unencumbering interest rate policy at the zero bound*, Jackson Hole Economic Policy Symposium, Federal Reserve Bank of Kansas City, Jackson Hole, Wyoming, 26–27 August.

Hicks J., (1969), Critical essays in monetary theory, *The Canadian Journal of Economics*, vol. 2, nr 1, pp. 141–144.

Ingves S., (2018), *Money and payments – where are we heading?*, speech at Stockholm School of Economics on 4 June 2018.

Ingves S., (2022), *Interview with Stefan Ingves, Governor of Sveriges Riksbank*, Obserwator Finansowy NBP.

International Monetary Fund, (2021), *Five Observations on Nigeria's Central Bank Digital Currency*, IMF Country Focus.

International Monetary Fund (2022), The Bahamas, *Staff report for the 2021 article IV consultation*, April.

Lagarde C., (2017), *Central Banking and Fintech—A Brave New World*? Bank of England conference on 29 September 2017.

Kosse A., Mattei I., (2022), *Gaining momentum – Results of the 2021 BIS survey on central bank digital currencies*, BIS Papers No 125.

Macias P., Stelmasiak D., Szafranek K., (2022), Nowcasting food inflation with a massive amount of online prices, *International Journal of Forecasting*, in press.

McLeay M., Radia A., Ryland T, (2014), *Money creation in the modern economy*, Bank of England Quarterly Bulletin 2014 Q1.

Narodowy Bank Polski, (2019), *Koszty instrumentów płatniczych na rynku polskim. Raport końcowy z projektu badawczego NBP*, March 2019.

Smets J., (2016), *Fintech and Central Banks*, presentation from the conference *Fintech and the Future of Retail Banking*, Brussels, 9 December 2016.

Soderberg G., (2022), *Behind the Scenes of Central Bank Digital Currency, Emerging Trends, Insights, and Policy Lessons*, International Monetary Fund Fintech Note 2022/004.

Sveriges Riksbank, (2022), *E-krona pilot Phase 2*, April.

Szpunar P., (2006), Międzybankowy rynek pieniężny, in: Pietrzak B., Polański Z., Woźniak B. (eds.), *System finansowy w Polsce*, Warszawa: Wydawnictwo Naukowe PWN, pp. 197–234.

5 Commercial banking

Drivers of accelerated digitalisation

Stanisław Kasiewicz and Lech Kurkliński

The aim of the chapter is to present an assessment of the state and drivers of digital banking development in the world, especially in Europe and Poland, during the 2000–2021 period. Changes in the digital sphere have been accelerated as a result of the COVID-19 pandemic and economic crisis. Special attention should be paid to the analysis of the maturity of the bank's transformation processes carried out for various categories and the identification of the forecasted trends in the development of the banking sector. Also, the most important challenges for banks are identified in the face of destructive competition from non-banking entities. The research is based on already published analyses and third-party sources, as well as the results of the authors' own research carried out in 2021 among banks, FinTechs, technology companies, and the scientific community in Poland.

5.1 The stage and drivers of digital banking development before the COVID-19 pandemic

Looking at the development of banking after 2000, two periods can be distinguished. The first one was covering the years 2000–2007/2008 and the second started after the collapse of Lehman Brothers. The critical point of this dichotomous division is the outbreak of the global financial crisis. In practically every crisis there is a catharsis, which is a premise for conducting a deep study on its origins, revealing the most important weaknesses and taking action to eliminate or reduce them. Very often it is the beginning of a new stage of development. This is what happened in the case of the banking sector.

The causes of the global financial crisis were primarily related to improper political and administrative interventions of the U.S. authorities in the real estate market, in particular, the adoption of a liberal mortgage granting policy to households with limited or even no creditworthiness. In the aftermath of the crisis, confidence in the banking sector dropped drastically and opened a new approach to financial services. Countering the dramatic effects of infecting the banking system through the subprime crisis, many governments have undertaken costly programmes to support strategically important banks. The financial burden borne by taxpayers has caused long-lasting changes to

DOI: 10.4324/9781003310082-9

the operating conditions of banks and enormous regulatory pressure from regulators. This led to the formation of a completely new face in the financial services market. The revolution in the sphere of information and communication technologies also came along. New technologies have not only become one of the factors shaping the financial services market but also have turned into a major driver of change. The effects have appeared in various spheres (Gasser, 2017, pp. 4–5):

5.1.1 Clients

The importance of physical contact with the bank has declined. Above all, this could be observed in the systematically decreasing number of bank branches, the reduction in their size, as well as the refocusing of their role. The nature of digital services enforced changes and adaptation to the customer journey in order to maintain constant contact with them (now remote, not physical) and ensure satisfaction with the provided services.

5.1.2 Operation models

The strong vertical integration of management processes between the front office and back office has weakened. The development of ICT enabled greater standardisation (e.g., open API interfaces) and opened a gate to "unbundling" many tasks, almost in all areas of bank operations. Atomisation of the value chain allowed the decentralisation of organisational structures, partnerships with other entities, and the creation of new operational and business models.

5.1.3 Revenue shaping models

Competition has increased not only between different banks but also among new players (FinTechs, BigTechs). New revenue models have emerged and new forms of revenue generation (e.g., fee-based or freemium) have been explored.

5.1.4 Digital banking platforms

The formula of operation as digital banking platforms gained more application opportunities. This presented a chance, especially for non-banking entities, to have a much wider presence in financial services, even without a banking licence.

5.1.5 Data-based banking

Access to and ability to use Big Data (both from internal sources and unstructured external information) have become extremely important, as they have an increasing impact on the design of new services, as well as increasing the operational efficiency of financial institutions or optimising risk management.

5.1.6 Banking value chain

More attention has been paid to the banking value chain and the opportunities to unbundle it. This has brought many non-banking companies into the game, especially FinTechs and BigTechs, such as Apple (Apple Pay app) or Google (Google Wallet). There was also an opportunity to intersect the "customer–bank" relationship with the instrumental use of banking institutions, treating them only as a "money warehouse" or donors of infrastructure or providers of selected products.

Even before the COVID-19 pandemic, there were predictions that 80% of financial institutions in their current form would go out of business or lose their ability to compete by 2030. McKinsey predicted that without appropriate remedial steps, the retail banking sector will shrink dramatically, with revenues falling to 40% by 2025 (HID IAM Solution, 2020; McKinsey, 2020).

5.2 The effects of COVID-19 on the functioning of banks and their competitors in the digital sphere

Initially, it was hard to believe that a relatively small phenomenon (a drop in the ocean) of the COVID-19 virus in China would be able to change the daily behaviours of individuals, society, the economy, and the banking sector in such a short time. At the beginning of 2020, the world was paralysed by a health and economic crisis and it is still unclear how long it will last. Its scale has overshadowed the global financial crisis from a decade ago. Regardless of the civilisational and economy-wide effects, banks have also felt the consequences. They have faced new challenges or seen the intensification of those already observed. The outbreak of the pandemic crisis came as a complete surprise to the public authorities, but also to economic actors, including banks. After the previous crisis, the management of the risk referred to as a "black swan" was perceived, but more theoretically than practically. As a result of the rapid spread of the pandemic, the decisions of public authorities were intuitive, uncoordinated, often irrational, and costly, as was later demonstrated by a drastic increase in inflation. A closed society, empty streets, airports, and factories created an atmosphere of fear, high uncertainty, and overwhelming helplessness. Despite the fact that the crisis situation has finally basically been brought under control and recovery is taking place, it is worth giving a closer look at how COVID-19 has affected the banking sector.

5.2.1 Macroeconomic environment and consumer behaviour

Most countries' economies experienced a collapse in economic growth at the beginning of 2020. In the second half of 2020 and in 2021 a fairly rapid economic "rebound effect" took place, but did not often exceed the levels from 2019. However, a return to normality is far from being achieved. This occurs at varying rates in different spheres, such as in transport services, tourism, hotels, catering, cosmetics, supply chains and anomalies in fuel markets, etc. This state of affairs was compounded by the outbreak of the Russian-Ukrainian war. This resulted in a significant weakening of positive trends (e.g., stimulating economic growth) and a strengthening of negative ones (e.g., fuelling the inflationary spiral).

The pandemic brought significant changes in customer attitudes. With the introduction of social distancing and remote work during the lockdown period the average consumer's life was limited to household chores. To a large extent, shopping shifted to the e-commerce industry and customers limited direct contact with banks as much as possible. Banks were forced to respond to these new conditions. Their digital transformation took a five-year leap forward in eight weeks (Agraval, 2021). The pandemic has accelerated changes in customer behaviour and expectations, forcing financial institutions to revise outdated ways of doing things and quickly implement innovations. Hence, the issue of leveraging the customer experience with redoubled force has become the focus of many banks (Kreger, 2020) as well as other financial services companies. Today almost every bank offers digital services. However, just having a mobile app or a web portal is no longer sufficient according to customer feedback. Customers demand services that they actually desire, threatening to give up their commitment and loyalty. They currently expect highly personalised communication and convenient and efficient service primarily on digital platforms (Kulahoglu, 2021).

5.2.2 Bank behaviour

After the outbreak of the crisis, banks quickly tried to enable the fastest possible customer access to banking services, for all those who had not yet used remote channels. The digital access capabilities of banks became important, and they were forced to adapt their operational systems to new conditions (e.g., remote work management and simplification of transaction processing). COVID-19 had an impact both on banks' relations with the environment and on the internal organisation of their work. First of all, it accelerated the processes of remote working and reduced the number of bank outlets, e.g., in Poland from March 2020 to October 2021, 15% of them disappeared (KNF, 2021). All this has accelerated the transformation process (McKinsey, 2021a). The pandemic has changed the way executives think about developing a digital strategy, and adequate business models, but also increased banks' resilience to disruptions arising in the market. The role of digital leadership has become an urgent necessity. Many banks have intensified the education of customers, on how to use ATMs safely and how to transact using cards, the Internet, and cell phones. In dealing with corporate customers, especially in the first stage of the pandemic, apriority was to recognise which industries would be impacted the hardest and which were likely to grow rapidly. The wider shift to digital channels has expanded the playing field for criminal groups, intensifying digital risks for individual and corporate customers. This has forced banks to counter these practices and customers to be more cautious.

5.2.3 Risk management

The course of the COVID-19 crisis has highlighted the importance of banks' communication systems with customers and risk management. The fact that some individual customers experienced the problem of digital exclusion cannot be ignored. It has become important for the banking sector from the perspective of losing reputation and trust, and competing in the digital environment. As far as the risk management system is concerned, the pandemic has confirmed the importance of, (a) appropriate modelling of dynamically changing phenomena, (b) having adequate risk management teams, (c) access to alternative data sources, (d) hybrid models (both simple and complex), and (e) monitoring a wide cross-section of information affecting significant risks (already known or new). This raises the challenge for banks not only to better identify risks but to be prepared for the emergence of low probability economically and socially impactful risks (the so-called "black swans"). Such situations may include the next pandemic, cyberattacks, domestic terrorism, sovereign debt crises, geopolitical and military tensions, supply chain disruptions, and others. Many of these phenomena have appeared (especially the Russian-Ukrainian war).

5.2.4 The impact of the crisis

The pandemic crisis has caused numerous negative effects, but also positive ones from the perspective of the development of the banking sector. The return to the state before COVID-19 will be slow, uneven, and impossible. Positive effects include the acceleration of the digital transformation of banks, giving more importance to the usage of new technologies, customer support offers, unprecedented forms of cooperation with other institutions to support social and environmental programmes, and the urgent need to develop new strategies and business models. This is demonstrated by McKinsey's (2021b) analysis, which finds that only 11% of surveyed companies believe their existing business models will be viable by 2023, while another 64% of respondents need to develop new strategies and business models to achieve digital transformation. The negative effects of COVID-19 from the perspective of traditional banks include the following:

- global GDP decline, the world economy contracted by 12% in Q1 2020 (Dewar, 2020);
- weakening of an important pillar of the banking business – payments. The global payments revenue declined by 5% in 2020, when it grew at an annual rate of 5% between 2011 and 2020, and even more importantly,

Table 5.1 Characteristics of the banking sector before and after the COVID-19 outbreak

Before the outbreak	*After the outbreak*
Branch banking and isolated digitisation	Integrated banking with a set of digital skills
An uneven and uncertain customer journey	A holistic process for digitalising the customer journey
Product-driven digital growth	Comprehensive, customer-focused intelligent transformation
Risk management based on credit scoring	Risk management based on data analytics
Permanent place of work for employees and in branches	Remote working and reduction of bank branch network
Competition between banks and customer generations	Competition between ecosystems
Business mentality as a priority	Socially responsible banking, sensitive to supporting the society

Source: Marous (2021)

banks' share of total payments revenue fell to less than 40% (McKinsey, 2021b). Competitors – FinTechs and BigTechs – have entered the arena more robustly;

- exposing weaknesses in the digital infrastructure used by many banks;
- the threat of bankruptcy of many economic entities (banks' customers);
- the necessity to implement processes of further restructuring and consolidation of banks;
- causing a decline in confidence in commonly used, traditional models by financial institutions;
- increasing uncertainty in the security of bank customers and thus undermining confidence in the banking system;
- a growing concern among banking personnel about the future of the banking industry as a whole and its employees, and a growing vulnerability in the battle for talent.

A summary of the characteristics of the banking sector before and after the outbreak of the COVID-19 pandemic is presented in Table 5.1. The changes taking place will have a profound impact on the operation and management of banks in the coming years, especially the success of their digital transformation.

5.3 Banks' digital transformation maturity

Reviewing the directions of the development of financial institutions clearly indicates that the focal point of any contemporary strategy and business model is the position of digital technologies. It shows the necessity to monitor the advancement of digital transformation processes in the banking sector, including assessing its maturity. This raises two dilemmas, which areas of digital transformation to choose for assessment (the banking sector as a whole, its main sub-sectors – e.g., retail banks, commercial banks, what types of technologies, factors supporting implementation – organisational culture). The second dilemma is the choice of appropriate maturity measures. According to the authors' opinion, the digital transformation of banks is determined in two ways, i.e., on the one hand by the activities of new competitors (external destruction, disrupting the existing way of functioning) and on the other hand by banks' independent decision-making (internal transformation). The evaluation of digital transformation maturity can be based on qualitative measures. The report of the "MIT Sloan Management Review" gives some examples. In a conducted study, 3,500 managers of service and manufacturing companies (29 industries) elaborated on this topic. Digital maturity was evaluated by the imagination of "… an ideal organization transformed by digital technologies and capabilities that improve processes, engage talent across the organisation, and drive new value-generating business models" (Kane, 2017, p. 3). The managers were asked to rate their companies. As recently as 2016, only 25% of responses indicated a high degree of this maturity among companies. Digital initiatives belonged to a key part of their business strategies. In contrast, 34% of companies were located in the early stages of digital development. They could be characterised more by plans and discussions about digital business rather than real actions. In addition, the length of the planning horizon, the scaling of digital experiments, the attracting talent, and the ability of digital leaders to implement the strategic visions were considered the main factors (Kane, 2017, pp. 3–4).

Identifying digital leaders can be achieved by determining what and how prevailing business practices and digital solutions give a competitive advantage. Deloitte's 2020 study reviewed the financial indicators (ROE, cost/income, ROA) of banks and compared them with selected features of digital maturity. The following areas were analysed to assess this maturity in banks: digital functionalities, preferred distribution channels (branches, Internet, and mobile), and perception of customer experience. Finally, four groups of banks were distinguished: digital laggards - latecomers, digital adopters, digital smart followers, and digital champions. Naturally, the latecomers were ranked lowest, while the leaders represented the highest level of maturity. The latter group offers a wide range of important functionalities, attractive to customers. Moreover, they set key trends and dominant practices. Most of the leading banks focus on retail activities. They are relatively small digital banks. Within the reviewed group 19% are "challenger banks" (Deloitte, 2020).

The external destruction of banks by competitors has been widely studied as well (MIT SMR, 2020; Vives, 2020). As recently as 2016, it was estimated that by 2020 as much as 28% of the banking sector and payment systems would be subject to destruction, with 22% of the threat affecting financial market sub-sectors such as Insurance, Asset Management, and Wealth

Management (PwC, 2020, p. 8). As a result of the pandemic, these changes have accelerated to some extent, but not to the level of the Cassandra forecast. Thus, the destruction of banks by the FinTech sector is progressing, which can be illustrated by comparing the share of the capitalisation of the 100 largest FinTech companies with the value of the 100 largest banks. It turns out this share in 2021 is 38% while in 2010 it was only 3% (CFTE, 2021, p. 14). This is a change of a revolutionary nature. However, the banks' defensive actions have also started to bear fruit. Digital bank customers in the United States already numbered 196.8 million in 2021, accounting for 75.4% of the population, and the latest estimates indicate that this share will reach 80.4% in 2025 (Phaneuf, 2021).

The level of maturity of banks can be examined by considering the degree of their commitment to customer expectations, through customer experience process analytics or by examining the degree of implementation of key technologies such as artificial intelligence. In 2020 47% of American business and IT leaders considered customer experience analytics their top priority (The Pointillist, 2020). A 2021 study by the Digital Poland Foundation found that artificial intelligence is used by 41% of financial and banking institutions in Poland (FDP, 2021, p. 38). The degree of advancement of banks' digital transformation was also the subject of the authors' 2021 research on the Polish market. The highest degree of advancement was assessed in the area of payments (see Figure 5.1). This opinion sounds somewhat paradoxical when FinTechs are gaining clear competitive successes precisely in this sphere. Adaptations to regulatory changes were also appreciated. Building partnerships with FinTechs/BigTechs and preparing for increased competition from them received weaker marks. Taking all respondents' answers into account, the digital transformation of Polish banks performed satisfactorily.

To have a more complete picture of the current state of the digital transformation of banks in Poland, it is worth adding the most important barriers to this process (excluding those strictly technological). They are related to market problems (market trends, intensifying competition, administrative actions unfriendly to banks, etc.), legal barriers, such as the high cost of regulatory burdens (EU and domestic), and the problem of mortgage loans in foreign currencies - a specific issue in several Central and East Europe. This was also compounded by fears of unpredictability by the authorities, such as the introduction of excessive protection for customers, especially borrowers when interest rates rise at the expense of banks (Figure 5.2).

In general, respondents' opinions focused primarily on external challenges for banks. Although banks recognised their own problems (23.5% of respondents) with their organisational nature (strategy development, business model adoption, leadership, etc.), these were not of primary importance. This was partly due to a certain degree of complacency about the level of technological complexity, which was evident in the weak perception of the threat from FinTechs and BigTechs (Kasiewicz, Kurkliński, Woźniak, 2021, pp. 103–122).

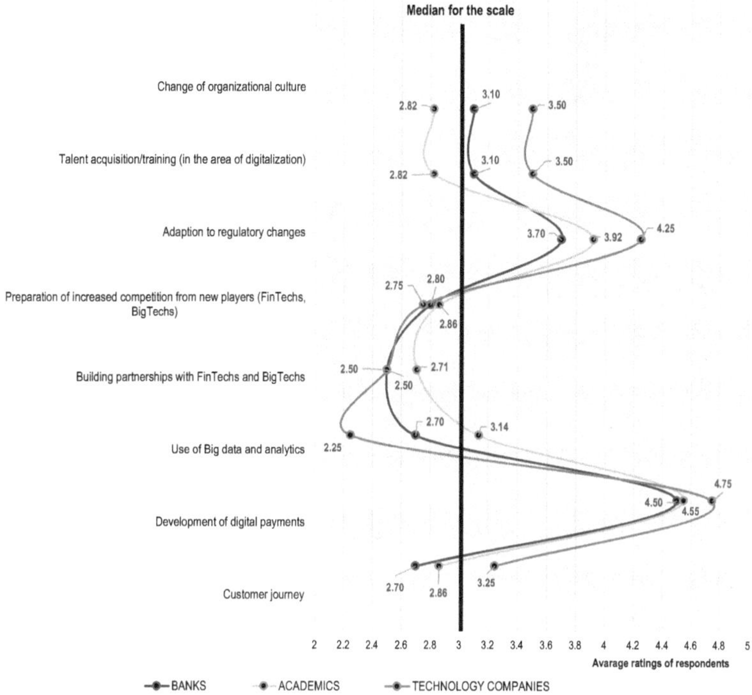

Figure 5.1 Areas of analysis on the current level of progress of digital transformation
The rating scale: 1 – the lowest, 5 – the highest
Source: Kasiewicz, Kurkliński, Woźniak (2021, p. 105)

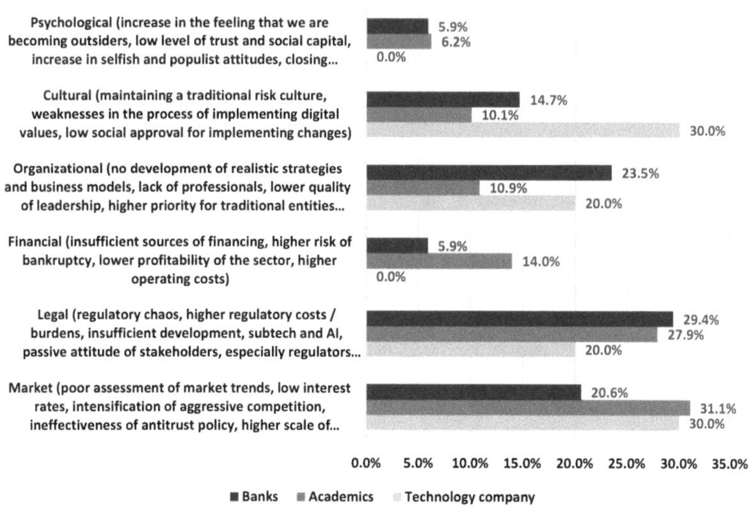

Figure 5.2 Key non-technological barriers to digital transformation (% of answers)
Source: Kasiewicz, Kurkliński, Woźniak (2021, p. 107)

5.4 Technological innovations and development trends in the banking services market

The wave of financial innovation is expanding as technological advances enable a deeper understanding of consumer behaviours and preferences. Realising how people buy, extract information, and use it for purchasing decisions is the foundation of actions for success for any type of business, including the financial industry. Customer behaviour analysis based on different data sources can help to reach the unbanked and underserved people. The financial innovations support satisfying increasing customer expectations. Products are more personalised and based on digital experiences. Also, digitalisation reduces the barriers to entry for new market players with new offers. How significant the scale of change made by modern technologies in the financial services market is presented in Figure 5.3.

Digital competition is highly dependent on prevailing trends. There are many studies on the direction of financial services. These diagnoses identify at least seven major trends (Marous, 2019):

5.4.1 Trend 1. High threat from BigTechs

After the global financial crisis, confidence in banks was severely shaken, but over time has recovered to relatively high levels (68%), as exemplified by the Polish market in early 2020. Unfortunately, as a result of the COVID-19 pandemic, it declined. In contrast, for companies categorised as BigTechs, these "pandemic" declines were minimal. In the longer view, their confidence is gaining slowly but systematically. This is due to offering customers convenience, quick turnaround times, and lower costs. Among the new players,

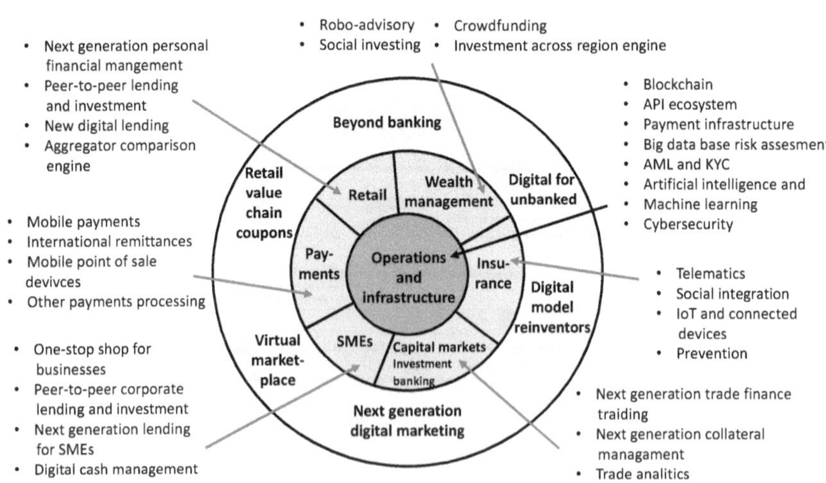

Figure 5.3 New trends in FinTech services
Source: Mohamed, Ali (2019, p. 23)

customers have the highest level of trust in financial services provided by Amazon (65%), with slightly lower levels of trust in Google (58%), Apple (56%), and Facebook (48%). There is no doubt that these giants will not give up the fight for greater market share in the coming years and therefore pose a serious threat to traditional banks (Kantar, 2020).

5.4.2 Trend 2. *Open banking* and expanding beyond traditional financial services

Expanding services beyond the traditional ones creates competitive opportunities for all banks receptive to innovative approaches. The concept of *open banking* unlocks opportunities for collaboration and partnerships with other companies through the extensive use of open API software. In the US, up to 44% of senior bank executives expect that non-financial products can generate 10% or more in profits. However, such openness is claimed only by a fraction of banks. In contrast, new competitors are much more active and effective in these areas (Marous, 2019).

5.4.3 Trend 3. Increasing levels of digitisation and a simultaneous decline in digital satisfaction

The appetite for increased digital functionality no longer encompasses only younger generations of consumers but is becoming more widespread, regardless of customers' age, education, and wealth position. This is accompanied by a decline in digital satisfaction, due to an increase in customer expectations. As always, especially in retail banking, pricing issues will play an important role, and with many services accustomed to being free, attempts to introduce fees will have a strong impact on customer opinions, especially in the age of social media ubiquity. Such an example was the initiative of one disgruntled customer who created the "National Transfer Day November 5 2011" initiative, when US banks lost 650,000 customers to credit unions within a month (Oremus, 2011).

5.4.4 Trend 4. Doing good is gratifying

The importance of pro-social activities of financial institutions is systematically growing. More attention is paid to providing transparent and fair services, enabling customers to become more financially literate, and offering innovative products for the economically disadvantaged or those from discriminated minorities, i.e., counteracting financial exclusion. The expected social attitude of banks, but also of their competitors, is also due to the increasingly severe effects of the occurrence of climate, environmental, and health crises or disasters, or the objectives articulated in the concept of sustainable development using Environmental, Social, and Governance (ESG) factors.

5.4.5 Trend 5. Bank's systemic weaknesses could cripple its growth prospects

In most countries (especially in Europe), banks have to operate in unfavourable macroeconomic conditions, bearing heavy regulatory burdens, heavy tax burdens, or experiencing the consequences of the COVID-19 crisis and the Russian-Ukrainian war. A large number of these banks have an obsolete IT infrastructure, which should be modernised as soon as possible. Unfortunately, some financial institutions may face significant barriers in overcoming these challenges due to insufficient resources to fund them, but also a lack of digital skills, or leadership. Continuing to maintain banking operations through slow, closed systems (main-frame IT systems) is far more expensive and less effective than the new competition from FinTechs, BigTechs, and challenger banks.

5.4.6 Trend 6. Risk mitigation – moving target

Adequate risk management in banks requires constant adaptation to market realities, technological changes, and other conditions. Understandably, this has always been the case, but current changes are occurring in dramatically shorter timeframes and multiple tracks. The level of uncertainty and discontinuity is growing, new "black swans" are appearing. Thus, it is no longer possible to speak of evolutionary change, but of abrupt or even revolutionary one (KPMG, ZBP, 2019; Skinner, 2021). Banks face new challenges of a very different nature, such as climate, security, political populism, and others. Surprising new regulatory requirements can cripple banks' operations to some extent. More pressure from customers is expected. This will require banks to have a more diverse and integrated team of specialists in social media, various risks, and crisis management.

5.4.7 Trend 7. Bankers' pessimistic job outlook

The attractiveness of jobs at banks is steadily declining, and they are finding it harder to draw in talent. Technological changes are forcing restructuring and downsising. There is a growing need to hire digital professionals, for whom almost all industries are competing, but the most successful are technology companies. Moreover, working in institutions with a traditional bureaucratic organisational culture is becoming less accepted by the younger generation.

The abovementioned trends indicate the direction of changes in the market of banking services. They also show areas of threats to banks and how dangerous are competitors. Digital transformation is not changing the main rule of competition – the customer is the king. That's why the greatest interest and involvement of management should focus on customer experience. Trends in this area include (Kreger, 2020):

- expanding the digital perspective,
- empowering an experience-based culture,

- overcoming the experience gap,
- enriching the experience with an emotional connection,
- setting up experience-driven key performance indicators (KPIs),
- switching from Intelligent Quotient (IQ) to Emotional Quotient (EQ),
- establishing consistency through product ecosystem,
- providing a contextual experience,
- teaming up with FinTech and technology companies,
- taking the value of customer experience to a new level.

Among the highlighted trends, it is particularly worth taking note of expanding the digital perspective, strengthening the culture based on customer experience, and moving from IQ to EQ. The need to broaden the digital perspective cannot be limited to customer experience alone but should include other actions taken in the back-office cells. Certainly, it cannot be done without developing a digital strategy and business model (presented in Chapter 7). It is also worth appreciating the growing trend in the wider use of the emotional factor of customers when it is already possible to measure their positive and negative emotions with high precision. On this basis, it is easier to look for solutions to increase the efficiency of banks.

5.5 Challenges for the banking sector

Traditional banking institutions are characterised by an obsolete IT infrastructure, high operating costs, inefficient processes, and inadequate culture. Therefore, banks face three major challenges, deepening digital transformation, adapting digital culture, and attracting or nurturing talent that can effectively impact the transition to highly competitive entities in a digital environment (Carbone, 2021; Liu, 2021; European Commission, 2021; OECD, 2020).

The key to effective transformation is to entrust bank management to a digital leader. Observation shows that an old management style and perception of the IT area still prevails, which does not determine the digital strategy, business model, and investment direction of banks. The most important characteristics of digital leaders include the following: clarity of vision, awareness of market changes, having an adequate strategy, customer orientation, ability to undertake collaboration, having a loyal and integrated team of employees, agility and flexibility in action, results in orientation, and willingness to learn and focus on achieving long- and short-term goals (KPMG, 2017, p. 11). Getting bank boards out of their comfort zone requires undertaking a fairly complex broad digital transformation programme covering areas such as (Marous, 2021):

- leadership in data and analytics,
- continuous improvement of customer service quality,
- consistent support for innovation,
- use of modern technologies,
- modernising systems and processes,
- convincing employees to accept digital solutions.

Without talented employees, it would be difficult for banks to gain a competitive advantage. In addition, salaries offered by banks are becoming uncompetitive compared to the offers of technology giants or large corporations. Therefore, banks cannot limit their own actions to acquiring talent from the market but should undertake a more complex process of training and shaping talent.

A very important aspect of digital transformation of banks is organisational culture, as this sphere is among the most important success factors (Kasiewicz, Kurkliński, 2020). A good culture integrates employees in achieving strategic goals and supports the effectiveness of applied business models. It affects the improvement of risk management, safety, growth of trust, reputation, honesty, and compliance with ethical principles. It creates an aura of a friendly institution for bank employees and customers. There are significant differences between the culture of a digital bank and traditional institutions. There are many reasons for these differences: the key features of the bank (e.g., a bureaucratic organisation, risk-avoiding attitude), the banks' competitive system (high barriers to enter the market), the cautious approach to carrying out the digital transformation, the stable value system, and the use of verified business practices. Primarily traditional banks have a formal approach to customers, a focus on financial performance, siloed operations, and especially a desire for stability and compliance with existing rules. In contrast, digital institutions place a high value on experimentation, collaboration, and partnership, and maximising the use of data and analytical techniques. Westerman, Soule, and Eswaran (2019) find that organisations based on new technologies pursue their competitive advantage through radical innovation activity, quick decisions under high uncertainty, openness and use of diverse information sources, and autonomy and informal forms of coordination for their employees. Nevertheless, it is important to state that not all practices of traditional banks should be eliminated, as the commitment to stability, integrity, and compliance with operating rules (formal and informal) should be nurtured and valued also in digital competition.

5.6 Conclusions

The main research problem is concentrated on the threat of traditional banks losing their dominant position in the financial services market in the coming years because of accelerated digitalisation. It was predicted by some reports from well-known analytical and consulting companies. The considerations carried out, based on the results of the latest studies, publications, and empirical research conducted by the authors in Poland, indicate that this will not happen, at least within the next five to ten years. Despite the described significant technological changes and acceleration of many processes concerning the banking sector caused by the COVID-19 pandemic crisis, the position of banks has not deteriorated drastically. The intensification of warning signals led to increased attention and the undertaking of certain steps by banks. The starting point should be the assessment of the maturity of the banking sector in the process of digital transformation. In this respect, the picture of the banking sector is mixed. Nevertheless, banks are quite involved in the process, although there is a large group of banks called digital laggards - latecomers. Apart from them, there are digital adopters, digital smart followers, and digital champions. These last two groups are also called challenger banks. There are also elements of complacency among some banks and underestimation of competition from new players, including FinTechs and BigTechs. The destruction of the banking services market occurs in two ways: by the actions of new competitors (external destruction) and by the strategies and business models of banks themselves (internal destruction). Both of these challenges are faced by banks. In order to meet them, it is worth taking into account the trends in the development of the banking sector, not only related to new technologies themselves, but to the broader social, cultural, demographic, environmental, political, and economic conditions that have been highlighted in this chapter. It is important to remember that although we are seeing a technological revolution, it is embedded in a particular environment.

Bibliography

Agraval V. (2021), *6 Ways Digital Is Transforming the Customer Journey in Banking*. The Financial Brand, April 28, https://thefinancialbrand.com/110823/digital-banking-customer-journey-experience-ai/ (15.12.2021).

Carbone B.V. (2021), *COVID, Legacy Banks and the Digital Competition*. Sopra Banking Software, September 3.

CFTE (2021), *CFTE's Fintech Job Report*. Centre for Finance, Technology and Entrepreneurship.

Deloitte (2020), *Digital Banking Maturity 2020*. Deloitte Digital, October.

Dewar J. (2020), *The Impact of the COVID-19 Pandemic on Financial Inclusion*. Nasdaq, Inc, April 27.

European Commission (2021), *Banking Package 2021: New EU Rules to Strengthen Banks' Resilience and Better Prepare for the Future*. Brussels, 27 October, https://ec.europa.eu/commission/presscorner/detail/en/IP_21_5401 (9.12.2021).

FDP (2021), *State of Polish API 2021*. Fundacja Digital Poland, Warszawa, April.

Gasser U. (2017), *Digital Bank 2025*, April.

HID IAM Solution (2020), *Staying Competitive in a Disruptive Banking Environment*, https://www.hidglobal.com/sites/default/files/documentlibrary/iams-approve-safe-disruptive-banking-eb-en.pdf (13.11.2022).

Kane G.C. (2017), *Achieving Digital Maturity. Research Report*. MIT Sloan Review, Deloitte University Press, 2017.

Kantar (2020), *Raport z wyników badań reputacji polskiego sektora bankowego*, Kantar Polska, Warszawa, Kwiecień.

Kasiewicz S., Kurkliński L. (2020), *Kultura ryzyka a cyfrowa transformacja banków w świetle pandemii COVID-19*. Wydawnictwo CeDeWu, Warszawa.

Kasiewicz S., Kurkliński L., Woźniak J. (2021), *Strategie i modele biznesowe banków wobec konkurencji ze strony FinTech-ów*, WIB, Warszawa (not published).

KNF (2021), *Dane miesięczne sektora bankowego (Monthly bank sector data)*, https://www.knf.gov.pl/?articleId=56224&p_id=18 (13.11.2022).

KPMG (2017), *Forging the Future. How Financial Institutions Are Embracing Fintech to Evolve and Grow*, https://assets.kpmg/content/dam/kpmg/xx/pdf/2017/10/forging-the-future-global-fintech-study.pdf (11.11.2021).

KPMG, ZBP (2019), *PSD 2 and Open Banking. Revolution or Evolution?*, Report.

Kreger A. (2020), *10 Digital Banking UX Trends that Will Drive Post-Pandemic Strategy*. The Financial Brand, December 21, 2020. https://thefinancialbrand.com/105206/digital-banking-ux-post-pandemic-trends-cx-experience-mobile-design/ (15.12.2021).

Kulahoglu Y. (2021), *Bad Habits that Stifle UX Innovation at Banks & Credit Unions*. The Financial Brand, January 18.

Liu E.X. (2021), *Stay Competitive in the Digital Age: The Future of Banks*. IFM Working Papers, February 19.

Marous J. (2019), *The Top 7 Digital Transformation Trends in Banking*, The Financial Brand, 7 October.

Marous J. (2021), *Digital Banking Transformation is a Journey, Not a Destination*, https://thefinancialbrand.com/107727/digital-banking-transformation-journey/ (23.12.2021).

McKinsey (2020), *FinTechnicolor: The New Picture in Finance*. McKinsey and Company. 08.03.2020.

McKinsey (2021a), *COVID-19: Briefing note #76*, McKinsey & Company. 13.10.2021.

McKinsey (2021b), *The New Digital Edge: Rethinking Strategy for the Postpandemic Era*. McKinsey Digital, May.

McKinsey (2021c), *The 2021 McKinsey Global Payments Report*. Global Banking Practice. McKinsey & Company, October.

MIT SMR (2020), *Disruption 2020*. "MITSloan Management Review". Special Collection. Spring.

Mohamed H., Ali H. (2019), *Blockchain, Fintech, and Islamic Finance*, Walter de Gruyter Inc., Boston/Berlin.

OECD (2020), *Can Market Studies Be a More Effective Tool for Tackling Emerging Competition Issues?* October 21.

Oremus W. (2011), *Should You Transfer Your Money to a Credit Union?*, https://slate.com/news-and-politics/2011/11/national-bank-transfer-day-does-it-make-sense-to-transfer-your-money-to-a-credit-union.html (7.01.2022).

Phaneuf A. (2021), *The Disruptive Trends & Companies Transforming Digital Banking Services in 2021*. July 28.

PwC (2020), *Financial Services Technology 2020 and Beyond: Embracing Disruption*. https://www.pwc.com/gx/en/financial-services/assets/pdf/technology2020-and-beyond.pdf (13.11.2022)

Skinner C. (2021), *Where Is the Banking Revolution?*, Chris Skinner's blog https://thefinanser.com, 2021/07 (18.08.2021).

The Pointillist (2020), *The Ultimate Guide to Growing Revenue with Customer Journey Analytics*. "MIT Sloan Management Review", https://www.pointillist.com/news/pointillist-cited-as-a-leader-in-journey-orchestration-platforms-by-independent-research-firm/ (16.11.2021).

Vives X. (2020), *Digital Disruption in Banking and its Impact on Competition*. OECD.

Westerman G., Soule D. L., Eswaran A. (2019), *Building Digital-Ready Culture in Traditional Organizations*, https://sloanreview.mit.edu/article/building-digital-ready-culture-in-traditional-organizations/ (15.05.2022).

6 Open banking

What does open banking open?

Marcin Kotarba

6.1 Introduction

The development of the financial sector would certainly put a smile on the face of the 14th Century Filippo Peruzzi, one of the founders of modern capitalism (GEO, 2014). The very idea of connecting economical systems to facilitate trade between communities specializing in various products and services has not changed for ages, but it has evolved stepwise toward more connectivity (linking more suppliers and consumers globally), more flexibility (new value propositions) and more technology, well seen in the digital revolution, where banks clearly hold a leadership position. At the same time, certain elements of the capitalistic system remain unchanged. The first and foremost is hosted in the name itself – it is about capital, the ultimate value of any venture. The capital serves three primary purposes of every human/organizational construct: survival, growth and consumption. It needs to be protected and accumulated, assuring all three purposes are balanced.

In the past, when the monetary systems were based on precious metals the protection of capital had an additional "physical" component. Storage and transportation of capital, e.g. in the form of gold coins, was oriented toward building safety, mainly by closing it in vaults, sturdy chests or armored vehicles. Generations of engineers worked on "closing" the capital in a way that would prevent unauthorized access. Other generations of thieves worked on "breaking into the vault" or bypassing the security systems, even making it to the Guinness Book of Records (Moneywise 2021). The legacy of banks being the trusted guardians of wealth has found its reflection in a highly digitized world of today, where capital is represented by data processed by financial institutions. Cyber security is a direct equivalent of the underground vaults, aimed at preventing the loss of now digital assets. It is therefore a heritage of setting up layers of barriers and closing the capital in allowing its usage only based on strict regulations and entitlements. In this context, the relatively new term "open banking" touches on a foundational paradigm of banks. Is it just a revolutionary buzzword aimed at creating a new revenue stream for consulting and technology companies or an actual change trigger that will bring innovation to the financial markets? Is it indeed going to bring value

DOI: 10.4324/9781003310082-10

by opening up new business opportunities, better customer service or solving some regulatory dilemmas? What does open banking open?

In this chapter, we are going to define the open banking concept, by looking at its ontology and understanding its value proposition for various participants of financial markets, focusing on banks and their clients, but reaching into other areas, such as technology used in finance or market regulation. We then cover a strategic evaluation of the concept, looking at opportunities and risks in its journey toward widespread adoption by the financial world. The discourse is focused on the European banking sector, which is considered the cradle of systematic open banking development. This situation can be mainly attributed to the PSD2[1] regulation of the European Union which forced the institutionalization of several building blocks of open banking, such as account information services (AIS), payment initiation (PIS) and strong customer authentication (SCA). PSD2 acted as a catalyst in the emergence of a new population of organizations – the third-party providers (TPPs) which grew from about 100 to 450 in less than two years (Mallick, McIntyre, Scott, 2021). This assisted development of a base open banking layer is followed by the outburst of "fintech", technology companies that create new value chains or enhance the existing ones with user-oriented, highly technologically advanced, non-regulated financial solutions. The growth in the number of fintech in the EMEA[2] region, between 2019 and 2021 had the highest dynamic (+160%) versus Asia-Pacific (+118%) and the Americas (+89%) (Norrestad Fintech, 2022) providing a view that the activation of "open" financial thinking in Europe is progressing at a high speed.

6.2 Open banking ontology

One of the first questions about open banking is to determine its nature and position within the economy, specifically within the financial system. Definitions found in the publications and business practice[3] cover a surprisingly broad spectrum of opinions, placing open banking in three main ontology clusters: strategic, business and technological.

On the highest level of abstraction, in a strategic sense, open banking is considered to be a **step in the ongoing development of the financial system**. Along the continuum of development, the most used terminology includes:

1 **evolution** – emphasizing the aspects of innovation, morphological changes and the expected increase in the intelligence of the markets and institutions,
2 **disruption** of current paradigms – pointing out the modification of value chains and market interactions, to the point where existing business models must be adjusted,
3 **new paradigm** – envisioning a design to give the customers more diverse and compelling value propositions,

4 **change trend/wave** – suggesting that open banking causes a global and unstoppable movement, which will leave a mark, either temporary or permanent, on the actors in the financial system.

All of the above points of view have their legitimate right to be high-level descriptors of open banking. However, the common element seen in all terms is related to "change". For the purpose of this discourse, we assume that this change can occur in all dimensions: creation, modification or removal of existing morphological elements of the financial system. As such these descriptions can be used only to signify the strategically significant emergence of sector activity, without talking about its actual content.

The second cluster brings together the business-relevant definitions and treats open banking as a **new business ecosystem**, established on various principles:

1 **high customization** and personalization of the products and service offer, achieved by a deep and instantaneous understanding of the client's financial situation and matching any needs with a wide product offer,
2 **client orientation** is built around the customer experience, ease of use and the comfort of usage of processes and tools, it may cover a refreshed process (e.g. simplified sales application) or the creation of a previously not available offer,
3 **data richness** suggests the collection of and widespread use of information to facilitate business processes,
4 **API-connected ecosystem** where new product combinations are offered by bringing together partners (or competitors) thanks to the usage of application programming interfaces (APIs).

The first three of the above descriptions are rather standard in the ontology of digitalization and fintech, providing limited value to capture the essence of open banking. However, the last point brings a strong message of a novelty coming from the fact that the connectivity within the ecosystem and between different ecosystems is based on the widespread usage of APIs. Although still referring to the business ecosystems it is already pointing to its technological core. This provides a solid bridge to the next cluster of online banking definitions, rooted in the technology, with the following examples:

1 **new technology platforms** that create an environment/infrastructure for building connectivity between market participants, increasing the level of multichannel access to products/services,
2 **technological third-party services** that come from beyond the world of banking, but are integrated into the financial ecosystem, here in a narrow sense open banking is also attributed to account aggregation (browsing the information of client products spread across many financial institutions),

3 **finance liberation through PSD2**- regulatory forced technological collaboration layer allowing for more open interactions, diluting the ever-present issue of captive banking,
4 **set of APIs for custom application development**, including software development and usage frameworks to register/sign-up, provide authentication and authorization schemes, create applications, test them, obtain approval and put them into production. The facilitation of API usage is supported by developer portals and partner networks allowing for collaboration and knowledge management.

The technological cluster of definitions appears to be the most convincing in highlighting the nature of open banking to stem from the API-oriented integration between market participants. One may immediately say that the entire financial system is already connected through similar technological interfaces, especially by online and mobile banking, in the area of payments (e.g. SEPA or Mastercard) or regulatory reporting feeds into central banks. As much as this is true, the aforementioned "traditional" connectivity is strongly based on proprietary interfaces that operate in a closed environment of financial institutions and selected integration partners. Open banking provides an additional layer of interfaces that are partially regulated but have no fixed boundaries other than the decisions taken by a financial institution (on the supply side) or the clients/consumers of such services (demand side). In other words, **open banking is a choice of a financial institution to change its business model to enable new direct technology-based interactions with market participants** raising a need for such interactions.

6.2.1 Open banking actors

Incumbent financial institutions are foundational actors in the open banking arena. These institutions, as managers and guardians of capital, are legal and regulated providers of asset and liability products, including their related transactional capabilities. This notion is crucial to the definition of open banking: the base of financial products remains with the regulated institutions, but what changes is the way they are offered and serviced. from this point of view, it is important to take a look at what impact open banking has on the actors and their connectivity in the financial system. Starting with the existing entities we can observe the following:

1 **Clients** (all segments):
  a have the option to start new connections with open banking vendors to optimize their financial management,
  b can build new interfaces with service providers, e.g. by developing custom online banking or finance management solutions.

2 **Financial institutions** (banks, investments funds, markets/exchanges):
   a are the providers of APIs as technical measures of accessing their processes in two modes:
      i mandatory (e.g. PSD2 based),
      ii voluntary, extending the API base for the benefit of the market and innovation,
   b create developer portals where APIs can be tested and implemented,
   c launch their own TPP ventures (e.g. ING Bank in Poland with the ING Uslugi dla Biznesu TPP registered as a non-bank corporation).

3 **Neobanks**[4] (branchless or mobile only, e.g. Revolut, Bunq) – same as with the financial institutions.
4 **All varieties of X-Tech** (Fin-, Reg- and Insur-tech) that participate in banking products of transactions:
   a develop new products based on the available APIs (e.g. account aggregation, pre-sales scoring, collections) by working with the TPPs,
   b launch their own TPP ventures,
   c integrate solutions within the ecosystem.

5 **Payment schemes** (cards, fund transfers, exchanges, cryptocurrencies, e-commerce) – same as X-Tech.
6 **Regulators** (national, cross-border, e.g. the EU):
   a shape the regulated open banking frameworks (e.g. required services) including the legal aspects, split of roles and responsibilities, market supervision and control,
   b provide directional guidance on the technical standards,
   c develop new internal teams that specialize in open banking themes,
   d popularize the usage of new banking products and services.

7 **Professional banking associations** or other financial service cooperation vehicles:
   a develop technical standards for APIs and other open banking technology,
   b facilitate the sectoral discussion on challenges in the open banking concepts (e.g. frequency of allowed account inquiries per TPP to avoid performance problems, digital trust management),
   c popularize the usage of new banking products and services, also by mobilizing the association members to an active "market maker role".

8 **Financial intermediaries/agents**:
   a large networks engage in development activities similar to X-Tech either via build or integration of open banking solutions,
   b individual agents remain outside of the APIs revolution if not able to technologically engage in the new solutions.

9 **Aggregators of financial information** and transactions (front runners of account integration, previously based on screen scraping and

controversial passing of user credentials) – same as X-Tech, however, their open banking solutions may enter a cannibalization conflict with the existing activities (e.g. PSD2 solves a previous dilemma).

10 **Outsourcing providers** for financial services performing selected processes (e.g. sales or aftersales) on behalf of an institution:
   a have the opportunity to rebuild their service offering around new open banking solutions to bring more efficiency into the process,
   b review the data exchange with their contract providers to verify options for further optimization.

11 **Non-bank institutions offering financial services** (e.g. consumer credit) - develop new products based on the available APIs (e.g. account aggregation, pre-sales scoring, collections) by working with the TPPs.

12 **Bigtech** (e.g. Google, Apple, Facebook): similar to X-Tech.

In addition to the above-listed existing actors, open banking became home to several new entities:

13 **TPP** of API services:
   a benefit from the open banking architecture to develop new products and services,
   b operate technological hubs managing data from various processes.

14 **Open Banking hubs** offering directory, standards and trust services for TPPs[5]:
   a onboarding: a standardized registration or licensing process for third-party providers and access to formalized standards (API/data, TPP verification, consent management, security (authentication, authorization, information protection), user experience guidelines for front-ends),
   b directory services: registry and routing services for TPPs with information on bank API locations,
   c third-party identification: electronic certificates for secure identification of TPPs,
   d digital identity: federated and decentralized digital identity services,
   e dispute management: unified incident reporting and dispute management services to manage customer disputes on behalf of the participants,
   f information dashboard: performance indicators, API reporting and analytics for participants,
   g unified access to accounts, identity services and payment processing.

15 **API Banks** take the API concept beyond most typical uses (e.g. PSD2) and create end-to-end API solutions that can be used to create a custom, component-based banking venture. For entities that hold a banking license and look for a simple banking setup, the API architecture provides the necessary modularity/flexibility to build the bank's IT out of the box, with customizations and proper branding.

The impact of open banking is clearly seen across the financial ecosystem and it would be difficult to argue that the change brought by it has a negative flavor. On the contrary, we are observing advancements in the ecosystem connectivity, innovation in products and regulation, and embracing the unavoidable – further digital revolution, including the challenges of trust and authenticity in new relationships and transactions.

6.3 Measuring open banking - KPIs

The next point to address is the state of the development of open banking, answering the question of whether it is a short-lived phenomenon where the initial splendor is later shadowed by the reality of business cases[6] or rather a change that will find a solid position in the financial system. Naturally, the survival of open banking in the PSD2 countries is in a sense guaranteed by EU law, but we have to remember that any solution that is not actively used by clients is subject to a brutal fate of "minimum mandatory" care and investment. In addition at this stage, it is not clear whether the many new TPPs will be able to survive and what consequences their exit may bring for the market. With the investment phase still in effect, we are unable to see whether the business models they deliver are financed by client revenue streams or startup investment funds. After all, many of the new ventures are chasing the mythical revenue streams with products and solutions that are not large cash generators (e.g. small transactional fees) and require the scale of business to deliver material revenues.

The measurement of the open banking market presence is still rudimentary and largely based on the PSD2 taxonomy. In the publicly available data of the EU and the United Kingdom (regulators, EU agencies, information provided on company websites) we can identify four primary measurement dimensions (KPIs)[7]:

1 **Number of open banking dedicated ecosystem entities - third-party providers (TPP)**: Account Information Service Providers (AISP) and Payment Initiation Service Providers (PISP),
  a According to Norrestad TPP (2022) in January 2021 there were 450 TPP registrations in Europe and 200 in the UK,
  b Based on the information from EBA[8], Belgian Fintech Banq manages a directory[9] of TPP, which as of April 2022 contained 466 entries[10]:
    i 29.61% established until 2018
    ii Highest number in 2019 (33.26%) due to the PSD2 due date in September of 2019
    iii Continued growth in 2020 and a significant slowdown in 2021 (only 7.51%).
2 **Number of bank APIs** offered to the public

With the research field focusing on EU banking and the regulatory nature of PSD2 we can assume that mandatory open banking functions (such as AIS/PIS) are provided by all regulated institutions to which the payment directive applies. Under this assumption, one of the key questions is to understand how broad is the coverage and whether it goes beyond the mandatory capabilities. The data collected by Banq[11] on the TPPs operating mainly in Europe, enhanced with the author's extended study of the API documentation present on the developer portals of banks, allows us to make observations on a diverse population of universal banks, savings institutions and cooperatives. The list was also optimized to remove payment-oriented fintechs (e.g. zoe.com or the credit cards specialist Capital One).

One of the primary challenges of this study is the granularity of API descriptions – some institutions bring together several APIs into one functional group (e.g. account services and transactions), while others keep a clear cut between information services. The content of the API groups also lacks transparency since PSD2 mandatory requirements are mixed with extended functionalities. Since the level of atomization cannot be fully compared without reaching for the technical specifications, it is advised not to interpret APIs as single functionalities, but rather as groups aimed at supporting a given area of data exchange or a business process. Although the observations made on this sample can only be considered general, they still provide several interesting insights and encourage further detailed functional studies to be conducted. Within the sample of 187 entities, the average number of services offered by the institutions is 3.6, with a minimum of 1, a maximum of 20 and a median value of 3. This is in line with the expectations that the majority of institutions started their open banking journey with PSD2. Having in mind the dilemma of disparate levels of atomization in API composition/description, it is proposed to look at the functional scope from the perspective of three clusters:

1. **Standard PSD2 API offer** - the grouping of API counts around the median (taking all institutions that are on the median plus the level before and after), shows nearly a Pareto balance, with the cumulative share of 76% of institutions belonging to this cluster.
2. **Extended API offer** – second cluster of institutions brings together all instances (27 institutions, 14% of total) where the API catalog contains between 5 and 9 functional areas.
3. **API leadership** – the last cluster contains 17 institutions (9% of the total), which individually offer more than 10 functional areas, and which in several cases go beyond core banking products.

The results indicate that API availability is largely concentrated on the basic, regulatory requirements, which could be an indication that without the PSD2 impulse, open banking would remain more of a technical concept rather than a fully functioning platform in the financial ecosystem. The third cluster shows bold innovators with a higher level of organizational mobilization and capital investments dedicated to the growth of open banking. The middle cluster contains organizations that are also on the open banking development path but possibly proceed at a slower pace due to less capital available for investments or simply to the application of the scouting strategy.

3 **Scope of API coverage** (# of connections)

The output of the previous analysis immediately calls for an introduction of another KPI that looks at the qualitative aspects of the APIs present on the market. In other words – apart for knowing that many institutions offer APIs, the evaluation of the open banking market must look into which functionalities (outside of the standard PSD2) are offered to the public. In order to illustrate this KPI, a detailed study of the APIs offered by 10 leading financial institutions[12] in Europe was conducted.

Every unique API function group was cataloged and mapped to the offering institutions. Several groups (especially being part of the PSD2) are fully comparable between entities, however, others are formed by linguistic and functional proximity (e.g. a reward platform is considered similar to the loyalty platform). The following insights can be observed:

1. The total number of API groups offered by these ten institutions is 207 and the number of unique groups is 102; the maximum per institution is 38 (Deutsche Bank) and the minimum is 11 (Erste).
2. The density of offerings shows that 64 groups (63%) are provided exclusively by 1 institution, 18 (17%) by 2 and 20 (20%) by 3 or more entities.
3. The most common API groups are built around the core PSD2 functionalities:
   a. AIS und PIS in the PSD2 version - offered by nine institutions,
   b. extended accounts (state, history, balance movements, cards), extended payments, instant payments – eight or seven institutions,
   c. places (branch, ATM, POS), online payments/e-commerce, account statements and customer data check - six or five institutions,
   d. FX exchange rates check, digital wallet (own or third party), list of cards, card details, notifications (events), consumer loan application, mortgage loan calculator, Know-Your-Customer check, trusted identity check, client registration, IBAN check – offered by four or three institutions.
4. Certain institutions have the same API group, but localized for respective locations (e.g. Erste has APIs for Austria, Romania and the Czech Republic). From the purely functional view, all these APIs will be similar (PSD2 oriented) but are adjusted to local technology or market cooperation standards.

5 For some institutions several APIs offer the same functional scope, but are split into separate code versions:
   a per segment (e.g. private or corporate),
   b per legacy system (e.g. products in different core banking or online banking systems).

6 "Global and wealthy" might not always mean " very open" – in the analysis, one of the leading positions in the open banking ranking is held by the National Bank of Greece, while giants such as HSBC did not make it to the top ten list. At the same time, Deutsche Bank is ranked at the top of openness while being a large, international institution. In this case, we can however argue that DB is rooted in the EU so it is thriving on the rich soil of the PSD2's homeland.
7 All institutions establish their own communities of expertise to facilitate API absorption and usage. Dedicated sections of the company profiles are offered, supplying technical documentation, user services, access to the test environment and go-live authorization. The portal names mainly (7/10) appeal to the development dimension ("developer portal") and 3/10 are API-oriented (API market, store, portal).
8 Selected institutions apply social media ideas such as the "likes" of individual APIs to build interest around usage and satisfaction. The like system in the example of BNP (as of 24.05.2022) shows that for 50 APIs offered (some duplicated per brand/architecture) the average number of likes is 8 and only 10 have more than 10 likes (maximum is 74), 17 have 2–9 likes, 16 has 1 like and 7 have 0. This provides directional evidence that there is a core API set (in this case the Pareto of 20% of the total) that brings a lot of utility to the market, while other APIs have limited popularity. Naturally, this simple observation refers to the social media view and not to any actual usage patterns.
9 Analyzing the nature of APIs we can identify 10 clusters:
   a **customer** - 17 APIs (16.7% of total),
   b **loans** - 17 (16.7%),
   c **transactions** (including also FX, Cash Management, Guarantees, and Money Market, but excluding pure payments) – 11 (10.8%)
   d **payments** - 10 (9.8%),
   e **accounts** - 9 (8.8%),
   f **investments** - 9 (8.8%),
   g **infrastructure** (e.g. tokens, authorization, document scanning and generation, biometrics) - 8 (7.8%),
   h **cards** - 5 (4.9%),
   i **insurance** - 4 (3.9%),
   j **product information** - 3 (2.9%).

In addition to the above, we can identify a cluster that groups all "special" items (nine APIs, 8.8% of total), covering exceptional and innovative solutions such as the blockchain registry, transparent account, loyalty and rewards programs, crowdfunding, ERP bank connection, social network platforms, job postings, translation services or even the regulatory information provision. All of these observations are a signal that open banking is reaching all client segments and products. At the same time, this "summarized" perspective does not mean all APIs are available from a single provider.

4 **Connectivity between the TPPs and banks** (# of connections)

Another interesting KPI to measure open banking is the number of connections that TPPs have with various financial institutions (mainly banks). According to the data collected by Nordigen, a leading Open Banking API integrator, their solution offers AIS connectivity to 608 financial institutions and is followed by Token (444), Klarna (403), Tink (394), Aiia (365) and Yapily (200) (Urbano, 2021). The measure of connectivity reflects the capability to run transactions across various channels, however without a view on which connections are actually active and with which intensity. For geographically set markets (e.g. within a country) the local provider may offer a far less number of connections globally, but enable full connectivity within the country ecosystem.

Further deep insight into the performance of open banking could be obtained based on the following indicators:

1 Number of TPPs' clients,
2 Number of transactions run by the TPPs (TTP view and bank view),
3 Volume (monetary) of transactions run by the TPPs.

Due to the business confidentiality of the above data, at this stage, there are no open information sources available for analysis. Unfortunately without a view of the transactional activity, the significance of open banking within the financial ecosystem cannot be quantified and requires further study. Public sources that offer information on the volume and number of transactions are mainly based on approximations or single examples.

6.4 Evaluation of open banking

In the context of the presented open banking insights we are able to formulate a view on the core question: what does open banking open? Below presented are the key opportunities that are being unlocked thanks to open banking, followed by the main threats that may be linked to its usage. Strengths are placed within the opportunities and weaknesses are documented in the threats, providing a simplified strategic evaluation of open banking.

6.4.1 Strengths and opportunities

1 **Product innovation** (e.g. account aggregation, advisory tools, product comparison).

2 **Service innovation** (e.g. outsourcing of parts of processes to partners with better user experience or higher process efficiency).
3 **Channel innovation** (e.g. fintech applications that allow to reach out to banking services).
4 **New business models** based on new products/services, new or improved channels/connectivity and reaching new client segments.
5 **Higher level of networking and communication** among ecosystem participants,
6 **Improved verification of threats** for the sector (e.g. client risk profile, default, availability of funds).
7 **Direct involvement of the Regulators**, actively involved in market liberalization and developing solutions that accelerate the digitalization of the sector.
8 **High standards of security and customer data protection** are built into the solution architecture from the beginning.
9 **Technical and market guidelines to streamline software development and interfacing**, however still not very precisely defined to allow for a better fit to a wider audience and higher experimentation capacity.
10 **Possibility for building custom online banking solutions by the clients themselves** / addressing the ever-present dilemma of building client online applications with required stability and scalability of standardized solutions versus the always growing customization expectations of the clients. With a broad set of APIs, clients may either integrate their internal systems or create more streamlined online banking functionalities.
11 **Increased level of competition**, especially between incumbents and the neobanks and fintechs, resulting in better conditions for the clients.
12 **Acceleration of digital transformation** by extending business models by definition with technology as its enabler.
13 Increased **exchange of ideas and best practices in coding** secure functional software and interfaces.[13]
14 Strong requirement for **advanced data management** acts as a catalyst of a positive change of legacy data management toward leaner and more agile configurations that can cope with precision and timing of interfacing with fintechs and other technology-based market participants.

6.4.2 Weaknesses and threats

1 **Limited participation of clients in the open banking models**, potentially stemming from:
   a insufficient trust in allowing TPPs to act on behalf of the client,
   b low perceived value of new products or services (e.g account aggregation was already possible and did not find a mass audience, due to trust issues and a limited pool of clients working with several financial services providers),
   c lack of promotion and marketing by TPPs and financial institutions.

2 **Overestimated business cases** that produce negative business value (financials collapsing due to insufficient scale or incorrect assumptions on sources of revenues).
3 New open business models pose a risk of **emancipation of existing clients** that were previously considered captive (due to a relative perception of account provider shift being a complex operation).
4 **Low level of client education** – the benefits of open banking are not clearly articulated (e.g. beyond the concept of account aggregation or against the biased thinking about "mythical fintechs offering innovative products for hipsters and not normal clients").
5 **Unforeseen cyber threats, fraud schemes or data protection breaches** that can surface after a longer time period and either go undetected (e.g. typical issue of small differences in transactions/trades) or create a massive attack on a large client base across many institutions.
6 **No common standards** – they need to be developed based on guidelines and require local coordination (e.g. in Poland the Association of Polish Banks moderated a "Polish API" initiative (https://polishapi.org/) to bring the sector toward higher interoperability.
7 **Initial motivation** to develop the open banking ecosystem seems to **have lost its spark**, previously highly moderated by the PSD2. Right now even very good open banking alliances and facilitators cease to update their dialog with the market with new content and meaningful advice.
8 API Banks or Bank-as-a-Service (BaaS) ventures, after a strong wave of investment and expectations of "disruptive power" **fail to deliver a competitive blow to the dominating market institutions** that also develop their digital and open capabilities at the comfort of strong capital positions and still fairly stable client bases.
9 In a composite, high-level view – the diversity and advancement of APIs offered by the banks is very broad, however **only a few institutions can claim to be "open banking attackers"** who built the API strategy into their overall strategic management.
10 **Limited amount of reciprocity**[14] **with respect to data sharing** – financial institutions are expected to be data and service providers while they are not easily granted access to TPP or other partner data (lack of bi-directional data exchange).

6.5 Conclusion

An old saying claims that "when some doors close, other doors open" encouraging a view that a significant change that "closes our old ways" is a step toward "new openings" and new opportunities. While looking at open banking we may paraphrase this statement into saying that open banking provides additional doors to the world, extending the current reality with new products, channel connections and client segments. This new door is highly sophisticated from a technological, API-based point of view. At the same time, this openness calls for special measures regarding the protection of both the security of the technology, but also the safety of the business model, potentially strained by selected revenue streams "going out the door" to third parties or competitors. In the securing of the business model, the core value chain built around capital and risk management must be retained and protected. This may mean that open banking will operate on the edge of value propositions, rather in their less regulated advisory, communication or user experience dimensions, without affecting the core, fully regulated competencies.

One of the key challenges for open banking will be linked to the future of trust in a continually digitalized world. At the same time, addressing this challenge in cooperative open banking models where the best banks work with the best TPPs and fintechs, the best software developers and system integrators – all under the support of the best Regulators seems to be the best option for the future. This highly knowledgeable, capital-rich and agile combination of organizations has the potential to turn the current challenge into a future competitive advantage. Digitalization is unavoidable - it brings progress and benefits to all participants in the financial market. Open banking is a practice ground to prepare for the next waves of digitalization, by simultaneously working on new and resistant infrastructure, modern products and processes (founded on the right legal frameworks) and user convenience strategies that combine sophisticated financial management with seamless transaction experience.

Open Banking without a doubt is an important evolutionary step for the financial ecosystems and banks in particular. It is also another step toward the further transformation of financial institutions into software/technology ventures, which retain their regulated core identity, while dynamically building up their connectivity internally and with the external world. Over the past decades we have seen a number of significant paradigm shifts in the world of financial management: moving from the "physical" world of gold, branches and advisors to money represented by database entries, fully digital banks and alternative value exchange mechanisms such as cryptocurrencies. All such changes lead to the opening of the financial sector for more sophisticated, widespread and flexible transaction schemes. As we move along the digitalization wave we can conclude that technology is a catalyst in opening up the sector and further digital advancement will provide further opportunities for new, innovative interactions within the financial market. While these digital advances will continue, the core mission of the financial sector – the organization of value exchange between market participants – will remain, with a focus on the protection of capital (represented in any form) and creating trusted relationships.

Notes

1 Payment Services Directive (EU) 2015/2366.
2 EMEA: Europe, Middle East and Africa.

3 Based among others on the following: Deloitte (2022), DeJong et al. (2017), Mallick (2021), PKO BP (2022) and websites of companies: Nordigen, Solarisbank, Mulesoft, finAPI.
4 A reference list of neobanks: https://neobanks.app/.
5 Description adopted from: https://www.openbanking.org.uk/directory/.
6 An example of such a situation is seen with the distributed ledgers (blockchain), where initial "hype" built significant expectations of radical system changes and at the end became just one variation of technology, without mainstream adoption (Baraniuk, 2020).
7 KPI – Key Performance Indicator, numerical/descriptive measure of events/states.
8 European Banking Authority, TPPs listings: https://www.eba.europa.eu/risk-analysis-and-data/register-payment-electronic-money-institutions-under-PSD2.
9 Banq: https://www.openbankingtracker.com/tpp-directory, state as of 2022.04.
10 In comparison to the data of Norrestad (450 TPP at the end of 2020), BANQ shows that 2021 was started with a cumulative number of 431 institutions, but this difference is considered irrelevant for the study.
11 Banq: https://www.openbankingtracker.com/api-directory, 2022.04.
12 Erste Group, OP Financial Group, Deutsche Bank, Akbank, BBVA, BNP Paribas, Barclays, Commerzbank, Santander and National Bank of Greece.
13 This advantage is pointed out by experts from the ZEB consulting company: https://www.bankinghub.eu/themen/open-banking-far-more-than-psd2.
14 Mentioned in a general text (company authored) on open banking by Deloitte: https://www2.deloitte.com/global/en/pages/financial-services/articles/open-banking-around-the-world.html.

Bibliography

Baraniuk, C. *Blockchain: The revolution that hasn't quite happened*, BBC Publishing, 2020, https://www.bbc.com/news/business-51281233

DeJong, B., Little, M., Gagliardi, C. *Open for Business, Accenture Strategy Report*, 2017, https://www.accenture.com/t20170629t215524z__w__/us-en/_acnmedia/pdf-56/accenture-strategy-digital-open-banking-pov.pdf

Deloitte. *Wie Open Banking die Finanzbranche transformiert*, 2022, https://www2.deloitte.com/de/de/pages/financial-services/articles/open-banking.html

GEO Epoche Nr. 69: Der Kapitalismus. *Wie ein Wirtschaftssystem die Welt eroberte*. Hamburg: Gruner Verlag, 2014, https://www.geo.de/magazine/geo-epoche/1548-rtkl-florenz-um-1300-die-ersten-kapitalisten

Mallick, A. *As Open Banking Gathers Momentum, Smart Banks Get Ready*, Accenture Blog, 2021, https://bankingblog.accenture.com/as-open-banking-gathers-momentum-smart-banks-get-ready

Mallick, A., McIntyre, A., Scott, E. *Catching the Open Banking Wave 2021 Report*, Accenture Banking, 2021, https://www.accenture.com/us-en/insights/banking/open-banking-moving-towards-open-data-economy

Moneywise, Editorial Team, 2021, https://moneywise.com/life/entertainment/the-biggest-bank-robberies-of-all-time

Norrestad, F. (Fintech) *Number of Fintech Startups Worldwide 2021, by Region*, Statista Online, 2022, https://www.statista.com/statistics/893954/number-fintech-startups-by-region/

Norrestad, F. (TPP) *Number of Open Banking Third Party Registrations in Europe Q4 2020, by Country*, Statista Online, 2022, https://www.statista.com/statistics/1214254/number-of-open-banking-third-party-registrations-in-europe-by-country/

PKOBP, *Open Banking Offer*, 2022, https://www.pkobp.pl/klienci-indywidualni/bankowosc-elektroniczna/open-banking/

Urbano, V. *Bank-by-Bank Comparison of Leading Open Banking Provider*, Nordigen, 2021, https://nordigen.com/en/blog/bank-bank-comparison-leading-open-banking-providers/

7 Techfins and the banking system

Rising battlefield

Stanisław Kasiewicz and Lech Kurkliński

The purpose of this chapter is to explain the advantages and weaknesses of the market players, their strategies, and business models in digital competition in financial markets. It requires the presence of the determinants of market success in the new age of rivalry and its essence. Regarding the rising battlefield between banks and FinTechs/BigTechs, the final result of this competition cannot be predicted precisely. It depends on the future actions of all stakeholders, not only market players but also other institutions like regulators, supervisory authorities, central banks, etc. Particularly this analysis should include the unpredictable regulatory policy and politicians' approaches.

7.1 The role, essence, and features of digital competition in the banking service market

The category of competition plays a prominent role in the considerations carried out in all macro and microeconomic analyses, as it determines the social welfare, efficiency, and stability of the entire economy, each particular industry, and individual companies. It influences the protection of clients' rights as well.

The category of competition in economics has evolved, including its interpretations. Various schools of economics have had different approaches to it. In the early period, competition was described in the language of military battles, but later more subdued forms started to dominate. Competition is defined as the process when market players compete with each other to conclude transactions by presenting more advantageous offers than others, achieving their interests in terms of price, quality, convenience, quality, etc. (Rosa, 2013). For financial services, at least two separate definitions of the term competition can be distinguished. The first one is described as classic (Bolt, Tieman, 2004; Neuberger, 1998; Northcott, 2004). It is connected with the "Structure – Conduct – Performance" paradigm (Bain 1951; Demsetz, 1973; Pawłowska, 2014). The analyses are limited to three sections: the subject structure of the market, the behaviour of market players, and the effects achieved by stakeholders. The second definition (called revision) undermines the mechanisms of competition through prices. It focuses on different rules in the conditions of oligopolistic rivalry, taking into account the dynamics of market changes.

DOI: 10.4324/9781003310082-11

Digital competition seems to be different from the traditional competition. It is reflected in the shaping of other rules, mechanisms, and accepted values, determining the performance of financial service providers. This also applies to the functioning of other market "organisers" (such as regulators, supervisors, central banks, and infrastructure institutions), having an impact on the rules of functioning, attitudes, behaviour, and decisions of market players. The key factors are based on the different mechanisms of the digital market formation and the specificity of its disruption. The boundaries between industries are blurring, while at the same time powerful development barriers related to external network effects emerge. This situation has roots in incurring very high initial outlays to achieve a profitable scale of effects. Market success requires building a capital-intensive IT infrastructure and architecture. It means there are relevant economic and technological barriers. They create monopolies willing to use high margins to ensure satisfactory rates of return. Moreover, the difference in digital competition lies in the possibilities of regulation as well. The traditional approach has been focused on the external evaluation of the sale of products/services and it hasn't dug into an enterprise interior, treating it as a "black box". In digital competition, the difference is indicated by the role of numerous applications and algorithms, which are hidden and protected, having unique value for a firm. They generate valuable benefits: increasing productivity, saving costs, stimulating connectivity and collaboration, encouraging innovation, or creating new revenue opportunities. Understanding of applications is highly difficult for regulators. They don't have access and possibilities to decipher the algorithms, crucial for leveraging these firms' market power.

At the US Congress, during anti-trust investigations against Amazon, Apple, Google, and Facebook, they indicated unfair practices used by these giants. For example, testimonies from the CEOs of smaller companies accused Google and Amazon of selling their Home and Echo smart speakers at discounted prices because they were not interested in profiting directly from this sale. The most important purpose of these corporations was to collect customer data and later earn by selling advertising and enriching databases (Del Rey, 2020). The BigTechs pricing policy is aimed at reducing competition (using differentiated margins, forcing consumers to sign unfavourable contracts in accordance with the "take it or leave it" rule, or applying non-transparent algorithms that are gainful for them).

There is no doubt that BigTechs have introduced breakthrough innovations to the market bringing significant benefits to customers and society and a high increase in share value for shareholders. At the same time, technology giants use their dominant market position to crowd out competitors, blocking other innovative companies to enter the market. This phenomenon is possible because of the weakness of supervisory institutions, especially in the area of mergers and acquisitions. This leads to the concentration in the digital market and its gradual monopolisation. It was estimated that Amazon accounted for nearly 40% of all U.S. e-commerce sales in 2019, and Facebook and Google together receive more than 60% of U.S. digital advertising revenue (Katz, 2021). BigTechs are very dexterous taking over innovations from smaller competitors by acquiring them. The giants have very robust R&D budgets with a high priority placed on this activity. Additionally, there is competition among the BigTechs themselves for the so-called neighbouring markets (Deller et al., 2021).

New technologies, such as artificial intelligence, the cloud, the Internet of Things, autonomous robots, blockchain, and Big Data, not only change the attitudes and behaviour of financial market stakeholders but above all have become an accelerator in the disruption of the traditional competition regime.

The main features of digital competition in the financial services sector are presented in Table 7.1. They were formulated on the basis of a reflection resulting from the query of academic literature, market observation, analysis of available reports, and the authors' own research.

Table 7.1 The features of digital competition in the financial services sector

	Characteristic
Main features	Digital technologies – main drivers for strategies and business models
	Digital processes, products, and communication
	Accelerators of growth – big data and artificial intelligence
	Digital leadership
	New values: innovation, speed, flexibility, openness, autonomy, responsibility
	Organisational culture, including risk culture
	Open API
Market	Concentrated market and prone to monopolisation
	New external competitors
	Lower entry barriers
	Crossing industry boundaries
	Bilateral and multilateral markets
	High volatility
	Unbundling of the banking value chain
Methods of winning the market	Platforms and ecosystems
	Network effects
	Anti-competitive acquisitions and mergers
	Intensive use of economies of scale
	Utilisation of the weaknesses of traditional anti-trust policy tools
	Aggressive attitude to a market
Customer	Weak protection of customer data
	Personalised offers
	Easier service provider switching
	Mosaic of benefits and weaknesses depending on customer position
	Different digital skills
Regulations	Delayed responses to the actions of tech giants
	Classic anti-trust tools are ineffective
	Problem of global integration of anti-monopoly policy
	Weak regulatory impact assessment

Source: Own study

Based on the common features of digital competition, the relationship between the market structure, protection of customer rights, and the regulatory system should be emphasised. The content of Table 7.1 shows that there are opportunities for market success and, on the other hand, there are numerous pitfalls leading to failure. The key is in diagnosing the interdependencies related to the factors of competition, material and intangible resources, and the adopted tools for winning in a market (HM Treasury, 2019; US House of Representatives, 2020; Crémer, de Montjoye, Schweitzer, 2019). The financial sector has undergone radical changes in recent years and now it is standing in front of a crossroads. On the one hand, it is still possible that traditional banks may maintain their strong competitive position as a result of taking adequate measures in line with the dominant trends in digital transformation. On the other hand, there is a risk that they will not cope with the disruption caused by new competitors and their market power will be marginalised.

7.2 Weaknesses and competitive advantages of banks versus FinTechs and BigTechs

Banks are very diverse in terms of their digital maturity. Their competitive position (i.e., the weaknesses and advantages) differ significantly from one another. Challenger banks focus on modernity and strive to fully adapt to the digital environment (Harrison, 2021). The opposite group – laggard banks maintain traditional IT infrastructure, stick to proven management principles, and avoid risky and costly transformation activities (Skinner, 2017). These two groups of banks define the spectrum of intermediate cases (Figure 7.1).

Primarily challenger banks build their market position by focusing on increasing market penetration. Traditional banks have a large and relatively loyal customer base. It means they are important market players. But this relatively comfortable position weakens their vigilance and aggressive attitude to competitors. Nevertheless, the banks' competitive struggle with FinTechs has already started. Currently, it takes place in almost all service categories

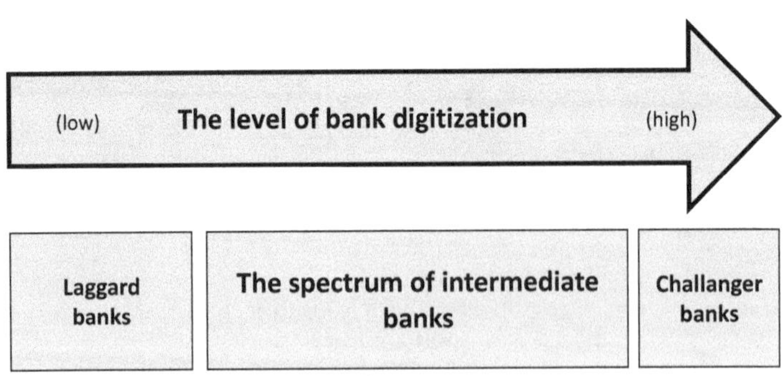

Figure 7.1 The level of banking digitisation

(Gimpel, Rau, Röglinger, 2018). So far, banks have strengthened the image of a "mainstay for finances", supported by values such as trust, reliability, tradition, and security, which remains a very important tool in their competitive strategy. However, these advantages are levelling slowly, a move that the COVID-19 pandemic crisis contributed to, to some extent. Because of new technologies, the pressure for change is rising. The majority of traditional banks are gradually entering the area of digital services. But this process is relatively slow and focused on a narrow range of activities – mainly related to offering basic services in the digital format (Deloitte, 2021). In the era of contemporary Revolution 4.0 and the growing market power of the so-called customers 4.0, it is not enough. Additionally, banks treat preparations for competing with FinTechs or BigTechs as a low priority (Kasiewicz, Kurkliński, Woźniak, 2021, p. 105).

The weaknesses of FinTechs (i.e., securing a scalable business, regulatory insecurity, innovation, and security trade-off, financing gaining, competition within the FinTech industry), as well as the strengths (i.e., prioritising utility and technological innovations, focusing on the provided quality – perfecting the "client's journey and experience" process, analysis of a selected market – a demand-based model of innovation, a flexible approach to business, experimenting, failure acceptance, adhocracy culture, lower regulatory restrictions), present the competitive position of FinTechs. But reviewing this comparison it looks like the advantages are overwhelming weaknesses. Such a juxtaposition for Tech Giants shows even bigger market power in front of bank rivals. Specifically, the attention should be focused on their strong predominance related to wide brand recognition, growing clients' trust, easy access to financing, a robust IT and R&D budget, hiring the best specialists, achieving economies of scale, using the effect of multilateral markets, huge databases and computing power, and advanced analytics. These competitive advantages are strongly ahead of banks.

7.3 Strategies and business models of major market players

The key role in the competitive fight between banks, FinTechs and BigTechs is played by strategies and even more by business models. For banks, the following development strategies can be drafted: reinforcing strengths, cancelling digital weaknesses as well as searching for new service markets. The strategies should be focused on building and improving digital potential. They have to focus on a customer experience constantly, which is (besides the strictly technological aspects) a precise adjustment to the clients' expectations (Figure 7.2). To achieve these purposes cooperation with certain FinTechs should be taken into consideration (Capgemini, 2020, p. 13).

The strategy of seeking new service markets integrates concentration on the clients' needs with striving for an improved market position. It can be addressed both to banks as well as FinTechs. The priorities shall include:

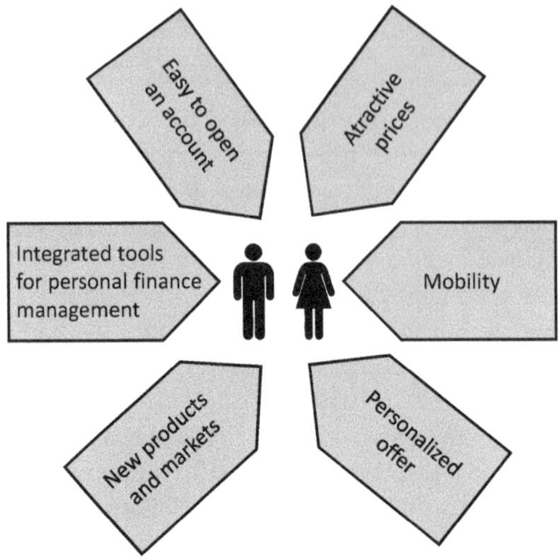

Figure 7.2 Customer experience as a chance of gaining competitive advantages

immersing the client in the process of creating/perfecting product offers that convert into clients' trust, engagement, and loyalty, guaranteeing support/education in case of more technologically advanced services and seeking new sources of income and cost (risk) rationalisation based on modern data analysis (Capgemini, 2020, p. 7). The analysis of digital financial services competition and then building strategies should lead in certain directions:

- moving towards digitalisation of all financial products with common usage of "cloud" solutions;
- the universal use of mobile devices without the need of installing complex applications;
- increasing the comfort of services and minimalising direct contact with financial institutions;
- increasing speed and flexibility of offered services;
- granting access to unstructured external data, perfecting the analysis and integration with internal data;
- considering scalability in activity;
- personalisation of services with acceptable profitability (Kasiewicz, Kurkliński, Woźniak, 2021).

As the activity horizon of financial institutions shortens, the significance of strategies declines, and an interest in business models rises. They present contents, structures, and management techniques, that allow for increasing value through the usage of existing business opportunities. They are the key source of value creation for the company and its stakeholders. They may favour or hinder the implementation of innovations (Genpact, 2016, p. 2). Gradually the market players started to understand the digital competition and the new market environment. Innovative business models are the answers to those challenges.

Till now banks have been characterised by a high percentage of "internal production" – maintaining high control and keeping most value chains "on their own turf". The average level of "own production" reaches 75% (Gasser, 2017, p. 8). It means that despite the changing attitude, banks are reluctant to use outsourcing. It results in poor efficiency related to a low level of operation standardisation. This picture is complemented by studies showing that at least 50% of all bank operations could be automatised. Therefore, banks will evolve towards intelligent automatisation, cooperation, and industrialisation (Gasser, 2017, p. 7). This process has been started. From this perspective, FinTechs are definitely more advanced.

The choice of a business model is impacted by a chain of values which consists of acquiring and keeping clients, financial consulting, product preparations, transaction processes, and others. A financial institution can rely on a selected fragment or consider all basic segments of a value chain. Because of expansiveness, the latter approach is harder to achieve in an efficient way. Different classes of business models that utilise the unbundling value chain concept are depicted in Figure 7.3 (ZEB, 2019).

The creation of business models relies on determinants (leverages) that impact incomes and costs. They are presented in Table 7.2.

The study of FinTech business models is still at a very early stage. They are based on the linking of two elements: a distinct specialisation together with a direct digital channel for easier financial transactions, better service

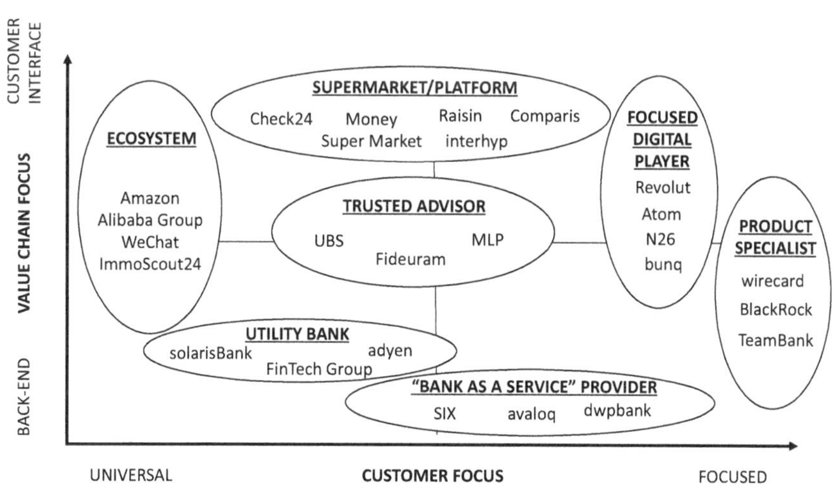

Figure 7.3 Bank business models archetypes

Table 7.2 Determinants in the sphere of income and costs in bank business models

Model type	*Income determinants*	*Cost determinants*
Ecosystem	• Premium payments • Direct income from sales • Income from third-party marketing	• Costs of acquiring members • Costs of realisation and servicing
Supermarket/ platform	• Brokerage commissions	• Costs of clients' acquisition
Trusted advisor	• Services and payments • Incomes from product owners	• Costs of consultant/service personnel • Product-related and risk-related costs
Digital specialist	• Commissions, premium payments	• Costs of clients' acquisition
Product specialist	• Income (interest, commissions)	• Product-related and risk-related costs • Marketing spendings
Public utility/ infrastructure provider	• Income (interest, commissions)	• Costs of platform/product development + operation costs
Banking as a Service (BaaS)	• Remuneration for the service	• Costs of platform/product development + operation costs

Source: ZEB (2019, p. 6)

availability, and better responses to clients' needs. The most active FinTechs have already left the start-up phase and are listed on stock exchanges and are currently undertaking an intensive expansion.

"Challenger banks" just like FinTechs adopt business models that significantly differ from traditional ones used by "laggard banks". Competitive threats generated by FinTechs, BigTechs, and "challenger banks" are particularly dangerous for smaller banks. New players offer their services mostly to retail customers and grant them "a digital proximity" (breaks the locality – the advantage of smaller banks). Additionally, the lesser group (consisting of a big number of laggard banks) has limited financial and human resources. It implies a need for seeking partnerships in order to survive. Meanwhile, the borderline between "challenger banks" and FinTechs becomes less clear in the progress of digitalisation.

A vast majority of banks are poorly prepared for a digital transformation. They have made-to-measure, but quite obsolete IT systems (mainly central banking systems CBS) that constantly need to be modified or updated. The desire for control led to the creation of inflexible solutions within competence silos. In such conditions, the IT infrastructure is rigid, costly, and hard to manage. After the global financial crisis, the requirements to adjust to the "regulatory tsunami" were prioritised, largely neglecting the support of IT. As a result – light and agile FinTechs have arisen.

New solutions (based on the cloud) like "Software-as-a-service" (SaaS), "Business-Processing-as-a-service" (BPaaS), and "Infrastructure-as-a-service" (IaaS) offer a high degree of standardisation and automation. They have started to be implemented into the banking services. The progress of efficiency can be achieved (cost/income ratio lower by 10/20 p.p.). Other advantages include (Porc, Frost, 2018, p. 10):

- *Accessibility*: readiness to apply when the need arises.
- *Elasticity*: quick adaptation to new requirements (market, technological, regulatory, and others).
- *Scalability*: burdens according to the "pay-per-use" rule, expenses are adjusted to the scale of activity.
- *Risk reduction*: for example, operational, resulting from i.e., the access to major reserve powers, the efficiency of emergency switches, and better preparation in the domain of cybersecurity.
- *Efficiency*: cost reduction.

A map of new solutions for banks is presented in Figure 7.4.

Joining the possibilities given by IaaS, SaaS, and BPaaS with the "open banking" concept created a new image of the financial services market. Technological and regulatory changes have opened a new path to innovative business models like "Banking-as-a-service" (BaaS), "Banking-as-a-platform" (BaaP), or "Banking-as-a-Marketplace" (BaaM).

In BaaS a licenced financial institution provides "white label" digital banking services. They are integrated with other companies' products usually not being subject to strict banking regulations. Provided services (reserved for banks) are offered without having a licence (Skaleet, 2021). The BaaS

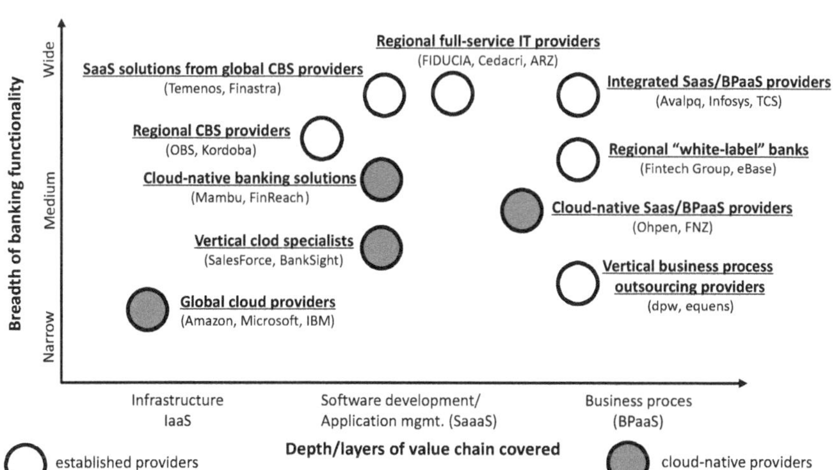

Figure 7.4 IT services providers for banks – solution spectrums

can be applied not only by digital banks but also global players providing universal banking services. The first group includes an American bank Green Dot (which cooperates with Walmart) or British Starling. The Continental-European example is the German Fidor Bank. Among global players, the most often named entities are American Bancorp or Spanish BBVA. The last one is considered to be one of the world's biggest innovators among financial institutions (Ciesielski, 2020).

BaaP is to a certain degree an inversion of BaaS. It allows for the creation of an ecosystem adjusted for clients' needs, where external FinTechs provide products for the bank. Then the products are offered as the bank's own. BaaP means that a bank does not have to be the "factory of all products". The newest technology allows for gaining a competitive advantage as the client has access to a wide array of financial innovations. Examples are N26 and Monzo Bank, both based on a new-generation IT platform (Accenture, 2020).

BaaM is related to BaaP, but in this case, the banking platform works similarly to Amazon. Thus, the term "Amazonization of financial services". For example, British Starling Bank (licences, but also using the BaaS model) offers a full array of financial services provided by third-party players i.e., in the spectrum of insurance, payments, or accounting. In BaaM the transactions between partners and consumers are easier, which created a net effect (Accenture, 2020).

The presented models can be applied selectively or joined into hybrid solutions. The crucial aspect of separating the producer and operator from the vendor. New players in the financial market (challenger banks and FinTechs) do not have issues with "historic legacy", obsolete business models, old IT systems, or high costs. They provide services better suited to their digital customers, which gives them a competitive advantage.

7.4 The unresolved market battle - the role of regulation

The current regulatory system presents a significant information asymmetry and an arbitrage in the banking services market. On one side there are strongly regulated banks and their inhibited development. On the other side (which can be described as moderate) there are small and medium FinTechs which comply with more relaxed restrictions and suffer less from administrative burdens. On the totally opposite side, there are Tech Giants that focus their efforts on claiming the largest part of the market. There are some efforts to remove anomalies in the digital market (i.e., UE Digital Services Act (DSA) or Digital Market Act (DMA)) – (European Commission, 2020a, 2020b). It is an open question: whether such regulations can be put into practice, as BigTechs possess great economic, technological, and political power. Summing up, the current regulatory gap is huge and should be a priority for country-level authorities.

For decades the financial sector was susceptible to technological innovations, but in the 21st century, the wave of innovations not only changes the rules and mechanisms of bank functioning but also has a significant impact on the economy. A question arose about whether those phenomena shall be regulated and if yes, then how. Generally, the regulators feared that introducing administrative restrictions would inhibit the development of innovations and therefore leaned towards the "wait and see" practice. They probably claimed that a small scale of FinTech activity would not cause market disturbances nor create a major risk of financial market destabilisation. Furthermore, they noticed the difficulties in creating regulations for highly diverse market entities. It turned out that granting freedom to FinTechs exposed two main market effects (Rodríguez, Ortún, 2020, p. 4). First, technology companies focused on those segments of the service value chain that was not strictly regulated. Second, newly created FinTechs stumbled across problems with achieving a sufficient level of operational scalability due to a lack of capital and high costs of client acquisition. As a result, the regulation of the FinTech sector was diverse and partial (Tanda, Schena, 2019, p. 84). This approach has begun to change, especially in the EU (Digital Europe, 2019, p. 5). It is visible due to the first legal acts (European Commission, 2016a, 2016b, 2016c, 2017), and publications and research from the European Commission's initiative (Carmona et al., 2018; Crémer, de Montjoye, Schweitzer, 2019). What is particularly interesting is that not much attention was originally paid to the significance of digital platforms. But it gradually led to a conclusion that administrative interventions are necessary. It does not mean that such platforms can function in a legal vacuum, they were subject to other regulations in such areas as consumer protection, copyright law, data protection, or general anti-monopoly acts (Dittrich, 2018, p. 6). A true breakthrough was the release of the European Commission's statement assessing the state of platform development as part of A Digital Single Market Strategy for Europe (2015).

The usage of self-regulation and co-regulation has been proposed which might often lead to achieving better results in terms of creating strings platform ecosystems in Europe. It led to greater efforts in digital market regulations (European Commission, 2016c). The key areas of interest for European regulators were not only global digital platforms run by American BigTechs, like Google, Amazon, Facebook, and Apple but also those run by Chinese ones (Bostoen, 2018; Regulation EU, 2019).

The COVID-19 pandemic outbreak found regulators working on key proposals on the issue. The changes in business processes have accelerated and the need for modifications in the spectrum of digital market regulations has become even stronger (EY, 2021a). The number of digital clients grew by 23% in comparison to the beginning of the pandemic (Hakkarainen, 2021). Grand projects for the digital market have been initiated (DSA and DMA) in the EU. A new ordinance for digital services (DSA) concerns the functioning of digital platforms. Another ordinance (DMA) concerns the negative consequences of platforms acting as "digital guardians" of a single market. Works on those two projects are progressing, but it is unknown when they will be completed.

7.5 Opportunities and threats for banks and FinTechs/BigTechs in the financial market

For competition in the financial services market, the processes of mergers and acquisitions are important taking into consideration the activity of banks and FinTechs/BigTechs. Theoretically, players with larger capitals (banks and BigTechs) are in a better position. However, in this area banks tend to be rather restrained. They do not participate in FinTech IPOs (presumably due to an aversion to higher-risk endeavours) and thus leave this field to venture capital funds and BigTechs. The difference in market prices of FinTechs and banks also plays a role, almost creating two separate worlds (Figure 7.5). Traditional banks have difficulties acquiring their way into FinTechs. It is the problem of the mandate as their valuation multiples (P/E ratios) are too low and synergies are likely limited.

The limited engagement of banks in the FinTech market manifests in the forms of partnerships or investing in minority holdings (Dealroom, 2019, pp. 35–37).

The opportunities for FinTechs (which are simultaneously threats to banks) can be linked to the following trends (Dealroom, 2019, pp. 14–30):

- FinTechs offer often bilateral services, while banks are dominated by unilateral ones;
- new regulations, especially PSD2, open access to data which was previously reserved for banks (development of the open banking concept);
- the prudential requirements regime keeps the phenomenon of regulatory arbitrage, restraining banks, and giving more freedom to FinTechs;
- broader usage of AI;

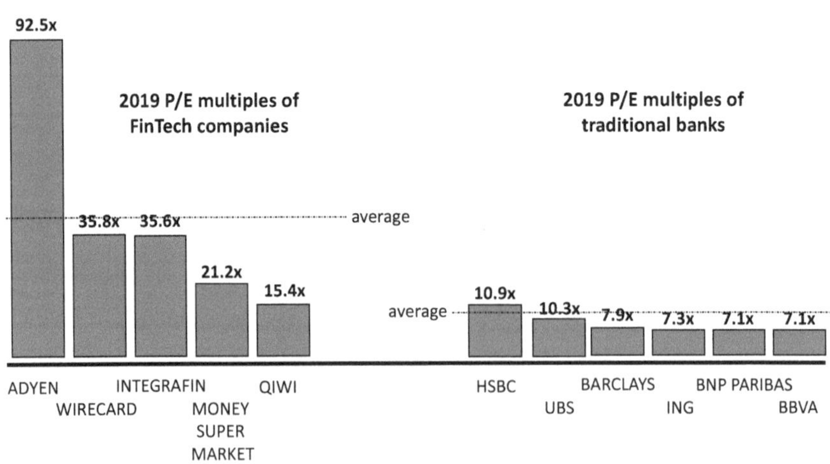

Figure 7.5 P/E ratios of FinTechs and traditional banks

- robo-advising platforms make resource management more accessible and tailored to individual needs –breaking with the "elitist" image of finances;
- cost challenges (mostly for banks) with limited possibilities of shifting costs to clients within price policies;
- extending the loan market with the usage of P2P (person-to-person) platforms and social investing;
- common usage of the"Internet of Things" (IoT) technologies for data mining and offering customised services;
- digital platforms supporting single services/products; online brokerage increases efficiency and scalability;
- faster processing and realisation of transactions (for example international transfers);
- intelligent contract solutions for decreasing transaction costs;
- integration of blockchain and crypto-assets with traditional financial and legal services;
- utilising "Augmented Reality" (AR) and "Virtual Reality" (VR) technologies for better customer service.

In the sphere of the greatest opportunities for banks in the competition race (based on a Polish market survey in 2021 – Figure 7.6) the strongest accent was put on supporting the creativity and innovativeness of employees. Therefore, banks should pay special attention to aspects of organisational culture. The major development opportunities for banks also include the expansion of the digital transformation level. The gap between clients' expectations and banks' preferences was also stressed.

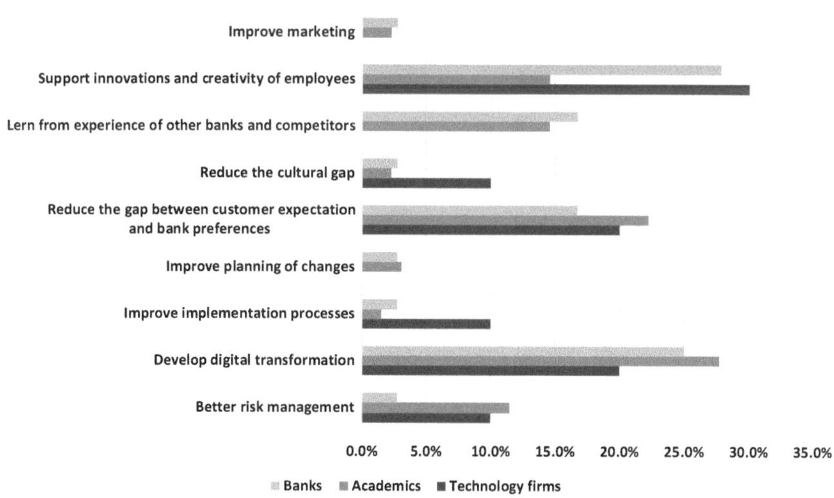

Figure 7.6 Areas of the greatest success chances for banks in the competition race (% respondent answers)

In the case of the growing significance of technology, the banks' chances to win against FinTechs are not an easy task. But this battlefield is not yet settled. Considering such criteria as owned technology and its usage, human and financial resources, and demand for services and market risk, the banks dominate FinTechs only in two areas (Figure 7.7). It relates to a more cautious introduction of innovative solutions to the market. Banks have relatively good staff, but they are gradually losing this asset.

The main threats for banks in terms of competing against FinTechs are as follows:

- insufficient utilisation of employees' potential – mainly innovative potential;
- fear of cooperating with FinTechs – perceiving this group as competitors, not partners.
- improper usage of the innovation budget (despite big financing possibilities);
- fear of rejecting innovations by current clients, slothfulness, cautiousness in their introduction, lack of openness;
- weaknesses in developing digital skills.

The opportunity and threat analysis for banks and FinTechs should serve as a warning primarily for the banking sector. The flagship advantage for banks – clients' trust – slowly decays. In this spectrum, BigTechs experience significant gains. If they commit to financial services, it might put banks in a very difficult situation. Available business models show that BigTechs do not need bank licences, have an access to a vast number of clients, know more about

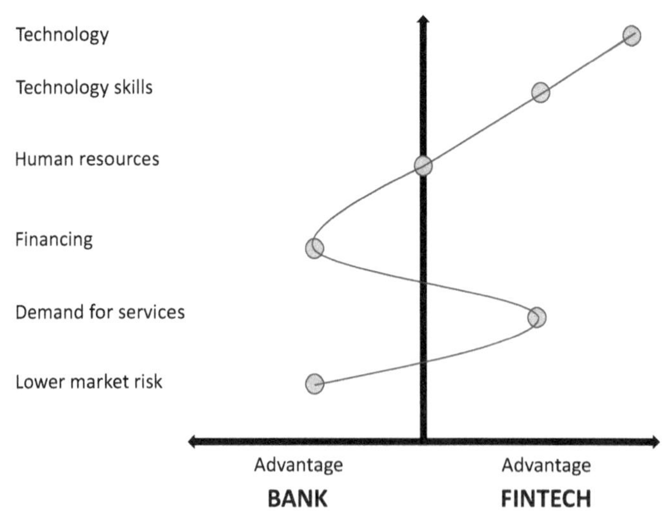

Figure 7.7 Competitiveness rating of banks in comparison to FinTechs

them than banks, acquire the most skilled specialists, and are leaders of the technology sector.FinTechs do not have such strong advantages over banks as BigTechs but are not deprived of them either. Therefore, they can contest a large portion of the market, which is already happening in the sphere of payments. However, banks are not yet in a losing position, but they need to undertake radical measures in order to minimalise the threats and maximise their opportunities.

7.6 Conclusions

The digital competition differs from traditional competition. Using advanced technology in the financial sector undermines the existing order. The current competition between banks, FinTechs, and BigTechs accelerated as a result of the COVID-19 pandemic. It concerns smaller banks to a larger degree. However, this phenomenon is smaller than prognosed by consulting agencies. The greatest threats to the traditional sector are related to challenger banks and BigTechs. The competitive potential of the latter is significant. Smaller FinTechs, due to capital, managerial limitations, and high partitioning, have not had such a big impact on the banks (with some exceptions). Despite those threats, banks present a certain degree of self-content regarding their competitive position. It is visible in the reluctance to undertake any major transformations of banks' IT systems. It seems like banks do not fully consider the consequences of new, changing conditions. The potential obligation to follow new very strict regulations could have a detrimental effect on competing in the market. FinTechs and BigTechs express concerns that future regulations might severely weaken their competitive advantages. BigTechs are already involved in politically "defensive" activities.

Generally, FinTechs and BigTechs have a larger number of potential competitive advantages over banks. But banks are not yet defeated if they adopt newer, more efficient strategies. Innovative business models are also important, as they created opportunities not only for banks' competitors but also for banks themselves. It turns out that there are many models that can be successfully used in the fight for the market. They are characterised by other determinants (leverages) of generating costs and expenses than the traditional ones.

Bibliography

Accenture (2020), *New business models for a new banking environment*, https://bankingblog.accenture.com/new-business-models-for-new-banking-environment (15.11.2021).

Bain J.S. (1951), Relation of profit rate to industry concentration: American manufacturing, 1936–1940. *The Quarterly Journal of Economics*, vol. 65, issue 3, pp. 293–324.

Bolt W., Tieman A. (2004), Banking competition, risk and regulation. *Scandinavian Journal of Economics*, vol. 106, issue 4, pp. 783–804.

Bostoen F. (2018), Neutrality, fairness or freedom? Principles for platform regulation. *Journal on Internet Regulation*, vol. 7, issue 2, pp. 1–19.

Capgemini (2020), *World Payments Report 2020*, https://www.capgemini.com/mx-es/wp-content/uploads/sites/24/2020/12/WPR-Hallazgos-Clave.pdf (17.12.2021).

Carmona A.F. et al. (2018), *Competition Issues in the Area of Financial Technology (FinTech)*, Study Requested by the ECON Committee, European Parliament, July.

Ciesielski M. (2020), *BaaS – czyli bankowość bez licencji*, https://www.obserwatorfinansowy.pl/bez-kategorii/rotator/baas-czyli-bankowosc-bez-licencji/ (15.08.2021).

Committee for the Study of Digital Platforms. Market Structure and Antitrust Subcommitte. Report, Stigler Center, Draft 15 May 2019.

Crémer J., de Montjoye Y.-A., Schweitzer H. (2019), *Competition Policy for Digital Era.* Final Report, European Commission.

Dealroom (2019), *The State of European Fintech, About Finch Capital*, October, https://dealroom.co/blog/the-state-of-european-fintech-report-2019-edition (20.12.2021).

Deloitte (2021), *Cyfrowarewolucja – bankipodczas COVID-19 – i co dalej?*, https://www.money.pl/banki/cyfrowa-rewolucja-banki-podczas-covid-19-i-co-dalej-6612402177173121a.html (15.05.2021).

Del Rey J. (2020), *6 Reasons Smaller Companies Want to Break Up Big Tech.* January 22.

Deller D. et al. (2021), *Competition and Innovation in Digital Markets.* BEIS Research Paper Number: 2021/040, March.

Demsetz H. (1973), Industry structure, market rivalry, and public policy. *Journal of Law and Economics*, vol. 16, issue 1, pp. 1–9.

Digital Europe (2019), *A Stronger Digital Europe. Our Call to Action Towards 2025.*

Dittrich P.J. (2018), *Online Platforms and How to Regulate Them: An EU Overview*, Policy papers, No. 227, Jacques Delors Institute Berlin, https://www.bertelsmann-stiftung.de/fileadmin/files/user_upload/EZ_JDI_OnlinePlatforms_Dittrich_2018_ENG.pdf (13.11.2022).

European Commission (2015), *A Digital Single Market Strategy for Europe (2015).* Brussels, https://eur-lex.europa.eu/legal-content/EN/TXT/PDF/?uri=CELEX:52015DC0192&from=EN (13.11.2022)

European Commission (2016a), *Online Platforms Accompanying the Document Communication on Online Platforms and the Digital Single Market*, Brussels, http://ec.europa.eu/newsroom/dae/document.cfm?doc_id=15947 (17.06.2021).

European Commission (2016b), *Online Platforms and the Digital Single Market. Opportunities and Challenges for Europe* (Communication from the Commission to the European Parliament, the Council, the European Economic and Social Committee and the Committee of the Regions No. COM(2016) 288 final), Brussels, http://eur-lex.europa.eu/legal-content/EN/TXT/PDF/?uri=CELEX:52016DC0288&from=EN (17.06.2021).

European Commission (2016c), *Report from the Commission to the European Parliament and the Council on the functioning of Commission Regulation* (EU) No 267/2010 on the application of Article 101(3) of the Treaty on the functioning of the European Union to certain categories of agreements, decisions and concerted practices in the insurance sector (No. COM(2016) 153 Final), Brussels, http://ec.europa.eu/competition/sectors/financial_services/iber_report_en.pdf (17.06.2021).

European Commission (2017), *Commission Delegated Regulation (EU) Supplementing Directive 2015/2366 of the European Parliament and of the Council with regard to Regulatory Technical Standards for Strong Customer Authentication and Common and*

Secure Open Standards of Communication. http://ec.europa.eu/finance/docs/level-2-measures/psd2-rts-2017-7782_en.pdf (17.06.2021).

European Commission (2020a), *Proposal for a Regulation of the European Parliament and of the Council on a Single Market for Digital Services (Digital Services Act) and Amending Directive 2000/31/EC*, Brussels, 15.12.2020.

European Commission (2020b), *Proposal for a Regulation of the European Parliament and of the Council on Contestable and Fair Markets in the Digital Sector (Digital Markets Act)*, Brussels, 15.12.2020.

European Commission (2021), *Banking Package 2021: New EU Rules to Strengthen Banks' Resilience and Better Prepare for the Future*, Brussels, 27 October.

EY (2021a), *2021 Global Bank Regulatory Outlook. Building a Better Working World*. EYGM Limited.

EY (2021b), *NextWave Global Consumer Banking Survey*, https://www.ey.com/en_gl/banking-capital-markets/how-can-banks-transform-for-a-new-generation-of-customers (7.01.2022).

Gasser U. et al., (2017), *Digital Bank 2025*, https://www.xupery.com/wp-content/uploads/2017/08/Digital-Banking-2025.pdf (13.11.2022).

Genpact (2016), *Banks Reimagine the Operating Model of the Future*, Whitepaper.

Gimpel H., Rau D., Röglinger M. (2018), *Understanding FinTech Start-Ups – A Taxonomy of Consumer-Oriented Service Offerings*, "Electron Markets", No. 28, pp. 245–264.

Hakkarainen P. (2021), *Digitalisation in European Banking: No Time Like the Present*. Keynote speech, Frankfurt, 23 November.

Harrison P.J. (2021), *What Is a Challenger Bank?*, https://thefintechtimes.com/what-is-a-challenger-bank/ (20.05.2021).

HM Treasury (2019), *Unlocking Digital Competition. Report of the Digital Competition. Expert Panel*, March, https://assets.publishing.service.gov.uk/government/uploads/system/uploads/attachment_data/file/785547/unlocking_digital_competition_furman_review_web.pdf (13.11.2022).

Kasiewicz S., Kurkliński L., Woźniak J. (2021), *Strategie i modele biznesowe banków wobec konkurencji ze strony FinTech-ów*, WIB, Warszawa (not published).

Katz M.L. (2021), Big Tech mergers: Innovation, competition for the market, and the acquisition of emerging competitors. *Information Economics and Policy*, vol. 54, March.

Komisja Europejska (2016), *Platformy internetowe i jednolity rynek cyfrowy*. Szanse I wyzwania dla Europy. Komisja Europejska, Bruksela, https://eur-lex.europa.eu/legal-content/PL/TXT/PDF/?uri=CELEX:52016DC0288&from=PL (13.11.2022).

Neuberger D. (1998), *Structure, Conduct and Performance in Banking Markets*. Working Paper, University of Rostock, Faculty of Economics and Social Sciences.

Northcott C.A. (2004), *Competition in Banking: A Review of the Literature*, Bank of Canada Working Paper, 2004-24, 2004.

Pawłowska M. (2014), *Konkurencja w sektorze bankowym*. CH Beck, Warszawa.

Porc P., Frost F. (2018), *Towards Banking-as-a-Service. Cloud-based Service Models and the Transformation of Banking*, ZEB, https://zeb-consulting.com/files/media/documents/2019-11/zeb_Topic_%20Towards%20banking_as_a_service_2018_EN.pdf (13.08.2021).

Regulation EU (2019/1150) of the European Parliament and Council of 20 June 2019 on promoting fairness and transparency for business users of online intermediation services, Brussels, https://eur-lex.europa.eu/legal-content/EN/TXT/PDF/?uri=CELEX:32019R1150&from=en (13.11.2022).

Robinson B. (2016), *4 Banking Business Models for the Digital Age*, Temenos, 27 October.

Rodríguez L.P., Ortún P.U. (2020), *From FinTech to BigTech: An Evolving Regulatory Response*, https://www.bbvaresearch.com/wp-content/uploads/2020/06/WP_From_FinTech_to_BigTech_an_evolving_regulatory_response_WB_.pdf (15.11.2021)

Rosa G. (2013), *Konkurencja na rynku – systematyka zagadnień [w:] Konkurencja na rynku usług transportowych*. C.H. Beck, Warszawa.

Skaleet (2021), *New Business Models for a New Banking Environment*, https://tagpay.fr/en/blog/new-business-models-for-a-new-banking-environment/ (15.08.2021).

Skinner C. (2017), *Which Banks Are Leading Digital (and Who Are the Laggards)?*, https://thefinanser.com/2017/09/banks-leading-digital-laggards.html/ (24.05.2021).

Social Science Space (2021), *Are Big Tech Companies Bad for Innovation?* Business & Management INK, 6 July, https://www.socialsciencespace.com/2021/06/how-does-competition-differ-across-digital-markets-and-between-national-and-regional-spaces/ (13.11.2022).

Tanda A., Schena C-M. (2019), *FinTech, BigTech and Banks*, Palgrave Macmillan, London.

US House of Representatives (2019) *Investigation of Competition Digital Markets Majority Staff Report and Recommendations,* Washington, 2020.

ZEB (2019), *Retail Banking Business Models – Defining the Future*, Banking Hub, 9 October, https://www.bankinghub.eu/innovation-digital/retail-banking-business-models (13.11.2022).

Part III

Digital insurance

8 Digitalisation of insurance

New values, new challenges

Jan Monkiewicz and Marek Monkiewicz

8.1 Introduction

To date, digitalisation of insurance has not been a popular subject for comprehensive academic papers or monographs. The studies that are available are mostly of a fragmentary nature, dealing with selected aspects of the new reality. This situation has started to change recently, however, with a good example being the research study by Eling and Lehmann (2018), which addressed the issue of the new developments in the insurance value chain resulting from digitalisation. Based on an extensive literature review from selected international databases for the period 2000–2017, they identified more than 80 scientific papers and expert studies dealing with digitalisation and its impact on the insurance value chain. The authors drew three principal conclusions from these studies: first, digitalistion changes the way in which insurers and consumers interact; second, digitalisation covers in principle all business processes; and third, digitalisation changes existing products and creates new ones, with a flagship example being the development of cyber insurance (Eling and Lehmann, 2018, p. 377).

A study by Christian Eckert and KatrinOsterrieder, available online in 2020, is of a similar nature. The authors examined 102 publications, collected in the same databases that Eling and Lehmann used, from the point of view of the application of selected digital technologies in the process of insurance digitalisation: big data, artificial intelligence, the internet of things (IoT), cloud computing and distributed data ledgers (Eckert and Osterrieder, 2020). The authors concluded that insurers are increasingly using new digital technologies in marketing, underwriting, and sales. Furthermore, another milestone development in this area was the first comprehensive monograph published by Bernardo Nicolettiin (2021).

Apart from academic works, another important source of knowledge arises from the studies prepared by experts representing institutions operating in the insurance sector, one of the most important of which is the Geneva Association, also known as the International Association for the Study of Insurance Economics. It recently released three topical reports: one addressed the issue of insuring hostile cyber activity (Geneva Association, 2022), another looked at the support provided by insurance companies for digital entrepreneurship

DOI: 10.4324/9781003310082-13

(Geneva Association, 2021), while the third focused on the impact of IoT on insurance business models (Geneva Association, 2021a). In addition to the output from the Geneva Association, the most important source of knowledge from the sector's expertise arises from the studies prepared by SwissRe, a leading global reinsurer, and analyst of global insurance trends. In recent years, these have addressed various issues, including the use of advanced analytics in insurance, data-driven insurance, and the application of machine intelligence in insurance processes (Swiss Re, 2015, 2019, 2020, 2020a).

The fourth important source of knowledge in the field of digital insurance is the work carried out by actors from the regulatory and supervisory system. Particularly important in this respect is the work of the International Association of Insurance Supervisors (IAIS), an organisation, which plays a central role in setting global standards for the insurance business. In recent years, it has published a paper on the use of big data analytics in the insurance product life cycle (IAIS, 2021) and an application paper on combating money laundering (IAIS, 2021).

In addition to the IAIS, the European Insurance and Occupational Pensions Authority (EIOPA) is another active participant in the discussion on digitalisation issues from the group of supervisory and regulatory actors. It published a number of studies between 2017 and 2021 on issues such as big databases, the new shape of the value chain (Eiopa, 2020a), cyber risk (Eiopa, 2019a, 2020a, 2020b, 2020c), and new business models (Eiopa, 2020, 2021). In 2021, it released a discussion paper on blockchain and smart contracts and a paper on artificial intelligence governance issues. In December 2021, it additionally published a paper on the digital transformation strategy of the EU.

Finally, it is also necessary to mention the extremely important role played by the studies, signals, and comments from the world's leading consultancies.

8.2 The new insurance business model: increased availability of data

The insurance sector relies on the processing of large amounts of information. This includes both personal data (e.g. from motor or life insurance) and non-personal data (e.g. from corporate insurance), and can either be structured data (in tables, forms, sheets, etc.) or unstructured data (in the form of notes, photos, or emails).

This data is used for a variety of purposes such as risk selection, marketing, product development, and claims management. In the traditional analogue insurance model, these data were collected by insurance companies mainly from their customers. This was a labour-intensive process involving the use of complex forms and the submission of a lot of information in paper form, which was then processed, classified, and stored.

Part of the data may also have come from common market databases organised by insurance companies and from public databases. In part, they may also have been provided by private databases, on commercial terms.

A survey conducted by Eiopa in 2018 covering 222 representative European motor and health insurance companies from its 28 member countries can provide evidence of some possible solutions in this regard (Eiopa, 2019b).

The results show that insurance companies use different types of data, depending on the needs of their business line, and the collected data come in different proportions from internal and external sources. The smallest share of internal sources was registered in geolocation data, data from bank accounts, population data, catastrophe data, and online media, i.e. where the direct presence of the insurer was limited. The share of internal sources in this population of companies was less than 30% of the total (Table 8.1).

The results also show that the insurance industry is now increasingly supplementing traditional data sources with new ones, mainly from social media and telematics, as well as internal resources, and that the share of data from third parties is growing. This concerns the use of new data sources, in particular traditional and social media, banking, other financial market entities, economic and social entities, public digital databases, and insurers' own resources, and involves the use of large databases and new analytical tools using artificial intelligence and cloud computing.

Table 8.1 Use of data in motor and health insurance for different business applications

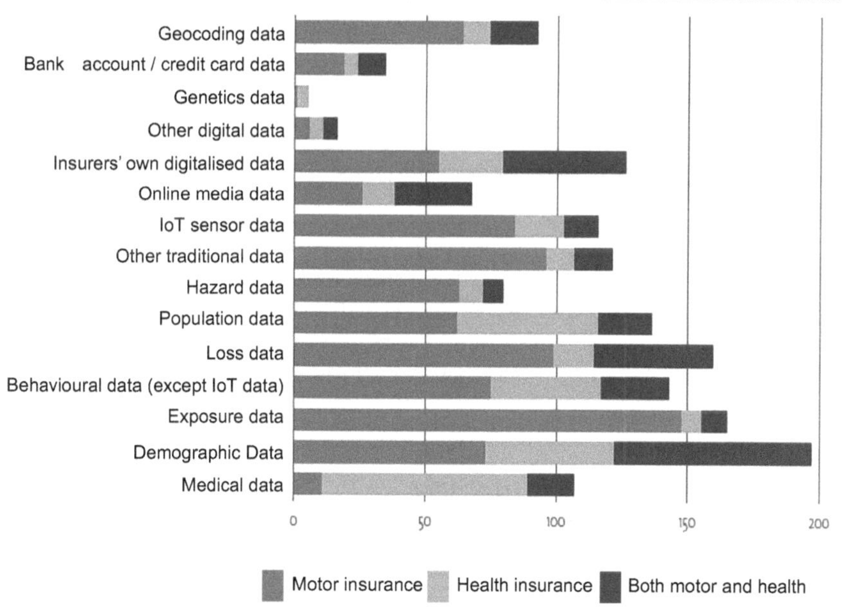

Note: Number of companies using different types of data in the EU in 2018 (out of 222 companies surveyed)
Source: Eiopa (2019b, p. 13)

Table 8.2 Traditional and new data sources used by the insurance sector

Traditional data sources	*New data sources enabled by digitalisation*
Medical data (e.g. medical history, medical condition, condition of family members)	**IoT data** (e.g. driving behaviour (car telematics), physical activity and medical condition (wearables).
Demographic data (e.g. age, gender, civil and family status, profession, address)	**Online media data** (e.g. web searches, online purchases, social media activities, job career information)
Exposure data (e.g. type of car, value of contents inside the car)	**Insurance firms' own digital data** (e.g. interaction with insurance firms (call centre data, users' digital account information, digital claim reports, online behaviour while logging in to insurance firms' websites or using insurance firms' app)
Behavioural data (except IoT data) (e.g. Smoking, drinking behaviour, distance driven in a year)	**Geocoding data** (i.e. latitude and longitude coordinates of a physical address)
Loss data (e.g. claim reports from car accidents, liability cases)	**Genetics data** (e.g. results of predictive analysis of a person's genes and chromosomes)
Population data (e.g. mortality rates, morbidity rates, car accidents)	**Bank account / credit card data** (e.g. consumer's shopping habits, income and wealth data)
Hazard data (e.g. frequency and severity of natural hazards)	**Other digital data** (e.g. selfie to estimate biological age of the consumer
Other traditional data (e.g. credit scoring, claim adjustment reports, information from the auto repair shops)	

Source: Own elaboration based on Eiopa (2019b, p. 9)

Traditional data sets are being supplemented to a large extent by new data sources (see Table 8.2), but at the current stage of development, data from the digitalisation of insurers' internal resources still seem to dominate.

In many cases, the use of additional data allows risks to be insurable that would otherwise be uninsurable based exclusively on traditional insurers' data (Swiss Re, 2015).

8.3 Digitalisation of the insurance value chain

The concept of the value chain was introduced into scientific discourse many years ago by Michael Porter in his seminal work on the development of competitive strategies (Porter, 1985). He defined it as a tool that allows companies to systematically analyse all their activities and interrelationships, which ultimately determine their competitive position in the market.

Porter's concept was addressed in principle not only to the analysis of manufacturing companies but has also been applied over time to the analysis of companies in other sectors, including those in the insurance business (EC, 2018; Eiopa, 2020a).

The value creation chain in insurance has generally been presented so far in terms of six basic activities: product management, sales/distribution management, underwriting, customer relationship management, claims management, and finally capital and asset management (see Figure 8.1). Product management includes two main activities: product development, i.e. its planning, design, and preparation of documentation, and its implementation and allocation to selected customer segments. In current European practice, product management processes are subject to far-reaching regulatory and supervisory interference, as reflected in the Insurance Distribution Directive (EU Directive, 2016).

Distribution encompasses the planning of sales processes and the management of sales channels, as well as the implementation of company policy in this area. It is also subject to a high degree of EU regulation.

Underwriting is the process of accepting risks for insurance, with the starting point being the defined acceptance policy. Underwriting deals with the analysis of the risk of the offer, and the process of its valuation and selection, as well as building the desired portfolio. Selection is an important element of the value chain, determining the profitability of the technical activity and the technical result of the insurer.

Customer relationship management encompasses all activities related to customer service, including contract administration and the handling of information, complaints, and requests, and is key to building customer loyalty.

Claims management, on the other hand, includes the management of the claims process, i.e. the receipt of claims information, the assessment of claims and payment of compensation, as well as the detection and prevention of fraud by customers and other stakeholders (suppliers, employees, etc.).

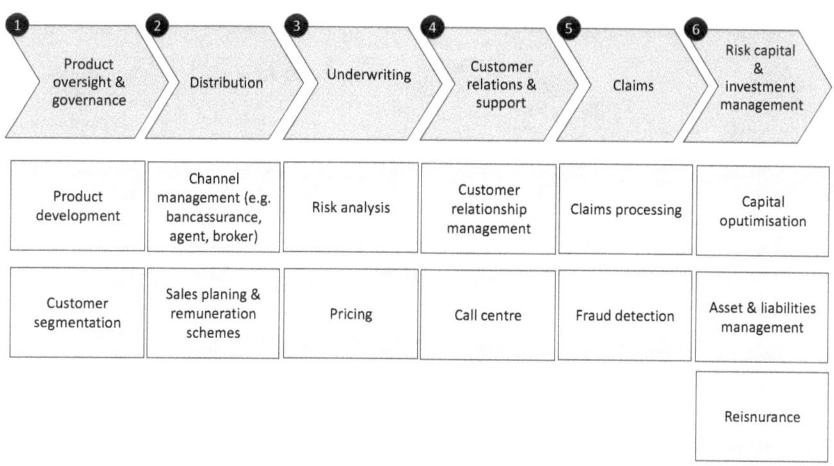

Figure 8.1 The insurance value chain
Source: EC (2018, p. 51)

Finally, the last element of the value chain includes risk capital management, reinsurance as a vehicle to protect against excessive risk, and asset management. Its importance, as a result of the new solvency and risk exposure measurement framework adopted recently in the EU insurance sector (Solvency II), is now particularly high (Regulation, 2019).

This description of the chain is simplified and static, while in reality, it is dynamic and interactive, with many links and interactions between the individual components. Product ideas, for example, may come not only from product cells but also from underwriting, marketing, and distribution.

The digitalisation of the insurance value chain is based on the application of various digital technologies at different points in the chain, which leads to a new way of connecting the real/analogue and virtual worlds (see Figure 8.2). The first group includes, in particular, artificial intelligence with machine learning, big databases, and IoT. The second group of technologies, in turn, includes distributed ledger technology, together with smart contracts and cloud computing technology. The third group includes very diverse component technologies, such as mobile devices and web applications replacing computing devices, chatbots, robo-advisers, video platforms (such as Skype, Zoom, etc.), video platforms (YouTube), websites, social media (Facebook) and instant messaging (Messenger, Whatsapp, etc.).

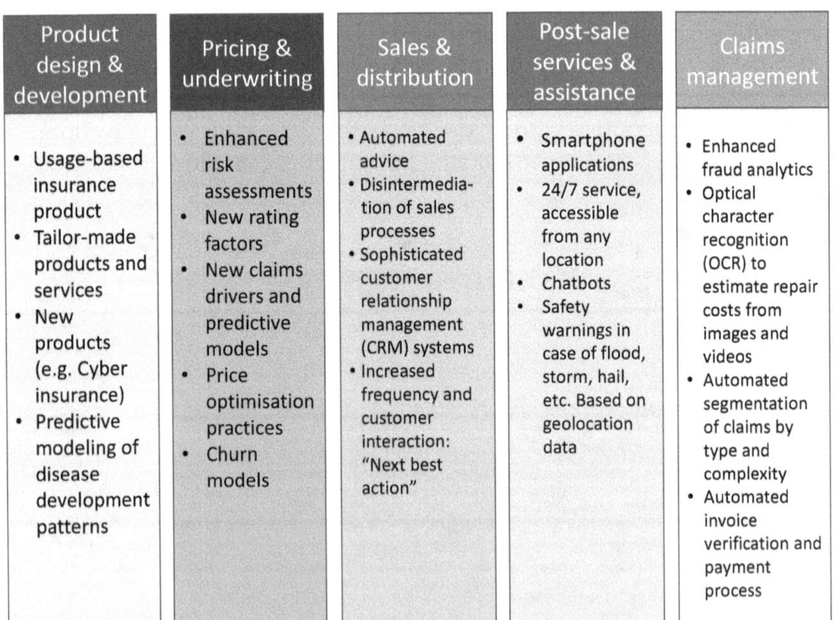

Figure 8.2 Digitalisation of the insurance value chain
Source: Own elaboration based on Eiopa (2020a, p. 10)

The use of digital technologies covers all the components of the value chain, although of course, this may occur in practice to varying degrees at different points in the chain. The most obvious is the impact of digitalisation on the wider customer relationship, i.e. product development, sales, after-sales activities, and claims handling. The second natural area where digitalisation has an impact on the value chain is the management of product offerings. The third is the automation of all internal processes taking place in the value chain, such as contract management, claims reporting, underwriting, etc. (Eling and Lehmann, 2018). A description of the changes taking place and their decomposition according to the components of the chain is not easy as the same changes and technological solutions (e.g. process automation, the use of artificial intelligence, etc.) may appear at different places in the chain.

As far as product management issues are concerned, digital technologies make it possible above all, as a result of the better availability of analytical data and the possibility to process them, to build offers that are much more personalised than in the past. Access to new data and conclusions from their analysis makes it possible to better identify the needs, expectations, and behaviour of customers. Such offers certainly include usage-based products, i.e. products based on monitoring customer behaviour and formulating an offer based on this knowledge. Product personalisation can also be based on better customer segmentation, which can be the result of using big data analytics (IAIS, 2020). Digitalisation also leads to the emergence of new types of products, not previously present, such as cyber risk insurance, drone insurance, or insurance on demand (instant).

Digitalisation in underwriting and pricing primarily leads to the better pricing of risks and their drivers, based on better access to the relevant data and processing possibilities. On the other hand, there are new opportunities to use predictive analysis techniques to create claims models. In addition, the digitalisation of this element of the value chain offers new opportunities for optimising insurance prices and activities aimed at retaining customer loyalty associated with pricing practices. It is also possible to shorten risk assessment and offer preparation by automating part or all of the underwriting process and using artificial intelligence methods for risk assessment.

Digitalisation in the field of distribution and sales enables, above all, better information interaction with customers through the use of hotlines, robo-advisers, or direct sales, as well as the use of many different distribution channels, thus applying the concept of omnichannelism. Digitalisation may also change the role of intermediaries as a result of the development of market comparison services.

Digitalisation in the area of after-sales activities makes it possible to maintain constant contact with customers on the 24/7 principle, namely, 24 hours a day, 7 days a week. This is possible through the use of both classic hotlines and also chatbots, or digital informants, which can prove to be particularly useful for carrying out customer satisfaction surveys or handling requests and complaints. Providing customers with a portal for after-sales self-service is also popular.

The digitalisation of the area of claims management is based on the use of many new technologies, in particular artificial intelligence and process automation.

There are also great opportunities to use computer vision technology to automate the damage assessment process on the basis of photos and videos, and also to use so-called Natural Language Processing (NLP) solutions. The first mechanism is used mainly in the area of motor vehicle damage, where the computer is "taught" to recognise the make of the vehicle and the damaged parts, while the second mechanism allows not only the analysis of information and data from documents but also the reporting of damage using chatbots and voicebots.

A particularly important role in digital transformation is played by the application in various insurance processes of the novel tool of big data analytics, combined with artificial intelligence. This impacts product design, sales and acquisition, pricing and underwriting, as well as product management processes, claims management, and customer interaction (see Figure 8.3).

The digitalisation of insurance is not only leading to changes within the insurance value chain but also to transformations in its wider environment, as a result of the new position given to outsourced activities and outsourcing,

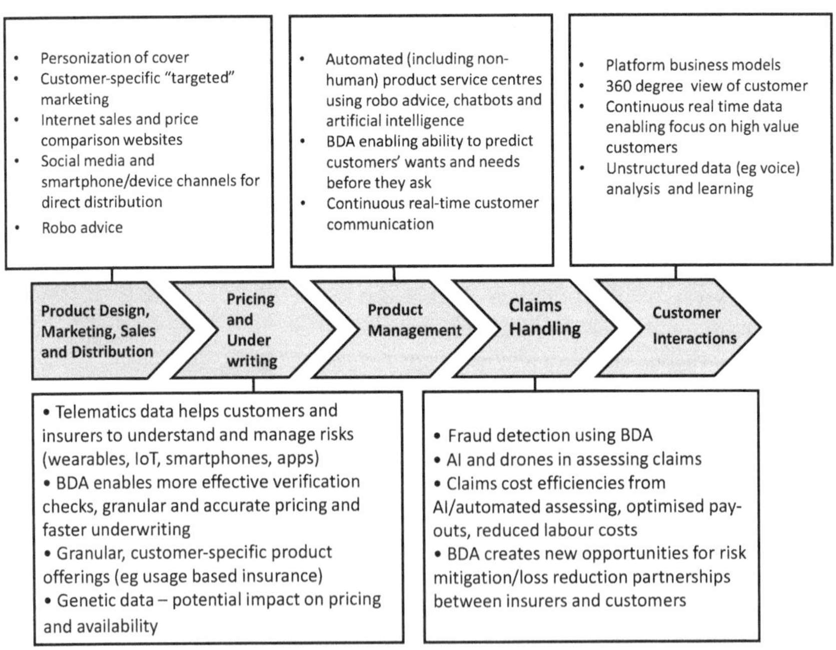

Figure 8.3 Big data analytics (BDA) and artificial intelligence across the insurance value chain

Source: IAIS (2020)

among other things. The use of outsourced services by the insurance sector is a long-established practice, but the use of new technologies is resulting in the much wider use of outsourced services as a result of the potential of technology companies, which are often able to handle certain value chain processes cheaper, faster and better.

This is also due to the activities of digital customers using different platforms, where the insurance offer is only part of a larger whole. This leads not only to increased organisational complexity in the value chain but also to increased regulatory complexity in the sector, as new providers may not be subject to the regulatory regime of the financial sector. This also creates new risks and challenges for supervisory systems.

8.4 Platformisation of the insurance business and the growth of ecosystems

The expansion of the value chain with ambient players may lead to a transformation of the entire business model towards a digital platform-based ecosystem (WEF, 2019). Its essence is that a stable business core mediates between a wide range of complementary products and potential users: customers, suppliers, advertisers and search engines, etc. The platformisation of economic life and finance is also increasingly visible in the insurance industry, providing new opportunities and creating new risks. Insurers can play different roles in this new model, either by building their own models and platforms or by joining existing platforms and ecosystems (Geneva Association, 2018). Platformisationintroduces completely new business models based on the decomposition of the value chain and the roles played by the different participants of the digital platforms. In principle, there are four of them: platform operators, platform suppliers, platform users, and platform advertisers. The platform operator defines the conditions and standards for participation on the platform, while the platform suppliers provide the goods and products traded on the platform. The platform users are the people using the services of the platform to purchase the products or interact with others and, finally, the platform advertisers purchase advertisements on the platform. Technically, platforms are thus essentially multilateral IT systems that connect participating physical persons and institutions to one another and to the operator of each system for the purpose of conducting financial transactions. Platforms differentiate from traditional business models in that they allow for interaction between the platform users, making it possible for them to derive network effects. These arise when the value that a user derives from a service or product increases with the number of other users (Figure 8.4). Platforms are a place for digital ecosystems, which may be defined as an interdependent group of actors which share the platform to achieve mutual benefits (Geneva Association, 2018).

All existing platforms can be classified into three groups: innovation platforms, which serve as a foundation on which others can develop complementary innovations, transaction platforms, serving as an intermediary, and hybrids integrating the two roles (Geneva Association, 2021).

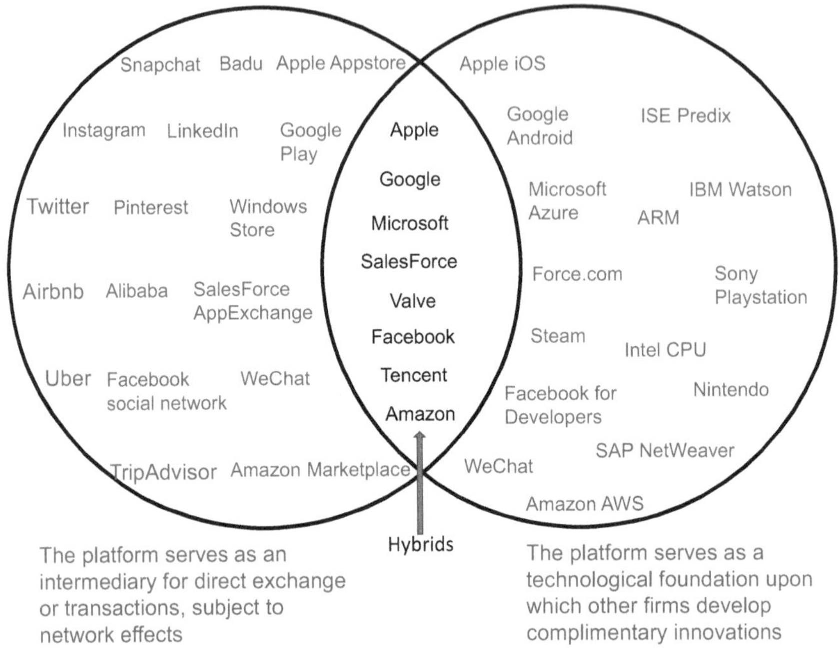

Figure 8.4 Basic platform types
Source: Geneva Association (2021)

The growth of platforms makes it possible to disaggregate and decompose existing insurance value chains. Specifically, it allows for the decomposition of both backup and front-line activities (see Figure 8.5).

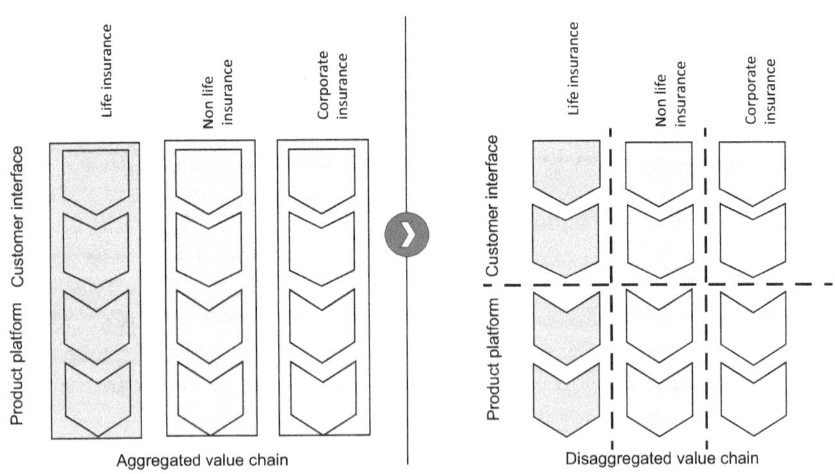

Figure 8.5 Transition from aggregated to disaggregated value chain
Source: Own elaboration based on BaFin (2018, p. 66)

It may therefore lead to the development of entire ecosystems. Generically, these are customer-centric networks located on the platform which offer products and services from different players. Large platforms like Amazon, Google, Facebook, and Tencent operate several ecosystems in parallel. These ecosystems may be particularly attractive for insurers as they challenge the traditionally passive and low-involvement way of interacting with customers. Within these ecosystems, insurers may play two completely different roles: either as a participant of an ecosystem or its orchestrator. Participation means, in essence, offering insurance products by integrating with the platform, while orchestration means bringing together several products and services from different participants onto one platform to satisfy the customers in a better way.

The growth of platforms and their ecosystems additionally requires sweeping changes to the regulatory and supervisory landscape (Arner et al., 2021) to keep things under control.

8.5 Open insurance

The digitalisation of finance has led, additionally, to the development of open banking, which in the EU is mainly associated with the modified directive on the development of payment services (PSD2 Directive). The essence of open financial systems is the possibility for data collected by individual financial institutions to be used by other, even competing, entities. The prerequisite for the use of that possibility is the condition contained in the EU General Data Protection Regulation (Regulation, 2016) stating that the owners of the data should consent to such access. In the Digital Finance Strategy recently adopted by the European Commission, building a common data space in the financial sector is one of its four main objectives. The Commission intends to present a legislative proposal on a new framework for digital finance by mid-2022, and it is highly likely that the new solutions will also include the insurance sector.

One of the few studies in this field is the discussion paper published by Eiopa (2021), which is a study on consultation with national supervisory authorities in the context of the regulatory intentions of the European Commission.

The document defines open insurance as an operating model involving access to, and the sharing of, personal and non-personal insurance data, typically through the use of application programming interface (API) technology. Viewed from the customer's perspective, this means access to, and the sharing of, insurance information between insurers, intermediaries, and third parties for service delivery and application development. It can also mean accessibility to a better connection infrastructure for customers to make choices in the market. This can consequently mean an improved market offer and a better fit with customers' needs.

The concept of open insurance combines the benefits of ecosystems and real-time data (Accenture, 2020, p. 3). While the concept of open insurance is new, the collaboration between insurers in so-called ecosystems or platforms is not new and has been around for several years. Most of us probably remember the beginnings of Assistance insurance, which has been around for at least 20 years. Insurers, by entering into cooperation with companies specialising in organising assistance or services of various specialists, could offer, as a part of an indemnity or a benefit, assistance in specific cases, creating specific added value for insured or injured persons.

However, today's platforms and the ecosystems they refer to are solutions that offer many more services and opportunities. They often offer the customer a range of products and services that are not insurance. These services sometimes have a preventative function, although that is not the rule, and sometimes they are simply products unrelated to the subject of the insurance or policy.

In the context of data transfer, two aspects are key here: (1) the transfer of data and the use of data provided by others; and (2) the offering of one's services and the use of other providers, often also outside the insurance industry. This is a shift from the traditional model of offering an insurance product to offering services (see also Swiss Re, Sigma 1/2020, p. 17).

8.5 Concluding remarks

The digitalisation of insurance is leading to significant changes in the insurance sector, both inside and outside insurance companies, and in their closer and more distant environment.

It is changing the insurance value chain and the business models used, making it possible to meet the requirements of customer-centricity and economically develop the personalisation of the insurance offer and the individualisation of protection.

Digitalisation also makes it possible to make extensive use of self-service in insurance processes by engaging customers accordingly. Today, it is not unusual for a customer to report a claim via a phone app or take photos of a damaged vehicle themselves, instead of waiting for an expert. It is also common for customers to have access to so-called customer zones, where they can change their data, pay premiums, extend their policy, or just report a claim. Nor should we forget the opportunities that digitalisation creates in the area of process automation, including intelligent automation using artificial intelligence.

References

Accenture (2020), *Open Insurance: Unlocking Ecosystem Opportunities for Tomorrow's Insurance Industry*, https://images.info.accenture.com/Web/ACCENTURE/%7B-34d3d948-6976-477d-942c-d5ee1b4b8446%7D_accenture-open-insurance.pdf?elqcst=272&elqcsid=196.

Arner, D. et al. (2021), *Governing FinTech 4.0: BigTech, Platform Finance and Sustainable Development*, ssrn/com/abstract+3915275, 2021.

BaFin (2018), *Big Data Meets Artificial Intelligence: Challenges and Implications for the Supervision and Regulation of Financial Services*, BaFin, 2018

Directive (EU) 2016/97 of 20 January 2016 on insurance distribution, 2016.
EC (2018), *Overview of the Fintech Sector: Challenges for the European Players and Possible Policy Measures at EU Level*, Final Report Prepared by Deloitte for the EC, EU, 2018.
Eckert, C. and Osterrieder, K., *How Digitalisation Affects Insurance Companies: Overview and Use Cases of Digital Technologies*, School of Business, Economics and Society, Friedrich-Alexander University Erlangen-Nürnberg, 1 October 2020.
Eiopa (2019a), *CyberRisk for Insurers – Challenges and Oppportunities*, Eiopa, 2019.
Eiopa (2019b), *Big Data Analytics in Motor and Health Insurance: A Thematic Review*, Eiopa, 2019.
Eiopa (2020), *Consultation Paper on the Proposal for Guidelines on Information and Communication Technology(ICT) Security and Governance*, Eiopa, 12.12.2020
Eiopa (2020a), *European Commission's Digital Finance Strategy consultation* – Eiopa's Draft Response, Eiopa, 22 June 2020.
Eiopa (2020b), *Eiopa Strategy on Cyber Underwriting*, 11.02.2020.
Eiopa (2020c), *Discussion Paper on The (re)insurance Value Chain and New Business Models Arising from Digitalisation*, Eiopa, 14 April2020.
Eiopa (2021), *Discussion Paper on Open Insurance: Accessing and Sharing Insurance-Related Data*, Eiopa, 2021.
Eling, M. and Lehmann, M. (2018), *The Impact of Digitalisation on the Insurance Value Chain and the Insurability of Risks*, The Geneva Papers on Risk and Insurance – Issues and Practice, 2018, pp. 359–396.
Geneva Association (2018), *Virtual Competition: Online Platforms, Consumer Outcomes and Competition in Insurance*, November 2018.
Geneva Association (2021), *Digital Entrepreneurship and the Supportive Role of Insurance*, September2021.
Geneva Association (2021a), *From Risk Transfer to Risk Prevention: How IoT is reshaping business models in insurance*, 26 May 2021.
Geneva Association (2022), *Insuring Hostile Cyber Activity: In Search of Sustainable Solutions*, 18 January 2022.
IAIS (2020), *Issues Paper on the Use of Big Data Analytics in Insurance*, February 2020
IAIS (2021), *Application Paper on Combating Money Laundering and Terrorist Financing*, 2021
Nicoletti, B. (2021), *Insurance 4.0: Benefits and Challenges of Digital Transformation*, Palgrave Macmillan, 2021.
Porter, M. (1985), *Competitive Advantage: Creating and Sustaining Superior Performance*, The Free Press, 1985.
Regulation (EU) 2016/679 of 27 April 2016 on the Protection of Natural Persons with Regard to the Processing of Personal Data and on the Free Movement of Such Data, 2016.
Regulation (EU) 2019/2088 of 27 November 2019 on Sustainability-Related Disclosures in the Financial Services Sector, 2019.
Swiss Re (2015), *Life Insurance in the Digital Age: Fundamental Transformation Ahead*, Sigma 6/2015, Zurich, 2015.
Swiss Re (2019), *Advanced Analytics: Unlocking New Frontiers in P&C Insurance*, Swiss Re Institute, Sigma 4/2019.
Swiss Re (2020), *Data-driven Insurance: Ready for the Next Frontier?*, Swiss Re Institute, Sigma1/2020.
Swiss Re (2020a), *Machine Intelligence in Insurance: Insights for End-to-End Enterprise Transformation*, SwissRe Institute, Sigma 5/2020.
WEF (2019), *Platforms and Ecosystems: Enabling the Digital Economy*, February 2019.

9 Internet of Things in insurance

Quo vadis?

Marta Kruk and Lech Gąsiorkiewicz

9.1 Introduction

Digital developments are having a significant impact on every sphere of the insurance sector. Technological innovations will also fundamentally affect the future of insurers, with their ability to use them potentially determining their ultimate success or failure.

Digitalisation changes the way that insurers and customers interact, covers all business processes, and creates opportunities to modify existing products and develop new ones, such as cyber insurance (Eling & Lehmann, 2018).

The totality of digital technologies used in insurance can be divided into three main groups: technologies for data acquisition and analysis, for data storage, and for communication and sales (Eling & Lehmann, 2018). The insurance sector bases its business on the processing of large amounts of information. According to a 2018 study by Accenture, data was key to decision-making at both operational and strategic levels for 80% of insurers (Accenture, 2018). Among the technologies used for capturing data, the Internet of Things plays a special role. It opens up new perspectives in terms of risk pricing, claims handling, identifying customers' needs and preferences, and managing customer relations, as well as activities aimed at preventing crimes to the detriment of insurers. The development of the Internet of Things will mark changes at every stage of an insurance company's value chain, consequently contributing to the emergence of new business models.

The aim of this chapter is to present selected issues related to the use of the Internet of Things in insurance. It contains definitions of the Internet of Things and its architecture, applications of the Internet of Things in insurance (areas of application of the Internet of Things in insurance, examples of the application of the Internet of Things in insurance, manufacturers of the Internet of Things ecosystem, and barriers to the application of the Internet of Things in insurance) and forecasts for the development of the Internet of Things in insurance.

DOI: 10.4324/9781003310082-14

9.2 The Internet of Things and its architecture

There are a number of definitions of the term 'Internet of Things' in information technology publications. K. Ashton, the British entrepreneur who is believed to have been the first person to use the concept of the Internet of Things, stated that it comprises objects equipped with appropriate sensors, combined with RFID (*Radio-Frequency Identification*) technology, which enables computers to observe, identify and understand the world without the limitations associated with man as an imperfect source of information (Ashton, 2009). According to M. Porter and J. Heppelmann, the Internet of Things emerged as a result of the growing number of smart, interconnected products and their capabilities. When characterising the Internet of Things, researchers refer to the technological sphere, emphasising that these are smart products that access the internet and consist of physical, intelligent elements (sensors, processors, data storage media, control mechanisms, and software) and elements enabling communication (ports, antennas, and protocols for wireless and wired data transmission) (Porter & Heppelmann, 2015). In turn, R. Dobbs et al. define the Internet of Things as sensors and devices placed in various physical objects in order to collect data, remotely monitor, make decisions, and drive optimisation processes in everything from manufacturing to infrastructure and healthcare (Dobbs et al., 2015). According to the McKinsey Global Institute, the Internet of Things comprises sensors and devices connected via a communication network to information systems, enabling the monitoring or management of the performance of the connected objects and machines (McKinsey, 2015). For W. Kokot and P. Kolenda, the Internet of Things is an ecosystem in which objects can communicate with or without human intervention (Kokot & Kolenda, 2015), while a similar opinion is also expressed by M. Grodner et al., stating that the Internet of Things is an ecosystem in which objects equipped with sensors communicate with computers (Grodner et al., 2015). European Research Cluster on the Internet of Things (IECR) defines the Internet of Things as a dynamic global network structure with self-configuring capabilities, based on standard and interoperable communication protocols in which the physical and virtual "things" involved have identities, physical characteristics and virtual personalities, use intelligent interfaces, and are seamlessly integrated into an information network (IERC, 2015). Finally, according to J. Krawiec, the Internet of Things is an infrastructure of connected entities, people, systems, and sources of information, with services processing information from the physical and virtual worlds (Krawiec, 2020).

An attempt to standardise the terms related to the Internet of Things was made by the Internet of Things Working Group, operating under the Minister of Digitalisation in Poland (Report, 2019), when it provided a technological, architectural, and business definition of the Internet of Things.

***Technological definition*:** The Internet of Things is a network connecting wired or wireless devices characterised by autonomous (with no human involvement) operation to acquire, share and process data, or interact with the environment under the influence of this data. It is a concept for building telecommunications networks and information systems with a high degree of dispersion, which can be used, among other things, to create intelligent control and measurement systems, analytical systems, or control systems in virtually every field of life, the economy, or science.

***Architectural definition*:** The Internet of Things is an IT architecture concept that enables the cooperation (interoperability) of various ICT systems supporting a variety of field applications, and is based on the following layers:

- *Equipment* – devices (or objects equipped with them), in particular sensors and actuators, as well as drivers, smartphones, tablets, laptops, or computers that are able to communicate and process data without any, or with limited, human involvement.
- *Communication* – a telecommunications infrastructure and network (wired or wireless), working on the basis of any data transmission standard of any range (in this case, the internet).
- *Software* – IT systems of IoT devices and software for data exchange, processing, system management, and security.
- *Integration* – a set of defined IT services ensuring software interoperability at all levels of architecture.

***Business definition*:** The Internet of Things is a system of business services using objects capable of collecting and processing information (interactions), networked together, providing interoperability and synergy of applications. Connecting IoT products/services allows for a better understanding of the consumer, environment, products, and processes, and enables the identification of relevant events and reactions for immediate optimisation or more precise personalisation.

The architecture of the tools that make up the Internet of Things solutions in the simplest terms is based on (Choroś, 2015):

- objects fitted with sensors and detectors (temperature, vibration, humidity, movement, etc.)
- and transmitters enabling communication, the receiving of commands, as well as the collection and transmission of information;
- IT systems and solutions that receive the data collected and transmitted by these objects, and are also the places where the data are processed and decisions are made (e.g. laptops, tablets, smartphones, and cloud computing);
- an infrastructure enabling communication, i.e. data transmission between objects (such as the Wi-Fi wireless network, Bluetooth, NFC, or the Z-Wave system, which is mainly used in building automation systems).

These tools enable analytical solutions to be implemented that process data and enable conclusions to be drawn and actions to be taken that generate business benefits.

Among the above-mentioned components, sensors play an important role in monitoring the condition of, and any changes to, the components that are the subject of insurance, as a result of which (Report, 2019):

- the catalogue of items subject to insurance will be expanded, making it possible to insure certain items, and their elements, that could not previously be insured due to the lack of mechanisms to verify the information about their condition and level of risk. The idea of metering different elements of everyday objects creates an opportunity to offer insurance for new products, such as insurance for bicycles or electric vehicles;
- the information about insured objects will be organised better since this information will come directly from the insured item itself rather than being the result of processing and classification by another entity;
- the precision of estimating the probability of events and the risks they generate will increase, as it will be based on a continuously growing pool of measurements;
- it will be possible to offer new products and services, developed on the basis of data obtained from new sources. Data from the Internet of Things will allow for the introduction of proactive actions after an event has occurred. It is understood that sensor data will enable insurance companies to respond in real time to events recorded by the sensors, such as sending roadside assistance when a vehicle breaks down or dispatching a plumber when indoor floor humidity levels rise;
- the settlement of claims will become easier and simpler as the insured will not have to report the damage. By analysing the data, the insurer will be able to deduce independently, on the basis of changes in the received parameters, that an insured event has occurred: such as breakage, flooding, or fire;
- it will be possible to prevent fraud against insurers by verifying actual data with the data received from the customer.

9.3 Use of the Internet of Things in insurance

The insurance sector has recognised the potential of the Internet of Things relatively recently, with the advent of commercial solutions based on the collection of information from data sensors.

9.3.1 Areas of application of the Internet of Things in insurance

Insurance activity can be considered in two aspects: static, as structural management, and dynamic, as process management not based on functions but on the optimisation of activities in across-section of implemented processes.

The process approach to managing commercial organisations (process management) is now the dominant paradigm within management. It is characterised by a change in the perception of the organisation from the classic one, based on the logic of specialisation and the grouping of similar functions to form larger units, to a new one, focused on organisational flows that gather resources from different fields around the creation of value for their customers, increasing the volume of sales and reducing the costs of their implementation. Processes are the basis for their improvement, and they include digitalisation.

The definition of a process as a chain of activities is contained in the works of R. Muller and P. Rupper, M. Porter, and M. Kunasz. According to Muller and Rupper, a process is a chain of activities aimed at producing a product or providing a service that meets the requirements of customers (Muller & Rupper, 2000). Meanwhile, Porter defines a process as a value chain in which the value involved in creating or delivering a product or service increases through the execution of individual activities. Each subsequent action performed in the process should add new value to the effect of the earlier action (Porter, 1985). Finally, according to Kunasz, a process is a sequence (network) of implemented activities aimed at transforming input into output, using the necessary resources with a focus on meeting the expectations of an external or internal customer (result), thus creating added value (Kunasz, 2011). The insurance value chain based on Porter's concept is shown in Figure 9.1.

The Internet of Things affects product offerings, distribution, underwriting, after-sales service, and claims handling, i.e. virtually every stage of the insurance value chain. Internet of Things technology is changing the way

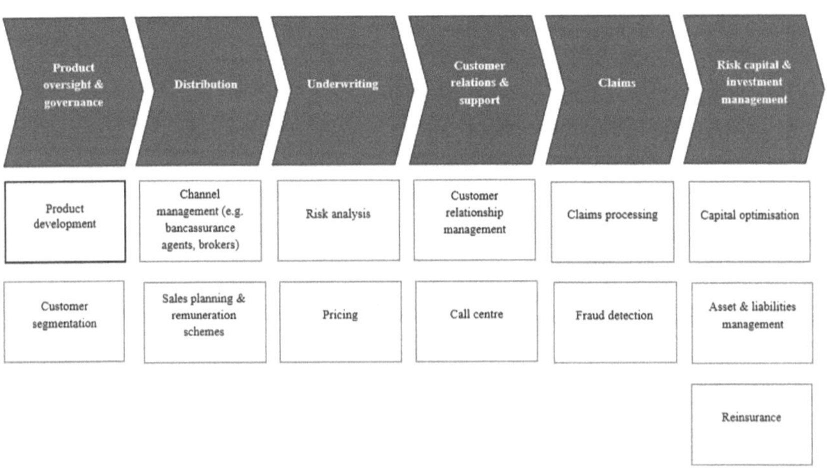

Figure 9.1 The insurance value chain
Source: European Commission (2019, p. 51)

insurance is priced and handled, and the way insurers are able to prevent and mitigate risks and associated losses. Insurers will increasingly use the Internet of Things to better predict and assess risk, streamline the loss adjustment process and create customised insurance products tailored to customers' individual needs. The areas of application of the Internet of Things, broken down by activities in the insurance value chain, are as follows.

9.3.1.1 Product management

The development of Internet of Things technology is creating opportunities for insurers to adopt new approaches to underwriting existing risks, and also to extend coverage to new, previously uninsurable risks (e.g. cyber insurance and instant insurance). The Internet of Things, thanks to the better availability of analytical data and the possibility to insure the processing of that data, allows offers to be created that are much more personalised than before. The data generated by the sensors, combined with the Internet of Things infrastructure, can be the basis not only for assessing the risk level of a given customer but also for indicating their current and future needs and helping to create insurance products based on the actual behaviour and habits of the insured (usage-based insurance). Product personalisation can also be based on better customer segmentation, which may be the result of the use of big data analytics (IAIS, 2020).

9.3.1.2 Distribution

Text recognition and generation systems allow some sales activities to be automated (e.g. via virtual assistants and chatbots) and, combined with customer relationship management systems and segment analysis algorithms, can help to identify optimal communication strategies. Access to new data and insights created by the Internet of Things allows us to better identify customer needs, expectations, and behaviours.

9.3.1.3 Underwriting

Underwriting today is redefining new sources of data that were inaccessible until relatively recently but today are opening up unlimited possibilities for improving underwriting models. In a broad sense, the Internet of Things, i.e. telematics devices installed in vehicles, smart sensors in homes, or various types of wearable technology, allows insurers' systems to be fed with a huge volume of data. The correct interpretation of that data and, above all, the generation of added value for the insurance business using them is a goal which, to be met, requires the use of automation and artificial intelligence tools (Kwiecień & Wawrzyniak, 2022).

The Internet of Things could change insurers' underwriting and pricing models. Insurance companies will be able to react dynamically to risk by taking advantage of the exponential increase in the amount of data generated by the Internet of Things. It has been suggested that the Internet of Things will enable insurers to shift from a reactive passivity to a proactive force, which in turn will reduce risk and thus mitigate, or even prevent, claim losses. In addition, new product portfolios will emerge due to the cyber-physical nature of insured assets. The cyber dimension of the Internet of Things makes it necessary to integrate cybersecurity into existing products, which will result in changes to product portfolios.

The implementation of Internet of Things solutions in insurance companies will have a significant impact on risk modelling. Combining different datasets – historical data and real-time Internet of Things data – will increase the possibilities for modelling and risk assessment capabilities. As the Internet of Things develops, more sophisticated cyber models will need to be developed to take into account direct and incidental cyber risks, as well as the operational risks arising from the use of new technologies. Furthermore, the collection and storage of Internet of Things data must take place within a specific legal framework, which will indicate precisely what kind of data may be collected and processed.

The Internet of Things offers insurance companies more precise risk management systems. Insurance companies can deploy the Internet of Things to monitor activities in real time in order to obtain realistic risk assessments and use the resulting data to avoid fraud.

Insurers can save a lot of money by implementing the Internet of Things in their operations. Automation minimises costs, which in turn helps insurance companies to lower premiums.

9.3.1.4 Customer relations and support management

Personalised insurance quotes, based on the Internet of Things, create a completely different relationship with customers. The insurer becomes a supportive entity for the customer, who is encouraged through specific incentives to adopt better behaviour. Newly offered products will be accompanied by business models based on platforms requiring a strategic partnership with technology suppliers (Lloyd's, 2018).

The availability of data, and the possibility for data analysis through digital technology, allow insurers to learn more about their customers. As a result, they can underwrite policies more accurately and detect fraudulent claims earlier.

9.3.1.5 Claims handling

Access to a significant amount of data, thanks to the Internet of Things, combined with the development of image and text analysis systems, enables loss adjustment processes to become automated. Dedicated apps allow users to upload a description and photos of the damage, which, once that data has been looked at and analysed, can then be priced automatically (Shang, 2018).

The use of Internet of Things devices in the case of medical devices monitoring people's health makes it possible to set devices (apps) that, in the event of significant or unfavourable changes in the person's condition, will allow the relevant alerts or notifications to be sent. With car insurance, the insurer can be notified of an incident by the automatic notification system, while for smart homes, connection to the internet or a mobile device ensures continuous monitoring of the insured property.

The Internet of Things will contribute to further evolution in the area of compensation as advances in safety technologies will affect the frequency of accidents. Improving safety standards and promoting compliance with safety rules will minimise the risk of accidents occurring, thus resulting in a lower number of claims, and also a lower propensity to take out insurance in the first place.

9.3.1.6 Capital and asset management

Data from the Internet of Things, and also from other sources connected with segmentation, prediction, and image recognition systems, can be used to assess the risk of structured investments.

9.3.2 Examples of the use of the Internet of Things in insurance

A number of companies have introduced solutions based on the application of the Internet of Things in their operations. Table 9.1 shows some examples of Internet of Things applications in insurance.

Table 9.1 Examples of IoT applications in insurance

Insurance company	*Examples of IoT applications*
Allstate, Discovery	It offers advanced telematics-based behavioural programmes linked to daily interaction with the insured. Insured people are rewarded for safe driving (Carbone, 2021).
Amodo, Croatia	It offers usage-based insurance, calculating premiums based on mileage data obtained from a mobile app (Kruk & Gąsiorkiewicz, 2022).
Anorak, United Kingdom	It launched a platform that automatically selects customised life insurance using advanced analytics and predictive models (Misionek, 2021).
AXA HL, USA	It offers the "Digital Risk Engineer" service, whereby customers receive alerts when a critical situation is detected in a building, enabling them to intervene quickly and prevent or mitigate the occurrence or extent of damage (Ritchie, 2020).

(*Continued*)

Table 9.1 Examples of IoT applications in insurance (Continued)

Insurance company	*Examples of IoT applications*
AXAMunich/RE HSB, Germany	Based on Internet of Things technology, it offers insurance services in the field of contractual liability protection for suppliers of machinery and equipment, and warranty protection for customers (Kruk & Gąsiorkiewicz, 2022).
Benefia 24.pl, Poland	It launched a service whereby customers can conclude a car insurance contract after scanning the QR code on the registration certificate using a mobile app (Misionek, 2021).
By Miles, United Kingdom	It offers usage-based insurance, calculating premiums based on mileage data extracted from vehicle systems (Kruk & Gąsiorkiewicz, 2022).
Church Mutual, USA	It equips insured properties with Internet of Things solutions to detect leaks and frozen pipes, and also to alert policyholders in real time to reduce potential losses. As a result, it achieved an above-average insurance renewal rate. This solution for 9,000 policyholders has cost $8.9 million since 2016, producing savings of $31 million by the end of 2020 (The Geneva Association, 2021).
Cuvva, United Kingdom	It offers car insurance allowing people to purchase cover for the hours when the car is in use (Misionek, 2021).
Cytora, United Kingdom	It has launched automated risk assessment processes in corporate insurance using machine learning technologies and access to public databases, which has contributed to improved insurance profitability (Misionek, 2021).
Discovery, South Africa	It offers Vitality health insurance, which rewards policyholders who lead healthy lifestyles (data is collected via devices monitoring customer activity) (The Geneva Association, 2021).
Ergo Hestia, Poland	The insurer first assesses the driver's driving style and then prepares an offer of reduced insurance premiums for private car owners (Kruk & Gąsiorkiewicz, 2022).
FloodFlash, USA	It offers flood insurance for properties using Internet of Things-based sensors to measure water levels inside the property. In the event of flooding or water inundation, compensation is paid out completely automatically (Misionek, 2021).
Generali, Italy	Using its many years of experience in telematics, it has introduced hardware solutions that provide drivers with real-time information about their driving style. The solutions used here improve driver skills and change driving habits, enabling improvements in road safety and a reduction in the number of accidents and insurance claims to be observed (The Geneva Association, 2021).
HDI Global, Germany	It uses the building, machinery, and equipment data generated from the Internet of Things technology to mitigate risk and offer both tailored insurance solutions and risk advice to customers (Ritchie, 2019).

Table 9.1 Examples of IoT applications in insurance (Continued)

Insurance company	*Examples of IoT applications*
Intact, Canada	It proposes solutions to prevent fires on farms, whereby customers purchasing equipment monitored by the technology provider receive discounts on the insurance of the monitored property (Kruk & Gąsiorkiewicz, 2022).
Ladder, USA	It offers term life insurance with a simplified quote and purchase process, as well as automated risk assessment (Misionek, 2021).
Lemonade, USA	It uses an automatic assessment of the circumstances of the damage, with the payment of compensation reduced to a matter of minutes (Misionek, 2021).
Liberty Mutual Insurance, USA	The insurer implemented a solution whereby the cost of home insurance was reduced after the installation of smoke alarms on the property to detect fire hazards (Misionek, 2021).
Link 4, Poland	It offers insurance based on telematics solutions that monitor the driving style of the insured. The policyholder can then receive a reward for safe driving in the form of a refund of part of the premium paid (Kruk & Gąsiorkiewicz, 2022).
Medallia, USA	It uses advanced algorithms based on artificial intelligence (analysis of customer interaction data), allowing for improved processes and increased customer satisfaction (Misionek, 2021).
Metromile, USA	It offers car insurance where the price of the insurance policy depends on the number of miles travelled (Misionek, 2021).
Neos, United Kingdom	It offers smart home insurance using internet technology to actively protect and insure the home (The Geneva Association, 2021).
Noblr, USA	It offers usage-based insurance by calculating the premium based on data about the car's usage obtained from a mobile app (Kruk & Gąsiorkiewicz, 2022).
People's Insurance Company of China, China	It uses the Internet of Things in insurance products related to lifting security. The data from the monitored equipment are transferred to the entities responsible for its maintenance, which results in an improvement in the quality of maintenance and a reduction in the failure rate (Kruk & Gąsiorkiewicz, 2022).
Progressive, USA	It introduced telematics-based car insurance that rewards good driving behaviour (Misionek, 2021).
PZU LAB and Ergo Hestia, Poland	Using Internet of Things technology, insurers provide industrial risk mitigation services to prevent industrial losses (Kruk & Gąsiorkiewicz, 2022).
PZU S.A., Poland	It offers the "Risk Pro" product for corporate clients – a solution that uses the Internet of Things and other digital technologies to monitor security levels in risk-critical areas of a company's operations, such as production, logistics, and machinery. A significant degree of monitoring takes place remotely (Małek, Monkiewicz, Monkiewicz, 2022).

(Continued)

Table 9.1 (Continued)

Insurance company	*Examples of IoT applications*
The Hartford, USA	It offers real-time risk mitigation solutions based on the Internet of Things to customers in the construction sector, with the cost of the technology split between the customer and the insurer depending on the share of the parties involved in the value of the service (Kruk & Gąsiorkiewicz, 2022).
Tokio Marine, Japan	It offers car insurance policyholders the possibility to have an AI-assisted camera fitted. This device automatically detects risky situations and warns the driver, thus reducing the probability of an accident and consequently the number of car insurance claims (Kruk & Gąsiorkiewicz, 2022).
Tractable, United Kingdom	It implements artificial intelligence-based solutions to analyse vehicle damage based on images (Misionek, 2021).
UnipolSai and Generali, Italy	These insurers use car telematics data at every stage of the claim (Carbone, 2021).
Vigo, Slovenia	It offers usage-based motorbike insurance, which requires a mobile app and also a monitoring device to be installed on the bike (Kruk & Gąsiorkiewicz, 2022).

Source: Own elaboration based on Carbone (2021), Kruk and Gąsiorkiewicz (2022), Misionek (2021), Ritchie (2020), The Geneva Association (2021), and Małek, Monkiewicz and Monkiewicz (2022)

9.3.3 Manufacturers of Internet of Things ecosystems

In view of the growing interest in the Internet of Things, a number of companies are producing ecosystems proposed for insurers. The world's leading companies operating in the Internet of Things insurance market are, by revenue: Microsoft Corporation, Accenture, Cisco Systems, Inc., Oracle Corporation, Wipro Limited, Capgemini SE, AerisCommunications, and Damco (Report, 2022).

Microsoft Corporation ($161 billion in revenue) – Microsoft Azure provides insurers with a solution to get started with the Internet of Things, adding sensors and smart devices, managing devices, analysing customer data, and leveraging insights to develop new business opportunities and revenue streams. With the Azure platform, insurance organisations can respond quickly to the data and adjust business processes and offerings as needed, ensuring revenue growth while reducing risk.

Accenture ($50.53 billion in revenue) – The Accenture Intelligent IoT Insurance Center in Rome helps insurers and fleet managers develop new services for their customers with a comprehensive portfolio of vertical solutions based on the Internet of Things, including:

- Fleet managers can use a telematics box to track cars, view their locations, monitor journeys, and collect data.

- Accenture's next generation of patented, enhanced AI-based features from Deep Learning AI will provide drivers with important signals to help them cope better with various driving difficulties (e.g. safe distances, overtaking, and traffic jams).

Cisco Systems, Inc. ($49.30 billion in revenue) – Cisco Systems, Inc., based in San Jose, California, is an American international technology conglomerate that develops, manufactures, and distributes telecommunications equipment, software, and other high-tech products and services. Central to the success of Silicon Valley, Cisco Systems, Inc. provides specialised technology in such areas as the Internet of Things, domain security, and energy management through several acquired companies, such as Webex, OpenDNS, Jabber, and Jasper.

Oracle Corporation ($39.07 billion in revenue) – Oracle IoT Cloud Service is a platform that helps companies make key business decisions by enabling them to connect to cloud devices, analyse data in real time, and integrate data with web services, enterprise applications, or other Oracle Business Intelligence Cloud Services.

Wipro Limited ($10 billion in revenue) – Wipro Limited is an Indian international organisation that specialises in IT, consulting, and business process outsourcing. Wipro Limited's Internet of Things solutions allows insurance companies to be more efficient, with greater security and better customer service. Examples of some of the IoT solutions developed by Wipro Limited include:

- a cloud-based Smart Vehicles platform that connects Original Equipment Manufacturers (OEMs), insurers, dealers and consumers to establish new revenue streams, including usage-based insurance (UBI);
- a cloud-based Smart Buildings platform that facilitates loss prevention by monitoring risk and handling claims in real time;
- providing real-time medical information through a next-generation smart device platform that offers preventive healthcare.

Capgemini SE ($6.67 billion in revenue) – Capgemini SE is an international IT advisory and service corporation based in France. In June 2021, the company partnered with Orange, Generali, and Sanofi to launch the Future4care project, which focuses on digital healthcare.

Aeris Communications ($110 million in revenue) – Aeris is a global technology partner that helps companies realise the benefits of the Internet of Things. Aeris' platform-based, scalable insurance solutions connected to the Internet of Things allow insurance companies to efficiently streamline their operations and offer customers a variety of helpful services. Aeris enables insurance companies to easily add new capabilities while changing the perceived and physical value of their products and solutions.

Damco ($79.6 million in revenue) – Damco helps insurance companies to simplify and accelerate the implementation of the Internet of Things in insurance – from health insurance to vehicle insurance. The company tailors its customer offering with a targeted strategy to streamline the complex Internet of Things ecosystem. It helps customers to start using Internet of Things technology to make effective data-driven decisions and improve customer service, thus reducing the cost of insurance claims.

9.3.4 Barriers to the use of the Internet of Things in insurance

The most important barriers that may significantly hinder the implementation and application of IoT-based solutions include issues related to security, data protection and privacy, interoperability, standardisation and integration, regulation, and the lack of sufficient staff with the right digital skills.

9.3.4.1 Security

Internet of Things-connected devices are getting smarter and the financial value of IoT data is growing. The widespread adoption of the Internet of Things will reduce the cost of sensors, thus enabling more and more business applications. Development cannot be stopped, which means that it's necessary to be prepared for an increase in security problems and challenges. The area of security is a key barrier to the implementation of Internet of Things concepts in organisations (Butun et al., 2019; Conti et al., 2018; Zdravković et al., 2018). According to research conducted by a number of companies, security concerns are the main limitation in the development of this innovative technology (DZone, 2018; KPMG, 2019; Microsoft, 2019; PwC, 2019). And security also remains a crucial issue in the meantime since, with the ever-increasing number of connected devices, the risk of cyber attacks on Internet of Things devices and unauthorised access to data is rising (Rot & Blaicke, 2017).

9.3.4.2 Data protection and privacy

Research carried out by a number of companies (Accenture Digital, 2017; Ernst & Young, 2015; McKinsey, 2015; PwC, 2019) indicates that the areas of data protection and privacy are among the most important factors influencing the development of the Internet of Things. A security vulnerability can be exploited by hackers to gain access to private data. Hence, there is a need to protect both product and user data (DZone, 2018; Porter & Heppelmann, 2014).

9.3.4.3 Interoperability, standardisation and integration

The Internet of Things is a complex ecosystem connecting devices, systems, and platforms from different manufacturers, distributors, and software developers, which can result in a lack of interoperability among the associated standards, norms, and tools. Data are the basis for insurance companies in all these business areas. The quality of the data collected, their consistency, and standardisation, are therefore particularly important. This is a prerequisite for implementing new, complex solutions and analytical models. It is especially crucial for insurance companies that intend to engage with third parties, as the lack of a comprehensive standardisation framework and the diversity of technologies being deployed will pose significant challenges to ensuring the integration of the Internet of Things environment.

9.3.4.4 Legal regulations

According to experts in the field, the existing regulations and laws are not adapted to the reality being created by new technologies, which may hinder the development of the concept of the Internet of Things in organisations (Ernst & Young, 2015). Considering that one of the pillars of the Internet of Things is the principle of decision-making without human intervention, it is important to ensure that these decisions do not violate consumers' rights, involve any kind of ethical risk, or be contrary to fundamental principles and human rights (EESC, 2018). With regard to the Internet of Things, the European Economic and Social Committee calls on European institutions and Member States (EESC, 2018):

- to ensure the protection of security and privacy by developing an appropriate regulatory framework with stringent controls,
- to put in place adequate resources and mechanisms for efficient coordination between the European Commission and the Member States in order to guarantee a coherent and harmonised application of both the provisions to be amended and the new regulations, while taking into account the international context,
- to monitor the development of new technologies related to the Internet of Things in order to guarantee a high level of security, full transparency, and fair accessibility,
- to oversee markets and ensure a level playing field for the deployment of the Internet of Things, avoiding the concentration of transnational economic power in the context of new technological actors,
- to secure the existence, implementation, and smooth functioning of a European system of collective redress that will make it possible to stop any such practices and obtain compensation, including in cases where the use of the Internet of Things causes collective damage or losses.

When talking about regulatory constraints, it is also important to bear in mind professional secrecy regulations for insurance companies, which can significantly affect the ability to build a coherent product offering with other entities within a certain ecosystem.

9.3.4.5 Lack of sufficient staff with the right digital skills

Another significant barrier relates to the use of huge volumes of data. Insurers do not have the right knowledge or sufficient skills to fully exploit the potential of the data coming from the Internet of Things devices (ACC-PIU, 2018). Dynamic technological development poses a challenge in terms of attracting qualified employees with digital skills (data analysis specialists or software specialists), and insurers are not only competing among themselves for employees with digital skills but also with companies from other industries.

9.4 Forecasts for the development of the Internet of Things in insurance

According to Mordor Intelligence, the global Internet of Things insurance market was valued at $28.96 billion in 2020, and it is expected to reach $184.82 billion by 2026, registering a CAGR (compound annual growth rate) of 40.08% between 2021 and 2026 (Mordor Intelligence, 2021). The growth in the global Internet of Things insurance market from 2021 to 2026 is shown in Figure 9.2.

Geographically, North America accounted for the largest share of the global Internet of Things insurance market in 2020, generating revenue of

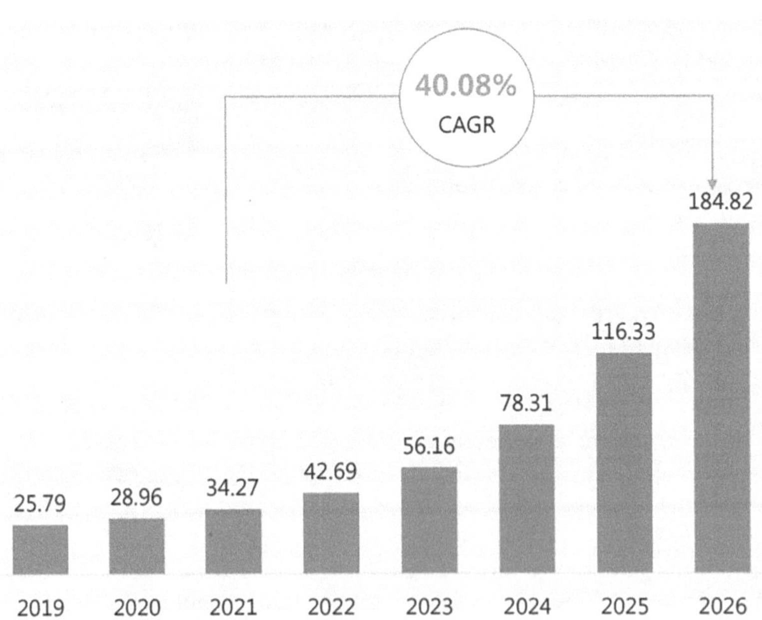

Figure 9.2 Global IoT insurance market (revenue in billions of dollars)
Source: Mordor Intelligence (2021)

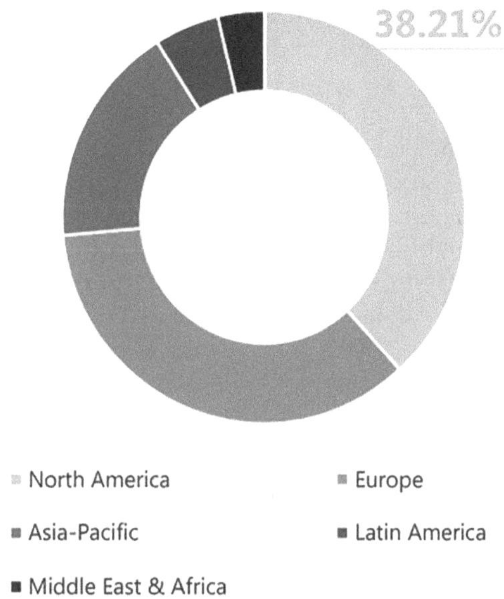

Figure 9.3 Global IoT insurance market geographically
Source: Mordor Intelligence (2021)

$11.07 billion, which represented a share of 38.21%. Meanwhile, Asia Pacific is projected to register the highest CAGR of 46.11% between 2021 and 2026 (Figure 9.3).

The Internet of Things can benefit insurance companies by reducing the cost of the claims handling process, leading to IoT devices reducing premiums by up to 25% (Mordor Intelligence, 2021). Insurers are aware that the time has come to make strategic choices about how to participate in the ecosystem.

By the end of 2019, insurers in North America and Europe had entered into approximately 27.5 million insurance policies linked to telematics tools, with 12.8 million policies in the European market alone. At the same time, the number of policies concluded in connection with telematics devices is predicted to rise to 44.5 million by the end of 2024 (Oiot, 2021). However, it should be noted that the dynamics of this growth will depend on the attitude of customers and their willingness to share detailed data.

9.5 Conclusions

Technological developments and changing customer expectations are the main drivers of innovation in the insurance industry. The rapid development of digital technologies, including the Internet of Things, will significantly affect the operations of insurance companies over the next few years. Insurers are recognising the huge potential of the Internet of Things technology, which is bringing about changes in the areas of the creation of customised insurance products, distribution, underwriting, customer relationship management, and the creation and management of claims.

Experience to date indicates that insurers are mainly investing in two areas related to digitalisation. The first is to improve the customer experience with the aim of increasing the company's revenue, while the other is to focus on cost optimisation through digitalising internal operations.

According to the published report "Digitalisation of the Insurance Sector in Poland", prepared by Accenture for the Polish Insurance Association, although most insurance companies are aware of the importance of the digitalisation process, they adopt different approaches to innovation and the implementation of new technologies. The authors of the report divided the companies into three groups: pragmatic traditionalists, digital followers, and diversified partners. The first group invests in point-of-sale digital solutions to improve current sales channels, while the representatives of the second group take a holistic approach to the subject of digitalisation, experimenting with various technologies, even those that do not currently have a business justification, in order to build the digital competence within their company for the future. The third group, meanwhile, builds ecosystems together with other partners, creating technology platforms, also in collaboration with companies outside the insurance industry (Accenture, 2018).

The implementation of new technologies in insurance, including the Internet of Things, is inevitable but it will bring a number of new challenges, which is why insurance companies should take important steps today to prepare for the digital transformation in this area. It is important to bear in mind that insurers will face a number of barriers of a technological, skills-related, and regulatory nature when implementing Internet of Things solutions.

References

Accenture, 2018. *Cyfryzacja sektora ubezpieczeń w Polsce.* [*Digitalisation of the Insurance Sector in Poland.*] Report Prepared by Accenture in Collaboration with the Polish Insurance Association. https://piu.org.pl/wp-ontent/uploads/2018/11/ACC_PIU_Raport-Cyfryzacja-Ubezpieczen-w-Polsce.pdf.

Accenture Digital and CXP Group, 2017. *Digital Industrial Transformation with the Internet of Things.* https://www.accenture.com/_acnmedia/PDF-49/Accenture-Digital-Industrial-Transformation-with-the-Internet-of-Things.pdf.

Ashton, K., 2009. That 'Internet of Things' Thing. *RFID Journal*, 22 June 2009. https://www.rfidjournal.com/that-internet-of-things-thing.

Butun, I., Österberg, P. & Song, H., 2019. Security of the Internet of Things: Vulnerabilities, Attacks and Countermeasures. *IEEE Communications Surveys & Tutorials*, 22(1), pp. 616–644. https://doi.org/10.1109/COMST.2019.2953364.

Carbone, M., 2021. *Let's Make Insurers Great Again*, Business Reporter, 11 June 2021. https://business-reporter.co.uk/2021/06/11/lets-make-insurers-great-again/.

Choroś, P., 2015. "Wykorzystanie analityki biznesowej w Internecie Rzeczy" ["The use of business analytics in the Internet of Things"] [in]: M. Grodner, W. Kokot, P. Kolenda, K. Krejtz, A. Legoń, P. Rytel & R. Wierzbiński (eds.). *Internet Rzeczy w Polsce* [*Internet of Things in Poland*], pp. 4–7. Warsaw: IAB Poland.

Conti, M., Dehghantanha, A., Franke, K. & Watson, S., 2018. Internet of Things security and forensics: challenges and opportunities. *Future Generation Computer Systems*, 78(2), pp. 544–546. https://doi.org/10.1016/j.future.2017.07.060

Dobbs, R., Manyika, J. & Woetzel, J., 2015. *No Ordinary Disruption: The Four Global Forces Breaking All the Trends*. New York: PublicAffairs.

DZone, 2018. *Internet of Things: Harnessing Device Data*. https://dzone.com/guides/iot-harnessing-device-data.

EESC, 2018. EESC - European Economicand Social Committee. *Trust, privacy and consumer security in the Internet of Things (IoT) (Own-initiative opinion)* [Zaufanie, prywatność i bezpieczeństwo w internecie rzeczy (Opinia z inicjatywy własnej)]. Brussels: INT/846-EESC-2018. https://www.eesc.europa.eu/en/our-work/opinions-information-reports/opinions/trust-privacy-and-consumer-security-internet-things-iot-own-initiative-opinion

Eling, M. & Lehmann, M., 2018. *The Impact of Digitalization on the Insurance Value Chain and the Insurability of Risks*. Geneva: The Geneva Papers on Risk and Insurance – Issues and Practice.

Ernst & Young, 2015. *Internet of Things: Human-Machine Interactions that Unlock Possibilities*. https://www.ey.com/Publication/vwLUAssets/ey-m-e-internet-of-things/$FILE/ey-m-e-internet-of-things.pdf.

Grodner, M., Kokot, W., Kolenda, P., Krejtz, K., Legoń, A., Rytel, P. & Wierzbiński, R., 2015. *Internet rzeczy w Polsce* [*Internet of Things in Poland*]. Warsaw: IAB Poland. https://www.emergenresearch.com/blog/top-10-companies-offering-internet-of-things-insurance-services-in-the-world.

IAIS, 2020. *Issues Paper on the Use of Big Data Analytics in Insurance*. February. https://www.iaisweb.org/page/supervisory-material/issues-papers.

IERC, 2015. IERC – European Research Cluster on the Internet of Things. *Internet of Things. Position Paper on Standardization for IoT Technologies*.

Kokot, W. & Kolenda, P., 2015. "Czym jest Internet Rzeczy". ["What Is the Internet of Things"] [in]: M. Grodner, W. Kokot, P. Kolenda, K. Krejtz, A. Legoń, P. Rytel & R. Wierzbiński (eds.), *Internet Rzeczy w Polsce*. [*Internet of Things in Poland*]. Warsaw: IAB Poland.

European Commission, 2019. Directorate-General for Communications Networks, Content and Technology. *Przegląd sektora Fintech: wyzwania dla graczy europejskich i możliwe środki polityczne na poziomie UE* [*Overview of the Fintech Sector: Challenges for European players and possible policy measures at EU level*], Publications Office. https://data.europa.eu/doi/10.2759/507164

KPMG, 2019. *The top 10 technologies for business transformation*. https://assets.kpmg/content/dam/kpmg/ie/pdf/2019/05/ie-top-10-technologies-for-business-transformation.pdf.

Krawiec, J., 2020. *Internet Rzeczy (IoT). Problemy cyberbezpieczeństwa*. [*Internet of Things (IoT): Cybersecurity Issues*.] Warsaw: Oficyna Wydawnicza Politechniki Warszawskiej (Warsaw University of Technology Publishing House).

Kruk, M. & Gąsiorkiewicz, L., 2022. "Internet rzeczy w działalności ubezpieczeniowej". ["Internet of Things in the Insurance Business"] [in]: L. Gąsiorkiewicz & J. Monkiewicz (eds.), *Finansecyfrowe. Perspektywa rynkowa*. [*Digital Finance:*

A Market Perspective]. Warsaw: Oficyna Wydawnicza Politechniki Warszawskiej (Warsaw University of Technology Publishing House).

Kunasz, M., 2011. *Process Management*. Szczecin: Economicus, p. 12.

Kwiecień, I. & Wawrzyniak, D., 2022. "Nowe technologie w underwritingu ubezpieczeń". ["New Technologies in Insurance Underwriting"] [in]: J. Monkiewicz, L. Gąsiorkiewicz, P. Gołąb & M. Monkiewicz (eds.), *Ubezpieczenia cyfrowe. Możliwości, oczekiwania, wyzwania*. [*Digital Insurance: Opportunities, Expectations, Challenges*]. Warsaw: PWN Scientific Publishers.

Lloyd's, 2018. *Networked World: Risks and Opportunities in the Internet of Things*, November 2018, published in November 2018. https://www.lloyds.com/~/media/files/news-and-insight/risk-insight/2018/internet-of-things/interconnectedworld2018-final.pdf.

McKinsey Global Institute, 2015. *The Internet of Things: Mapping the Value beyond the Hype*. https://mck.co/2D5v5Qq.

Małek, A., Monkiewicz, J. & Monkiewicz, M., 2022. "Ubezpieczenia w świecie cyfrowym: nowe uwarunkowania i wyzwania". ["Insurance in the Digital World: New Conditions and Challenges"] [in]: J. Monkiewicz, L. Gąsiorkiewicz, P. Gołąb & M. Monkiewicz (eds.), *Ubezpieczenia cyfrowe. Możliwości, oczekiwania, wyzwania*. [*Digital Insurance: Opportunities, Expectations, Challenges*]. Warsaw: PWN Scientific Publishers.

Microsoft, 2019. IoT Signals: Summary of Research Learnings 2019. https://azure.microsoft.com/en-us/resources/iot-signals.

Misionek, R., 2021. *Cyfryzacja w ubezpieczeniach*. [*Digitalisation in Insurance*]. Seminarium Zakładu Finansów Wydziału Zarządzanie Politechniki Warszawskiej. [Seminar of the Department of Finance, Faculty of Management, Warsaw University of Technology].

Mordor Intelligence, 2021. *Global IoT Insurance Market – Growth, Trends, COVID-19 Impact, and Forecasts (2021–2026)*. Hyderabad: Mordor Intelligence.

Muller, R. & Rupper, P., 2000. *Process Reengineering*. Wrocław: Astrum.

Oiot, 2021. https://oiot.pl/telematyka-przyszloscia-ubezpieczen-iot/.

Porter, M., 1985. *Competitive Advantage*. New York: Free Press.

Porter, M. E. & Heppelmann, J. E., 2014, *How Smart, Connected Products Are Transforming Competition*. Harvard Business Review.

Porter, M. E. & Heppelmann, J. E., 2015, *How Smart, Connected Products Are Transforming Companies*. Harvard Business Review, October.

PwC, 2019. *IoT Survey: Speed operations, strengthen relationships and drive what's next*. https://www.pwc.com/us/en/services/consulting/technology/emerging-technology/iot-pov.html.

Report, 2019. *IoT w polskiej gospodarce*. [*IoT in the Polish Economy*]. Grupa Robocza do spraw Internetu rzeczy przy Ministerstwie Cyfryzacji. [Working Group for the Internet of Things at the Ministry of Digitalisation]. Warsaw: Ministry of Digitalisation in Poland.

Report, 2022 ID: ER_00121. *Top 10 Companies Offering Internet of Things (IoT) Insurance Services in the World*. https://www.emergenresearch.com/blog/top-10-companies-offering-internet-of-things-insurance-services-in-the-world.

Ritchie, D., 2019. *Schneider Electric and HDI Global in IoT Collab*. Continuity, Insurance & Risk Magazine. https://www.cirmagazine.com/cir/SchneiderElectric-and-HDI-Global-in-IIoT-collab.php?utm_source=jsrecent.

Ritchie, D., 2020. *AXA XL launches IoT tool for monitoring building health.* Continuity, Insurance & Risk Magazine. https://www.cirmagazine.com/cir/2020092401.php.

Rot, A. & Blaicke, B., 2017. *Bezpieczeństwo Internetu Rzeczy. Wybranezagrożeniaisposobyzabezpieczeńnaprzykładziesystemówprodukcyjnych.* [*Security of the Internet of Things: Selected Threats and Security Measures on the Example of Manufacturing Systems.*] Zeszyty Naukowe Politechniki Częstochowskiej. Zarządzanie. [Scientific Notebooks of the Częstochowa University of Technology. Management], 26, pp. 188–198. DOI:10.17512/znpcz.2017.2.17

Shang, 2018. *Applying Image Recognition to Insurance.* Society of Actuaries. https:/www.genevaassociation.org/sites/default/files/research-topics-document-type/pdf_public/in_the_digital_age_01.pdf.

The Geneva Association, 2021. *From Risk Transfer to Risk Prevention – How the Internet of Things is reshaping business models in insurance.* May 2021.

Zdravković, J., Zdravković, M., Aubry, A., Moalla, N., Guedria, W. & Sarraipa, J., 2018. Domain framework for implementation of open IoT ecosystems. International Journal of Production Research, 56(7), pp. 2552–2569. https://doi.org/10.1080/00207543.2017.1385870.

10 Telematics in motor insurance

New opportunities and challenges for insureds[1]

Marek Monkiewicz and Adam Śliwiński

10.1 Introduction. Telematics – nature and application

The term "telematics" was first used in 1978 by Simon Nora and Alain Minc in a report entitled "L'Informatisation de la société" (Nora et al., 1978), commissioned by the French Prime Minister in response to the development of computer technology and the beginning of the information age.

Telematics is a combination of the achievements of two fundamental fields – computer science and telecommunications. Its development has become possible with the development of digital technologies and the availability of the Internet. It can be defined as

> telecommunications, IT, information and automatic control solutions tailored to the needs of the real systems operated (...). Real systems are installations created for a specific activity together with their administration, operators, users and environmental conditions, including both the natural, economic and formal-legal environment.
>
> (Wydro, 2005)

Operating information systems allow the collection and management of specific data. Through the use of teletransmission systems, these data are transmitted remotely in real time.

The most important features of telematic systems include, above all, their applicability to distributed physical systems, also where real-time contact between their users is required. In addition, telematic systems enable the interoperability of various types of electronic equipment and integrate their software. It is also possible for users to react almost immediately while maintaining the security of the collected data and information. These systems can also be improved and upgraded relatively easily as technology advances. However, one of the most important functions of telematics is the ability to handle and process large amounts of data and information for a predefined purpose. For example, the location and movement of objects or the pricing of a service, as is the case in insurance.

DOI: 10.4324/9781003310082-15

As already mentioned, the technological development in recent years, both in terms of devices enabling the collection of specific data and their transmission, has influenced the expansive development of telematics and its use in many areas of life, including in insurance. Analysing the literature on the subject, one can distinguish several basic areas in which telematics is used. These include areas such as (Wydro, 2005):

1 Transport, including urban transport,
2 Logistics management,
3 Medicine,
4 Agriculture,
5 Librarianship,
6 Household,
7 Finance (banks, insurance).

Logistics and transport are the most important areas where telematics is widely used. Road transport telematics concerns the transport of people and cargo. Transport-Spedigree-Logistics (TSL) is in common use. The application of telematics in transport is primarily aimed at improving the efficiency of the process by optimising costs, improving safety and reducing the negative impact on the environment. In transport and logistics, telematics systems use data from GPS, measuring devices and transport monitoring equipment. For example in rail transport, RFID (Radio-Frequency Identification) is used to optimise processes (Lewiński et al., 2019). Using digital technology, this system enables the detection of the precise location of transported goods. At the same time, the use of radio waves eliminates cabling, thus reducing the cost of the process. A similar application is Real Time Location System (RTLS) (Kampczyk et al., 2013). One of the most interesting applications of telematics is in the field of medicine. In this area, telematics provides necessary information in the treatment process. Using appropriate systems and devices also allows the patient to contact the doctor via teleconferencing. Telematics and its use in medicine are becoming increasingly common. Many entities are being established to provide services at a distance. These services involve, for example, the exchange of disease data or enabling remote connection with a doctor. The global telemedicine market could be worth USD186 billion by 2026 (it was USD14.6 billion in 2018). Undoubtedly, the COVID-19 pandemic has accelerated the development of telemedicine.

Other interesting applications of telematics systems are library telematics, operational telematics, home telematics and postal telematics. Library telematics refers to the system equipment of library resources enabling the search and remote access to the required works. Operational telematics refers to scientific research carried out through the use of remote, highly specialised research laboratories. The term can also be used in the medical field for specialised operations carried out remotely. Home telematics refers to solutions for remote control and management of the home or office. For example, home telematics includes the so-called smart home system. Within the system solutions, the user is able to control lighting, heating, water resources, etc. while, for example, being away from home or the office. Home systems are becoming more and more common. They also make it possible to maintain security and keep an eye on the house in the absence of the hosts. Postal telematics, on the other hand, is the possibility of integrating postal systems by making use of the possibilities for long-distance data transmission. At the same time, postal telematics includes all systems that allow optimisation of postal services, such as for example mail tracking, information on availability of mail at the collection point, etc.

Agriculture remains an interesting application area for telematics. Today, it is rare to find small farms focused on industrial production. Farmers are entrepreneurs managing often huge agricultural production enterprises. Telematics is often an indispensable tool for enabling work and improving production efficiency. In agriculture, telematics mainly concerns machines and equipment used in agriculture, telematics concerns mainly machines and devices used in running a farm. For example, autonomous tractors equipped with a range of sensors that collect data and allow remote control of the work process. Using the data, intelligent machines correct their own course by optimising, for example, fuel consumption or working time required to complete a task on a given section of the farm. Telematics systems make it possible to exploit the full potential of the farm's machinery and optimise operating costs.

Telematics is also widely used in finance, both in banking as well as in insurance. Generally, the concept of telematics in finance refers to the situation of performing certain financial activities remotely, without the need for a physical meeting with a representative of the financial institution.

In insurance, the term telematics refers to the way an insurance contract is concluded or the way a premium is calculated. Telematics is currently used by insurers primarily in the context of tariff systems in motor insurance (Kuryłowicz, 2021). There are also emerging applications of telematics in other types of insurance.

10.2 Telematics in motor insurance

Motor insurance is one of the areas where telematics is increasingly used. The origin, development and implementation of telematics in insurance processes date back to the 1970s. At that time, traditional rating methods based on the probability of an insurance accident were criticised. This was due to the fact that insurance companies' revenues were falling as a result of the uncompetitive offerings. People who used the vehicle intensively paid the same premium as those who used the vehicle occasionally. This problem was to be eliminated by making insurance tariffs dependent on the real distances covered by the insureds. Two systems of premium calculation were proposed. The first one consisted in including the premium in the price of fuel. The second involved cooperation between companies and tyre manufacturers (Kuryłowicz, 2021). However, these systems did not work, mainly due to the fact that the rule of balance between premiums and benefits was not observed. At the same time, the inclusion of the insurance premium in the price of fuel rewarded vehicles that consumed less. An effective solution turned out to be the installation of special metres, which could monitor driving style in real time and count the kilometres driven. The start of style monitoring gave rise to Usage Based Insurance (UBI). One of the first companies to offer a telematic premium calculation system was the American insurer Progressive. It initiated a pilot programme called Autograph. The programme consisted of calculating premiums based on data sent by GPS installed in pilot-insured vehicles. Further developments in technology have made the device for collecting data and transmitting it to the insurer increasingly efficient and cheaper to operate.

There are currently a number of different UBI tariffing schemes. In addition to traditional tariffing, where no telematics solutions are used, there are such tariffing systems as:

- PATP – pay-at-the-pump – the insurance premium is added to the price of fuel;
- PPM – pay-per-mile – these are systems that do not use telematics, but where the premium is partly or wholly based on vehicle distance data (reported by the insured);
- PAYD – pay-as-you-drive or PAYG – pay-as-you-go – the tariff provides for mileage-based premiums, and distance data is collected, aggregated and transferred using telematics solutions;
- PHYD - pay-how-you-drive – insurance where telematics allows analysis not only of mileage but also of the driving style of the drivers of a vehicle, characterised by variables such as the speeds they reach, the types of roads they take or the time of day they use the vehicle, The telematics system can analyse not only the mileage but also the driving style of the drivers of a vehicle, characterised by variables such as the speed they reach, the type of roads they travel on or the time of day they use their vehicle;
- PAYS – pay-as-you-speed ("pay when you speed") – the tariff provides for a system of financial penalties in the form of a reduction in the discounts granted when insured persons exceed the speed limit.

The above tarrifs systems are used by insurance companies all over the world. Examples of companies from selected countries and their systems are presented in Table 10.1.

The use of telematics-enabled UBI by insurers offers potential benefits for both insurers and customers (policyholders). For example, according

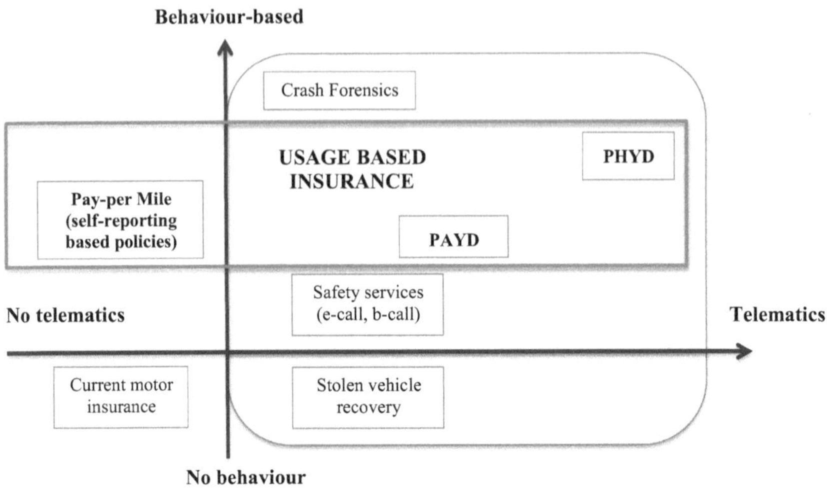

Figure 10.1 Types of premium pricing systems in motor insurance

Source: Husnjaka S., Perakovića D., Forenbachera I., Mumdzievb M., Telematics System in Usage Based Motor Insurance, 25th DAAAM International Symposium on Intelligent Manufacturing and Automation, DAAAM 2014

to Accenture, it enables insurers to improve risk selection, conduct more sophisticated underwriting and fraud analysis, reduce claims costs and improve customer understanding. As a result, the latter are more satisfied with the services provided by insurers and thus show greater loyalty to these establishments (Accenture, 2014). In the case of customers, they can count on greater price transparency, personal influence (control) over the amount of insurance premiums, greater safety of participation in traffic, and especially lower and more affordable insurance premium prices.

For example, Liberty Mutual in the USA offers the possibility of a premium discount ranging from 5% to 30%. The condition is the entry of the insured into the RightTrack programme. Telematics technology collects data on driver behaviour, and then communicates it to the insurance company. Liberty Mutual offers policyholders the opportunity to use the RightTrack telematics tracking device and/or mobile app to share their driving data during a 90-day review period.[2] After the period ends, Liberty Mutual leverages the data harvested by the device and/or the app to determine the discount a policyholder will get. The better your driving behaviour, the larger your discount will be applied. Despite the fact that the maximum available discount is 30%, most drivers seem to earn an average discount of 10%–15%. Similar programmes exist in other companies. The programmes differ in details but the core idea for all of them is to look at the possibility of minimising the premium.

Table 10.1 Examples of UBI solutions implemented in selected countries by specific insurers

Insurance company	*Country*	*Name of the UBI program*	*Insurance concept*	*Technology platform*	*Data transmission*
AIOI [8]	Japan	Pay as you drive	Distance-based vehicle insurance	G-book (telematics subscription service provided by Toyota Motor Corporation)	Mobile data service
Aviva [9]	Canada	Autograph	Insurance is based on traditional parameters with several levels of risk within 24 hour period	Device connected to vehicle diagnostic port	Universal serial bus
AXA [10]	Italy	Autometrica	Distance-based vehicle insurance	GPS-based	Mobile data service
Generali [11]	Italy	Protezione Satelitare	Insurance is based on traditional telematics parameters	GPS-based	Mobile data service
AXA Winterthur [12]	Switzerland	Crash Recorder	Recording events	Event-data recorder	Data retrieved from event-data recorder
MAPFRE [14]	Spain	YCAR	Insurance is based on traditional telematics parameters with several levels of risks within 24 hour period	GPS-based	Mobile data service
RSA Insurance Group [15]	United Kingdom	More Than Green Wheels Insurance	Insurance is based on traditional telematics parameters with several levels of risks within 24 hour period	Device connected to vehicle diagnostic port	Mobile data service
Uniqa [16]	Austria	Safeline	Insurance is based on traditional telematics parameters with several levels of risks within 24 hour period	GPS-based	Mobile data service
WGV [17]	Germany	Young & Safe	Insurance is based on traditional telematics parameters with several levels of risks within 24 hour period	GPS-based	Mobile data service

Source: Husnjaka S., Perakovića D., Forenbachera I., Mumdzievb M., *Telematics System in Usage Based Motor Insurance, 25th DAAAM International Symposium on Intelligent Manufacturing and Automation, DAAAM 2014*

Table 10.2 UBI tariffing using telematics – potential benefits for insurers and customers

Insurers	*Customers*
• Better risk selection • Better fraud analysis, fraud detection and lower fraud costs • Lower value of compensation payments • Lower claims handling costs • Automation and improvement (enhancement) of key insurance processes (cost and time) • Higher customer satisfaction (happiness), retention and loyalty • Improvedcustomerinsight and understanding • Improved reputation and brand, particularly in relation to policy issues such as safety and the environment • Moving away from purchasing insurance only for the provision of a service in the event of a claim, towards the provision of a wide range of continuously tailored services with added value for the customer	• Increased price transparency • Degree of autonomy and personal control over insurance premiums • Lower and more affordable insurance premiums, especially for younger drivers • Reassuring parents of teenage children • Overall safety improvement: better guidance, reduced frequency and "severity" of incidents • Faster assistance and support after an incident • Value-added services, including more efficient fuel consumption and vehicle maintenance, as well as tailored discounts and packages for appropriate lifestyle and behaviour • Morepersonalisation • Rewards (benefits) for loyalty

Source: Accenture, *Insurance telematics: A game-changing opportunity for the industry,* 2014, p. 8

A detailed list of potential benefits for insurers and customers in relation to UBI is presented in Table 10.2.

Telematics in motor insurance is developing unevenly in individual countries around the world. The next section focuses on the analysis of the survey conducted by the authors in European countries. The basic aim of the survey is to determine the development potential and the basic directions of telematics development.

10.3 Directions of telematics evolution in motor insurance in the light of pan-European survey

10.3.1 UBI global trends

Global UBI market size exceeded USD30 billion in 2020. It is estimated that the growth rate will be over 20% Compound Annual Growth Rate (CAGR) between 2021 and 2027.[3] There are a number of factors that drive the development of new technologies application within the insurance industry, especially auto insurance. For example cars with remote diagnostic features. Growing demand for remote diagnostic technology throughout the automobile industry is likely to boost the industry's growth. The use of remote vehicle diagnostic systems using data-driven technology is gaining more traction in the automobile sector mainly because of the increasing complexities of vehicles. The remote diagnostic technology brings a safety mechanism that would make available the vehicle to be monitored and controlled using a remote operator. All of that features would make the UBI market grow. The COVID-19 pandemic has also had a visible influence. The COVID-19 pandemic resulted in restrictions on the movement of vehicles across the globe. The unstable global economic conditions owing to the pandemic supported consumers to avoid buying new auto insurance policies. After recovering from the COVID-19 outbreak, the consumers realised the benefits of UBI insurance over traditional insurance with regard to the high premiums charged by insurance companies for unused vehicles. It is estimated that the total market size of UBI at the end of 2027 will exceed USD127 bn.

Implementation of new UBI solutions by major participants operating in an industry might strengthen their position in the market. For instance, in March 2021, Hyundai Motor America introduced the UBI program to promote safe and secure driving habits among drivers. This new UBI approach helped the company to offer better control over insurance costs to vehicle owners. This also helped the company to enhance safe on-road driving behaviour. Some experts predict that up to 20% of all vehicle insurance in the USA will incorporate some form of UBI within the next five years.[4] According to the National Association of Insurance Commissioners, predicted growth is being propelled by technological advances, which continue to substantially improve the cost, convenience, and effectiveness of using telematics devices.[5] The question arises what are the forces of development of UBI in Europe. In the next subchapter, the authors are trying to answer the question by describing the results of survey research done across representatives of chosen motor guarantee funds and national bureaux.

10.3.2 Telematics in Europe – survey results

In the period of May–July 2021, the authors carried out a survey on the application of UBI in selected European countries. This has been done with the participation of representatives of motor guarantee funds in the Protection of Visitors System or national offices in the Green Card System, from 18 selected European countries, i.e. Austria, Belgium, Belarus, Bosnia and Herzegovina, Bulgaria, Czech Republic, Estonia, France,

Germany, Ireland, Lithuania, the Netherlands, Poland, Russia, Serbia, Slovakia, Turkey and Ukraine. The cooperating national bodies were asked nine detailed questions:

1 on the possibility of using telematics-based insurance in the country;
2 on the presence of special regulatory setup;
3 on the possibility of the selection of UBI and classical contract;
4 on the driving forces generating the use of UBI;
5 on the level of UBI usage among all clients;
6 on the level of UBI usage among individual clients, corporate non-fleet clients and corporate fleet clients;
7 on the level of UBI usage among various categories of vehicles;
8 on the work in progress regarding spreading UBI usage;
9 on the work in progress regarding regulatory take up of telematics.

According to the information provided in most of the analysed countries (14 out of 18), product offerings are available to customers in the domestic motor insurance market where insurers use UBI with telematics. In these countries, customers are free to choose whether to conclude a motor insurance contract and calculate the premium in the traditional way (e.g. based on customer-related factors such as the age of the vehicle owner, the period of holding a driving licence, the estimated mileage of the vehicle, single/instalment premiums, the number of damages and the role in the events, the value of the damages caused, etc., and vehicle-related factors such as the type and make of the vehicle, the solenoid capacity, the year of production, the place of registration, etc.) or in the UBI mode using telematics. However, only one insurance company in Slovakia currently offers this type of product, while in Russia and Turkey, UBI with the use of telematics is currently not available under the obligatory third-party liability insurance of motor vehicle owners (for example in Turkey it applies only to AC insurance). Only in Belarus, Bosnia and Herzegovina, Bulgaria and Serbia, it is currently not possible to buy telematics policies. The reason is not however in the insurance regulations but on the side of insurers who, for various reasons, have not decided to launch this type of product offer in these markets. The common denominator of the above countries is that none of them is a developed market representative. Hence, insurance companies seem to prefer the traditional way of concluding contracts and calculating (tariff) premiums. At the same time, in none of the above 18 countries, there is a special regulation implemented, which covers the issue of UBI using telematics. Among the answers (on a scale of 1–5 points) to the question about the reasons, which have a decisive influence on the fact that the customers of insurance companies decide to use UBI with the use of telematics, the most points were given to the reduction of insurance premium (a total of 55 points from 12 respondents), then the respondents indicated a reduction in other costs associated with the use of a vehicle (e.g. lower mileage, lower fuel consumption, etc.) (29 points), greater driver safety (promoting a smooth driving style, not exceeding speed limits, avoiding congested streets and peak traffic) (28 points), and greater passenger safety (22 points). According to respondents' own estimates (no in-depth national market analyses available on this topic), the use of UBI using telematics in motor insurance is not popular in their countries. Even in countries such as Belgium, Estonia, Ireland or the Netherlands (22% of the countries participating in the survey), where the estimated percentage is the highest, only 1%–5% of motor vehicle owners nationwide use this type of solution. In countries such as the Czech Republic, France, Lithuania, Poland, Slovakia, Turkey and Ukraine, the percentage is even lower <1% (39% of respondents). In the remaining countries either respondent did not (or were not able to) provide a response or this solution is available in the respective national market. The low uptake of UBI using telematics in motor insurance is confirmed by the respondents' answers to further more detailed questions in this regard. Regardless of whether the criterion is the entity signing the insurance contract (individual, corporate-non-fleet and corporate fleet customers) or the type of vehicle (passenger vehicles and heavy goods vehicles) – the most common answer was that <5% of customers (Belgium, Czech Republic, France, Lithuania, Germany, Slovakia, Ukraine) opt for this solution. The only exceptions to this rule are Ireland, the Netherlands and Poland. In the case of the first country, the very high proportion of corporate clients (with 10 or more vehicles) and those using trucks is striking. In Ireland, more than 50% of these customers conclude UBI contracts using telematics. This is because it serves the purpose of better and continuous risk monitoring and there is no inherent conflict/dilemma for natural persons customers to share information about their privacy and personal data with insurance companies. In the Netherlands and Poland, the above reasoning remains also valid. In both countries, the use of telematics ranges between 5% and 30% of customers, in the Netherlands, it applies to both non-fleet and fleet corporate customers and cars and trucks, while in Poland, according to the respondent, it applies only to fleet corporate customers. Overall, at least in the group of the above 18 countries analysed, the short to medium-term (up to three years) prospects for the uptake of the UBI solution with the use of telematics seems to be low. This is because all respondents indicated that at the moment there are no legislative actions planned in their countries in this area. In fact, there are no plans or projects in this area also There are also no plans or projects in this area at the level of the insurance sector itself (Tables 10.3a and 10.3b).

Table 10.3a Survey on the application of UBI in selected European countries

		Austria	*Belarus*	*Belgium*	*Bosnia and Herzegovina*	*Bulgaria*	*Czech Republic*	*Estonia*	*France*	*Germany*
1	Is it generally possible to use telematics –(UBI) within motor insurance in your country?	Yes[1]	No	Yes	No[1]	No[1]	Yes[1]	Yes[1]	Yes[1]	Yes[1]
2	Do you have special regulation(s) on telematics (UBI) within motor insurance in your country?	No[2]	No	No	No	No	No[2]	No[2]	No	No
3	Does the client in your country choose the way in which the insurance contract will be concluded as well as the way in which the insurance premium will be calculated (in a traditional way or with the use of telematics (UBI)?	Yes[3]	No	Yes[1]	No	No	Yes[3]	Yes[3]	Yes	Yes
4	Which premises have decisive importance and determine, that insurers' clients use telematics (UBI) in motor insurance, while concluding insurance contracts in your country? Please estimate this in a scale from 1 to 5, where 1 means a low impact on the client's decision to use telematics (UBI), while 5 means a great impact	4					4	4	2	

a	Lowering insurance premium (direct lowering of the costs/price of the insurance contract)	5	5		5	5
b	Lowering other costs connected with vehicle's use (i.e. ex. rationalisation of vehicle's use, lower mileage, lowering fuel consumption, etc.)	3	2		3	3
c	Greater passenger safety	3	2		2	2
d	Greater safety of the driver (promoting smooth driving style, not exceeding speed limits, avoidance of crowded streets and peak hours, etc.)	3	2		2	2
e	Others, if so, please enumerate and assess each of them on an above-mentioned scale from 1 to 5:		–			
5	To what extent/level do insurers' all clients use telematics (UBI) within motor insurance in your country?	5				2
a	<1% of all clients conclude insurance contracts with the use of telematics (UBI)			Yes[5]	Yes[3]	

(*Continued*)

		Austria	*Belarus*	*Belgium*	*Bosnia and Herzegovina*	*Bulgaria*	*Czech Republic*	*Estonia*	*France*	*Germany*
b	1-5% of all clients conclude insurance contracts with the use of telematics (UBI)			Yes				Yes[5]		
c	6–9% of all clients conclude insurance contracts with the use of telematics (UBI)									
d	10–30% of all clients conclude insurance contracts with the use of telematics (UBI)									
e	31-50% of all clients conclude insurance contracts with the use of telematics (UBI)									
f	>50% of all clients conclude insurance contracts with the use of telematics (UBI)									
6	To what extent/level do insurers'' clients (divided into individual clients, corporate-non fleet clients and corporate fleet clients) use telematics (UBI) within motor insurance in your country?	6					6	6	4	
a	Individual clients – private persons conclude insurance contracts via the use of telematics (UBI):									
a1	very rare (<5% of clients)			Yes			Yes		Yes	Yes

a2	rare (5–30% of clients)						
a3	often (31–50% of clients)						
a4	very often (>50% of clients)						
b	Corporate non-fleet clients conclude insurance contracts via the use of telematics (UBI):						
b1	very rare (<5% of clients)		Yes	Yes		Yes	Yes
b2	rare (5–30% of clients)						
b3	often (31–50% of clients)						
b4	very often (>50% of clients)						
c	Corporate fleet clients (with 10 or more vehicles)						
c1	very rare (<5% of clients)		Yes	Yes		Yes	Yes
c2	rare (5%–30% of clients)						
c3	often (31%–50% of clients)						
c4	very often (>50% of clients)						
7.	To what extent/level do insurers' clients (divided into given categories of vehicles) use telematics (UBI) within motor insurance in your country?	7		7	7		
a	Passenger cars						
a1	very rare (<5% of clients)		Yes	Yes		Yes	Yes
a2	rare (5%–30% of clients)						

(Continued)

		Austria	Belarus	Belgium	Bosnia and Herzegovina	Bulgaria	Czech Republic	Estonia	France	Germany
a3	often (31%–50% of clients)									
a4	very often (>50% of clients)									
b	Trucks/lorries			2						
b1	very rare (<5% of clients)								Yes	Yes
b2	rare (5%–30% of clients)									
b3	often (31%–50% of clients)									
b4	very often (>50% of clients)									
8	Are there any developing plans or programs for spreading/ increasing the market share of telematics (UBI) within motor insurance in your country?	No[8]	No	No[3]	No	No[2]	No[8]	No	Yes[5]	3
9	Are there any plans to establish and implement any regulations on telematics (UBI) within motor insurance in your country? If so, when are they expected to be introduced?	No[9]	No	4	No	No[3]	No	No	No[6]	No

Source: Own researches with the participation of representatives of motor guarantee funds in the Protection of Visitors System or national offices in the Green Card System; May–July 2021.

Austria

1 appr. 2016

2 However in Motor Third Party Liability (MTPL) insurance, insurance terms and conditions must be presented to the Austrian Insurance Supervisory Authority in general.

3 Only some insurance companies offer telematic contracts. Clients can choose their contracting partner and between offered products.

4 We do not have figures concerning the above. However, it is my view, that lowering the premium is the most frequent decision criterion.
5 We do not have data in order to provide the above information.
6 We do not have data in order to provide the above information.
7 We do not have data in order to provide the above information.
8 Still increasing telematics seems not to be the main goal of Austrian insurers.
9 Not to our knowledge.

Belgium
1 We filled in "yes" because the client is allowed to refuse UBI but then this will influence the setting of the premium
2 We have no information about UBI in trucks.
3 Since 2015 the topic appeared in our market but there seems to exist rather limited enthusiasm at this moment, so we think that an increase is not to be expected.
4 We have no information at all about this question.

Bosnia and Herzegovina
1 Unfortunately, telematics –(UBI) is not in use in our country. Although there are many benefits, we are still in the waiting process for implementation.

Bulgaria
1 Based on the information we have from ABZ (the Association of Bulgarian insurers) there are no insurance companies, for the time being, working with UBI.
2 There were some projects or plans in some of the insurance companies for development in this area, but no real results or application exists to the best of our knowledge.
3 The same goes for answering your questions on the current legal framework or future developing plans.

Czech Republic
1 Approx. 2010. Premium calculation is fully deregulated after 2003, when these methods are generally allowed. On the other hand, technical development and especially customer's demand have been developing gradually.
2 The only regulation comes from MTPL law that MTPL premium has to be calculated in a sufficient way in order to meet all liabilities including Bureau contributions. This process is controlled by a supervisor that is Czech National Bank.
3 The client is free to select any product according to his/her preferences based on the offer given to insurers.
4 We do not have any data or survey on this topic, however, I would assume that the greatest motivation from the side of the client would be a lower premium.
5 Indicative estimate based on market information.
6 No exact data, just an estimate based on the very low penetration of telematics.
7 No data, just an assumption.
8 This is up to individual companies.

Estonia

1 In our country, it is possible to use UBI with the use of telematics from the early 2000s.
2 As the tariffication is free and every insurer has the possibility to use different calculation methods for their premiums.
3 Insurance companies are free to choose whether or not to use UBI with the use of telematics.
4 The client can choose if the selected insurer provides the possibility.
5 No information.
6 It is difficult to estimate as insurers do not have to provide/declare/disclose such information, but it is definitely less than 5%.
7 Possible users might be fleet, who have "black boxes" on board
8 No information.

France

1 In France, the calculation of contributions in the UBI system using telematics has been possible since around 2008.
2 UBI telematics is mainly used for the most risky driver profiles (young drivers), and it is expensive. Insurance companies try to promote other profiles and services linked to telematics.
3 These are estimates. No data available.
4 Estimated figures. No data available
5 These topics are not discussed within the federation. However our members are considering any solution that might increase/hold their market share.
6 General Data Protection Regulation (GDPR) rules are fit for UBI and vice-versa. Since the beginning (2000), the regulatory body that enforces data privacy law watched closely the development of UBI. This authority stated for example that insurers were not allowed to have access to raw driving speed as such data would enable them to establish driving rule infringements which they are not allowed to.

Germany

1 Telematics in Germany – since the early 2010s.
2 Certified numbers are not available, but an educated estimate would hint at a low percentage, perhaps about 1%.
3 There may be internal considerations within some insurance enterprises, but these are not communicated to us.

Table 10.3b Survey on the application of UBI in selected European countries

		Ireland	*Lithuania*	*Netherlands*	*Poland*	*Russia*	*Serbia*	*Slovakia*	*Sweden*	*Turkey*	*Ukraine*
1	Is it generally possible to use telematics (UBI) within motor insurance in your country?	Yes[1]	Yes[1]	Yes[1]	Yes [1]	Yes [1]	No	Yes [1]	Yes[1]	Yes[1]	Yes
2	Do you have special regulation(s) on telematics (UBI) within motor insurance in your country?	No	No	No	No	No	No	No	No[2]	No	No
3	Does client in your country may choose the way in which the insurance contract will be concluded as well as the way in which the insurance premium will be calculated (in a traditional way or with the use of telematics(UBI)?	No	Yes	Yes	Yes	Yes	No	Yes		Yes	Yes
4	Which premises have decisive importance and determine, that insurers' clients use telematics(UBI) in motor insurance, while concluding insurance contracts in your country? Please estimate this in a scale from 1 to 5, where 1 means low impact on client's decision to use telematics (UBI), while 5 – great impact.	2	2	2	2				3		
a	Lowering insurance premium (direct lowering the costs/price of the insurance contract)	3	5	4	4	4		5		5	5

(*Continued*)

		Ireland	Lithuania	Netherlands	Poland	Russia	Serbia	Slovakia	Sweden	Turkey	Ukraine
b	Lowering other costs connected with vehicle's use (i.e. ex. rationalisation of vehicle's use, lower mileage, lowering fuel consumption, etc.)	3	2	1	2	2		3		2	3
c	Greater passenger safety	2	1	1	1	2		3		2	1
d	Greater safety of the driver (promoting smooth driving style, not exceeding speed limits, avoidance of crowded streets and peak hours, etc.)	5	1	1	1	3		3		2	3
e	Others, if so, please enumerate and assess each of them on an above-mentioned scale from 1 to 5:							52			
5	To what extent/level do insurers' all clients use telematics (UBI) within motor insurance in your country?			3					4	2	
a	<1% of all clients conclude insurance contracts with the use of telematics (UBI)		Yes[3]		Yes			Yes		Yes	Yes
b	1%–5% of all clients conclude insurance contracts with the use of telematics (UBI)	Yes		Yes							
c	6%–9% of all clients conclude insurance contracts with the use of telematics (UBI)										

d	10%–30% of all clients conclude insurance contracts with the use of telematics (UBI)							
e	31%–50% of all clients conclude insurance contracts with the use of telematics (UBI)							
f	>50% of all clients conclude insurance contracts with the use of telematics (UBI)							
6	To what extent/level do insurers' clients (divided into individual clients, corporate-non fleet clients and corporate fleet clients) use telematics (UBI) within motor insurance in your country?						5	
a	Individual clients – private persons conclude insurance contracts via the use of telematics (UBI):							
a1	very rare (<5% of clients)	Yes	Yes	Yes	Yes	Yes		Yes
a2	rare (5%–30% of clients)							
a3	often (31%–50% of clients)							
a4	very often (>50% of clients)							
b	Corporate non-fleet clients conclude insurance contracts via the use of telematics (UBI):							
b1	very rare (<5% of clients)		Yes		Yes	Yes		Yes
b2	rare (5%–30% of clients)	Yes		Yes				
b3	often (31%–50% of clients)							

(Continued)

		Ireland	Lithuania	Netherlands	Poland	Russia	Serbia	Slovakia	Sweden	Turkey	Ukraine
b4	very often (>50% of clients)										
c	Corporate fleet clients (with 10 or more vehicles)										
c1	very rare (<5% of clients)		Yes					Yes			Yes
c2	rare (5%–30% of clients)			Yes	Yes						
c3	often (31%–50% of clients)										
c4	very often (>50% of clients)	Yes[2]									
7	To what extent/level do insurers' clients (divided into given categories of vehicles) use telematics (UBI) within motor insurance in your country?							3	6		
a	Passenger cars										
a1	very rare (<5% of clients)	Yes	Yes		Yes			Yes			Yes
a2	rare (5%–30% of clients)			Yes							
a3	often (31%–50% of clients)										
a4	very often (>50% of clients)										
b	Trucks/lorries				3						
b1	very rare (<5% of clients)		Yes					Yes			
b2	rare (5%–30% of clients)			Yes							
b3	often (31%–50% of clients)										
b4	very often (>50% of clients)	Yes[3]									
8.	Are there any developing plans or programs of spreading/increasing the market share of telematics (UBI) within motor insurance in your country?	No	No	No	Yes	No2	No[1]	Yes[4]			Yes[1]

9	Are there any plans to establish and implement any regulations on telematics (UBI) within motor insurance in your country? If so, when are they expected to be introduced?	No	No	No	No[4]	No3	No[2]	No	No

Source: Own researches with the participation of representatives of motor guarantee funds in the Protection of Visitors System or national offices in the Green Card System; May–July 2021.

Ireland
1 Telematics (UBI) within motor insurance in Ireland started in the 2000s.
2 In general while telematics is a feature in the commercial/fleet space where it doesn't tend to feature too widely in the private market. Where it does exist it tends to be a product targeted towards the youth.
3 As above in point 2.

Lithuania
1 In Lithuania, the calculation of contributions in the UBI system using telematics has been possible for several years.
2 The estimation of impact is based on personal opinion.
3 Generally speaking, UBI with the use of telematics is a very phenomenon in Lithuania. The entire response to the survey and the estimates presented are based on information that the Lithuanian Motor Insurers Bureau (which is, inter alia, the Lithuanian car guarantee fund) obtained from interviews with some of the largest players in the motor insurance market.

Netherlands
1 Telematics within motor insurance in the Netherlands started in 2010 (the date for start is an estimation)
2 Safety is an issue in particular in fleet management.
3 Telematics for insurance is still on a very modest level in NL and we do not expect a strong increase in the next years.

Poland
1 In our country, it is possible to use UBI with the use of telematics in motor insurance since 2017. In the case of fleet insurance, it could have happened earlier, but it will be rather difficult to get to this data.
2 The above answers apply to individual clients. Entrepreneurs probably have other priorities – for example, when insuring the fleet, cost optimisation and increased safety are more important for them.
3 Such data is unlikely to be collected anywhere. Estimated it would probably be more than 5%.
4 One of the parliamentary committees deal with this subject – however, it was not to be regulated by law.

Russia

1 Telematics (UBI) motor insurance in Russia was started in 2011, but customers can only opt for voluntary excess over and above the compulsory excess.

2 Russian compulsory MTPL does not use telematics. There are no plans for developments on the level of the insurance market or for any new Russian legislation. We also do not have information regarding the application of UBI.

3 As above in point 2.

Serbia

1 To our knowledge, there seems to be no specific plan to introduce telematics in Serbia. There are some rather unofficial "rumours" concerning dash-board cameras, but it is a far cry so to speak.

2 As above in point 1.

Slovakia

1 In our country, it is possible to use UBI with the use of telematics in motor insurance since 2015. In practice, however, telematics is possible in Slovakia through one insurer only.

2 Assistance after a road incident.

3 In our country, it is possible to use UBI with the use of telematics in motor insurance only for vehicles weighing <3.5 thousand kg.

4 Many insurers evaluate the use of telematics.

Sweden

1 There are insurance companies that started around 2010 with applications that could influence motor insurance. Around the year 2015, a special digital insurance policy was introduced.

2 We cannot find any special demands or rules on this type of product, compared to the traditional products. It is unclear as to how many companies have a product like this, and what we have found is some information from Insplanet: https://www.insplanet.com/forsakring/bil/digital_bilforsakring/. The products can be described as digital insurance, without involving measuring or information of real data.

3 When it comes to statistics it is also difficult. NTF (*The National Society for Road Safety – a non-governmental organisation which works to improve road safety*) made a study in cooperation with Paydrive some years ago. https://ntf.se/nyheter/2018/digital-forsakring-halverar-antalet-fortkorningar/.

4 As above in point 3.

5 As above in point 3.

6 As above in point 3.

Turkey

1 The general impression is that the use of telematics is very limited in Turkey. It is used exclusively in casco (own-damage) policies. Some insurers have concluded a special agreement with car-makers to establish the driving patterns of policyholders but it is applicable only for a certain car model.

2 Policyholders do not prefer telematics because the premium discount is not big enough, competitors offer more discounts even without telematics.

Ukraine

Promotion (advertising).

10.4 Conclusions

In light of the above analysis following final observations could be provided:

1. UBI with the use of telematics is a different system from the traditional one for the construction of motor insurance premium rates. Despite the fact that in some countries its origins can be traced back to the 20th century, while in many countries it has been developing for more than ten years, it is still complementary to the traditional offer. Even in countries with a high penetration rate of telematic policies (Italy, USA), on average 80%–90% of motor insurance policies are issued based on traditional tariff systems.
2. The spread of UBI using telematics globally and in Europe is progressing more slowly than the forecasts presented. A good example in this regard is, for example, Deloitte's 2016 predictions, according to which the estimated penetration rate of telematics policies in motor insurance in Italy and the UK at the end of 2020 should be 27% and 23%, respectively. Meanwhile, in reality, it does not exceed 20% (Italy) and 5% (UK) (Deloitte, 2016). This is also evidenced by the authors' own research, in which the vast majority of UBI penetration rates using telematics do not exceed 1%. The reasons for this are mainly to be found in the lower actual (than declared) willingness of customers to allow online monitoring of their driving style and insufficiently high benefits (premium refunds) in relation to customer expectations offered to customers by insurers.
3. Some exceptions to rule 2 are corporate fleet customers. However, this is primarily the case in highly developed countries with a well-developed and innovative motor insurance market (e.g. Belgium, Ireland, the Netherlands, UK), where in some of them the telematics market penetration rate oscillates around 50%. Employers in this area, however, are particularly keen to ensure that company vehicles are used for the right purposes at full cost optimisation (fuel, repairs, servicing, etc.). They may even be enthusiastic about the idea of online monitoring
4. To the greatest extent, UBI using telematics is developing in countries where there is state regulatory support, such as in Italy (public model), and in countries where the wider players in the insurance sector and beyond (i.e. insurers, including insurtechs, industry organisations, telematics platforms and operators) are actively involved in the uptake of such solutions, such as in the UK (market model). Additional premises that favour the development of telematics in motor insurance are large differences in the price of insurance (before and after the application of UBI using telematics and the high level of insurance crime (extortion of damages, vehicle theft) and the targeting of telematics solutions at the youngest drivers. It is they who are its most grateful recipients and beneficiaries. In fact, all the above-mentioned four premises are present in both Italy and the United Kingdom.

5 In the future, UBI using telematics should spread most among young drivers and corporate customers with fleets of vehicles.
6 In the medium term (3–5 years) there is a chance that UBI, using telematics, will be more widespread worldwide than it is today. This may be influenced by the COVID-19 pandemic (which has made drivers in many countries realise that having pay-as-you-drive policies for periods when you do not use or use your vehicle much less frequently can be an interesting alternative to traditional policies), the rapidly advancing digitalisation, or the increasing proportion of the total population of the next generation increasingly familiar with or even born into digital reality.
7 Global studies suggest a CAGR of 20% on average per annum between 2020 and 2027. Literature studies indicate that the most widespread use of UBI using telematics in motor insurance is in North America and Europe (from other continents, noteworthy individual markets as in Africa: South Africa, in Asia: Singapore and China, in Australia and Oceania: Australia) (Dharani et al., 2018). In 2019, the two aforementioned continents accounted for a total of 27.5 million policies (of which 14.7 million were issued in North America and 12.8 million in Europe). In terms of individual markets, countries where UBI using telematics is relatively widespread compared to other countries include Italy, the UK, USA.

Notes

1 Both Marek Monkiewicz and Adam Śliwiński are professors in Institute of Risk and Financial Markets at the Warsaw School of Economics.
2 https://www.valuepenguin.com/right-track-liberty-mutual-insurance-review#whatis-righttrack (access 21.05.2022).
3 https://www.gminsights.com/industry-analysis/usage-based-insurance-ubi-market.
4 https://ims.tech/opinion/usage-based-insurance-program-usa/ (accessed 29.05.2022).
5 ibidem.

Literature

Accenture, 2014, *Insurance telematics: A game-changing opportunity for the industry,* 2014.

Bain & Company, 2016, in: Dang TMJ., *The impact of telematics on the motor insurance landscape and on customer behaviour in the case of Italy,* Bachelor Thesis, University of Zurich, 2017.

Deloitte, 2016, *European motor insurance study. The rise of digitaly-enabled motor insurance,* November 2016.

Dharani S., et al., 2018, *Telematics: Poised for strong global growth,* McKinsey&Company, Mckinsey Center for Future Mobility, April 2018.

Friedman S., et al., 2014, *Overcoming speed bumps on the road to telematics. Challenges and opportunities facing auto insurers with and without useage-based programs,* A research report by the Deloitte Center for Financial Services, Deloitte University Press, 2014.

Husnjaka S., et al., 2014, Telematics system in usage based motor insurance, *25th DAAAM International Symposium on Intelligent Manufacturing and Automation, DAAAM 2014*. Vienna.

Kampczyk A., et al., 2013, The concept of using RFID technology in the inventory of rail transport infrastructureelements, *Zeszyty Naukowo-Techniczne Stowarzyszenia Inżynierów i Techników Komunikacji RP*, Oddział W Krakowie, materiały konferencyjne nr 3/2013k.

Kuryłowicz Ł., *Telematyka ubezpieczeniowa jako instrument przywracania równowagi na polskim rynku ubezpieczeń komunikacyjnych (InsuranceTelematics as an Instrument for RestoringBalance on the Polish Motor Insurance Market)*, Oficyna Wydawnicza SGH, Warsaw 2021, s.72.

Lewiński A., et al., 2019, Technologie Informatyczne Jako Metoda Poprawy Funkcjonalności Towarowych Kolejowych, Prace naukowe Politechniki Warszawskiej, *Transport*, Z 125, 2019.

Nora S, et al. 1978, *L'Informatisation de la société*, La Documentation Francaise, Janvier 1978.

Otonomo, 2020, *What European consumers think about new insurance offerings based on car data*, June 23.

Tusa S., 2018, *Will Italy mandate telematics in insurance?*, April 16, 2018.

Wydro K.B., 2005, Telematics – meaning and definitions of the term, *Telecommunications and Information Technology* 2005, no. 1–2.

11 Big data analytics in insurance

What is on offer

Daniel Szaniewski

11.1 Introduction

Acquiring, storing, processing and analyzing information in the era of globalization and computerization has become a particularly important aspect of the activity of business entities. The dissemination of digital technologies contributed to the exponential growth of the amount of generated data, which is distinguished by high diversity, complexity and poor structuring. This data is called Big Data, and managing it is one of the biggest challenges that the insurance industry has to face today. Big Data has contributed to the transformation of processes, organizations and many aspects of the insurance sector. Progressing digitization allowed insurance companies to thoroughly analyze consumer behavior and their lifestyle. This knowledge is invaluable in the improvement and development of new methods of risk identification and evaluation; moreover, it enables insurers to cover new risks, offer products better suited to the market needs and raise the standard of advisory services provided in the field of loss prevention. However, the new reality also brings with it serious concerns regarding, in particular, privacy, segregation and potential customer discrimination, and the protection of competition in the market.

11.2 Big Data – concept

The term Big Data was first used in the mid-1990s by John Mashey, a former Chief Scientist at Silicon Graphics. Originally, it related to the handling and analysis of large data sets. This definition has evolved very dynamically – thanks to Doug Laney in 2001 the term Big Data began to be identified with data characterized by a large volume, the speed of its generation and diversity (Kitchin, McArdle, 2016). In the literature on the subject, there are many attempts to define the concept of Big Data. Some of them are listed in Table 11.1.

Big Data is nowadays characterized by a set of features called 10V. In addition to volume, speed and diversity, the features of Big Data include the widely understood variability, also identified with the multidimensionality

DOI: 10.4324/9781003310082-16

Table 11.1 Selected definitions of Big Data

Definition	*Source*
"In a recent decade, the term "Big Data" has become a symbol of a revolutionary breakthrough in the field of data processing. Initially it literally meant "data bulks". The meaning gradually expanded and currently it includes: huge data volumes, technologies of data processing and use, methods for information searching in data bulks."	Kostyunina (2018)
"Extensive data sets, primarily in the characteristics of volume, velocity and/or variety, that require a scalable architecture for efficient storage, manipulation, and analysis."	NIST (2015)
"Big Data is commonly understood as the use of large-scale computing power and technologically advanced software in order to collect, process and analyse data characterised by a large volume, velocity, variety and value"	OECD (2017)
"Technology that engages big data is complex, opaque and often uninterpretable"	OECD (2017a)
"Big data refers to data sets that are too large or complex to be dealt with by traditional data-processing application software [...] Big data analysis challenges include capturing data, data storage, data analysis, search, sharing, transfer, visualization, querying, updating, information privacy, and data source."	Wikipedia (2022)

of Big Data (variability), low data reliability (veracity), low validity, and susceptibility to cyberattacks. In addition, Big Data is characterized by a short useful life of data, which makes it unprofitable to archive such large data sets (volatility), the difficulty of visualization and business value (value). The publications devoted to Big Data are dominated by numerous comparisons and definitions, the authors of which pay special attention to the need to use non-standard methods when collecting, processing, analyzing and visualizing this data (cf. further Kostyunina, 2018; OECD, 2017a).

11.3 Application of Big Data in the EU insurance sector

The insurance business is based on the analysis and understanding of data in order to effectively evaluate insurance risk. Actuaries and insurance specialists depend on the results of these activities in their everyday work. Therefore, it can be said that data is one of the most important factors necessary to conduct business in the insurance sector. Big Data does not necessarily translate into useful information that enables decisions and actions to be taken. The real benefit of Big Data lies in the effective extraction of useful information and its integration with other data sources.

According to research conducted in 2019 by European Insurance and Occupational Pensions Authority (EIOPA), Big Data tools based mainly on

AI and machine learning were actively used by 31% of the surveyed insurance companies. Big Data solutions were a field for experimentation for 24% of insurance companies, and 28% had no plans to use them in the future. Big Data was usually used only in part of the insurance value chain, and companies using Big Data in all their processes constituted a definite minority of entities present on the market.

The insurance sector adopts Big Data solutions more slowly than the banking sector (cf. further OECD, 2017, 2017a). It can be assumed that the nature of business activities of both types of institutions is responsible for this state of affairs. Due to the history of bank accounts, banks have a much larger source of continuously provided information about their customers. In the case of insurers, this contact is usually limited to two moments in time – the conclusion of the insurance policy and the possible occurrence of an insured event.

Insurance entities have used or experimented with Big Data mainly in the areas of claims management (including fraud prevention) as well as service valuation and insurance risk analysis. In the former, Big Data tools were used by 35% of respondents, and in the latter – by 30%. Almost every fourth surveyed insurance company used Big Data techniques in the area of sales and distribution. Insurers indicated that Big Data had the greatest impact on the valuation of services and underwriting – approximately 30% of respondents agreed with this statement. The three-year forecast showed that Big Data involvement will increase in all areas of the value chain. This trend was especially noticeable in the fields of premium setting, risk analysis and claims management (see Figures 11.1 and 11.2).

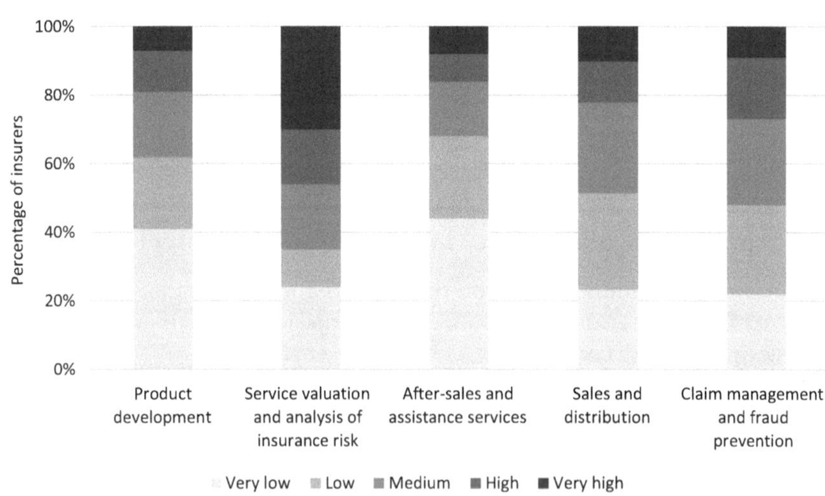

Figure 11.1 Assessment of the impact of Big Data on the value chain of insurance companies in 2019

Source: EIOPA (2019)

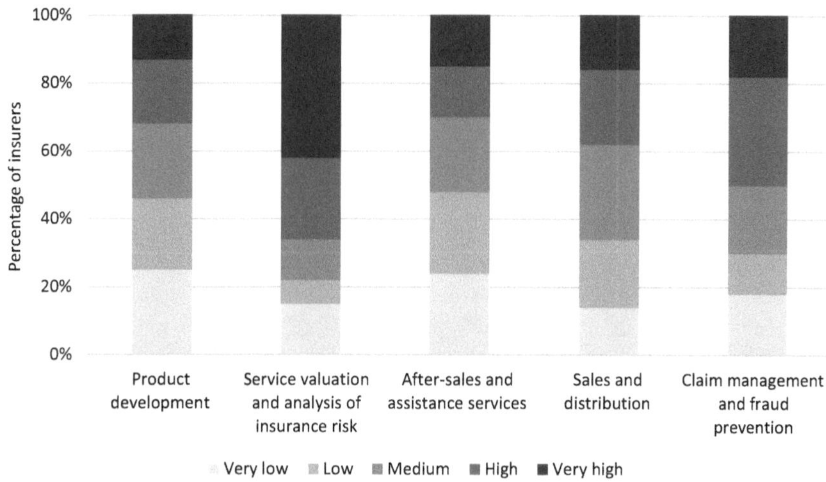

Figure 11.2 Assessment of the impact of Big Data on the value chain of insurance companies – forecast 2020–2022
Source: EIOPA (2019)

The use of Big Data allows insurers to introduce usage-based insurance products. Examples of such products are motor, health and life insurance proposals, based on the measurement of the insured's behavior and the insured's environment in order to assess the risk and estimate the value of the insurance premium. Based on Big Data technology, German insurers have developed the so-called telemetry tariffs used in car policies (IAIS, 2020).

In 2019, less than 20% of companies declared the use of Big Data in the motor insurance segment. In the case of health insurance, this percentage was only around 3%. If insurers have already used Big Data solutions, they were responsible for no more than 10% of the gross premium. The share of this type of insurance product in the gross premium is expected to increase in the coming years (see Figure 11.3).

The potential benefits of using Big Data in the area of sales and distribution result primarily from increasing the level of understanding of customer needs and verification of the characteristics of a given brand in order to meet consumer expectations. This results in a gradual improvement in the interactions between the enterprise and the client, especially in the area of digitization of financial products and services (cf. further Zillner et al., 2014). French insurers used Big Data in building a multi-channel distribution strategy, which was aimed at providing clients with convenient interaction with the insurance company (IAIS, 2020). Another example of using Big Data in sales and distribution is the so-called robo-consulting. In 2019, only 2% of insurance companies used robo-advisors, i.e. advisors based almost entirely on algorithms and decision trees. As many as 25% of establishments declared

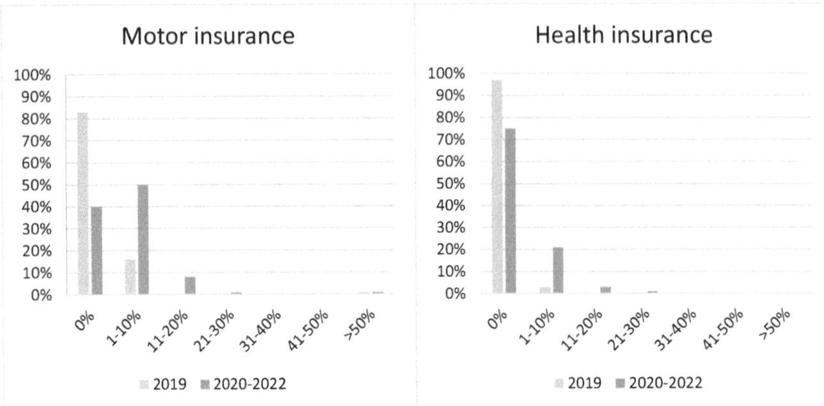

Figure 11.3 The share of motor and health insurance using the measurement of the behavior of the insured and their environment to evaluate the risk and estimate the value of the premium in the gross premium of insurance companies

Source: EIOPA (2019)

their willingness to use robo-consulting by 2022 (EIOPA, 2019). Insurance companies have found their application for robo-consulting mainly in simple insurance products, such as car insurance. In conjunction with Big Data, it has become possible to develop more complex products, e.g. since 2017, insurers from the Netherlands have been using robo-advice in the development of disability insurance (IAIS, 2018).

Solutions in the area of after-sales services have gained much greater recognition in the insurance market, thanks to the so-called chatbots. Virtual assistants are primarily used to answer the most frequently asked questions by consumers (the so-called FAQ). In 2019, 12% of insurers actively used solutions in this area, and 42% planned to introduce them within a three-year time horizon (EIOPA, 2019).

Big Data allows you to expand the possibilities of claims management as well as the detection and prevention of fraud in the insurance services industry. Financial institutions have always been exposed to the risk of extortion, both from individuals and from organized crime organizations. Additionally, in the time of the COVID-19 pandemic, insurance companies have noticed an increase in fraud attempts (EIOPA, 2020). According to the Swiss Insurance Association, 10% of reported losses in Switzerland were fraudulent. On the other hand, research on the German insurance market showed that approximately 9% of notifications in motor, third-party and property insurance are inconsistent. In 2017, insurers estimated that losses from the activities of insurance frauds amounted to EUR 4–5 billion per year (IAIS, 2020). As of 2019, insurers used Big Data primarily in the detection of fraud (over 60% of insurance companies) and the automation of processes related to handling payments on claims (over 50% of insurers) (EIOPA, 2019). The first of these issues is presented in Figure 11.4.

Most insurers have claims assessment tools that use machine learning algorithms in models trained to find patterns of potential fraud based on selected attributes, e.g. accident location, number of previous claims, etc. Based on this data, each claim is assigned a fraud probability rating (claims scoring). Often, in conjunction with this solution, insurance companies use algorithms based on a set of rules to assess claims. These algorithms are designed to search for anomalies by automatically comparing e.g. scanned invoices to assess whether they fall within the range of previously defined values (anomaly detection). In health insurance, German insurers use applications that allow the submission of claims and their processing based on photos of receipts. Big Data is also used in agricultural property insurance – damage evaluation is based on photos taken by drones (IAIS, 2020).

Big Data also leads to changes in the approach to insurance risk. The ability to analyze big data allows insurers to create more realistic mathematical models. In the Netherlands, insurers use an external IT company to estimate the replacement value of a home in non-life insurance (IAIS, 2020). Thanks to the use of Big Data, insurance will no longer rely only on a retrospective (statistical) approach, but will also start to rely on predictive behavioral analysis. The system for determining insurance premiums may experience a similar transformation in the future from a static model to a dynamic model, which will be updated with a frequency depending on the changing risk profile of each client. The use of Big Data for the purpose of determining premiums and risk assessment is therefore the source of the greatest controversy.

With the increase in competition and customer awareness on the market (e.g. thanks to the use of price comparison websites), insurance companies were forced to compete in the area of premiums. Traditionally, insurers classify their

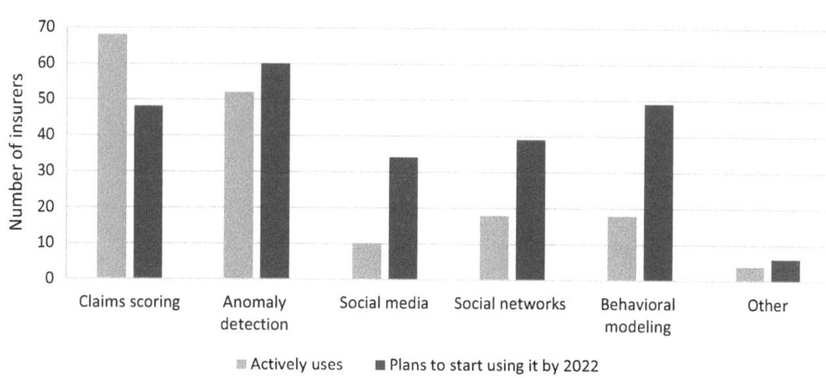

Figure 11.4 The use of Big Data in the detection of false claims
Source: EIOPA (2019)

clients into categories with comparable levels of risk. Based on these categories, they set appropriate rates of insurance premiums, obviously creating more expensive insurance policies for the highest risk categories in order to be able to compensate for the higher probability of an insured event occurring. The information provided by the insured person himself and derived from statistics are the basis of these estimates. Valuation of services based on models using Big Data helps both in the segmentation of risk and in calculating the cost proportionally to the risk of a specific client, strengthening the upward trend in the number of risk segments of insurance companies (see Figure 11.5).

Online insurance comparison websites in the Netherlands prove that insurers are increasingly exploring the possibility of applying dynamic prices and even dynamic characteristics so that both the amount of the premium and the insurance conditions are defined "on demand" (IAIS, 2020).

The digitization and use of Big Data can significantly reduce insurance costs due to the automation of processes across the entire value chain of insurance companies. Big Data could help reduce information asymmetries, which are believed to be the main factor causing insurance ineffectiveness. In addition, Big Data should allow for the creation of new insurance products (analogous to individual insurance) and cover the risks that were previously considered uninsurable (Kuryłowicz, 2017).

The key to achieving the benefits offered by Big Data is the quality of the obtained data. Nowadays, data obtained by insurers from public data collections are constantly gaining importance. These data are primarily aimed at increasing the detection of frauds. An example of this type of solution is digital driver registers integrated with police databases implemented in Great Britain in 2001. Insurers also see significant potential in data from social media. In 2016, one of the first applications of this type appeared on

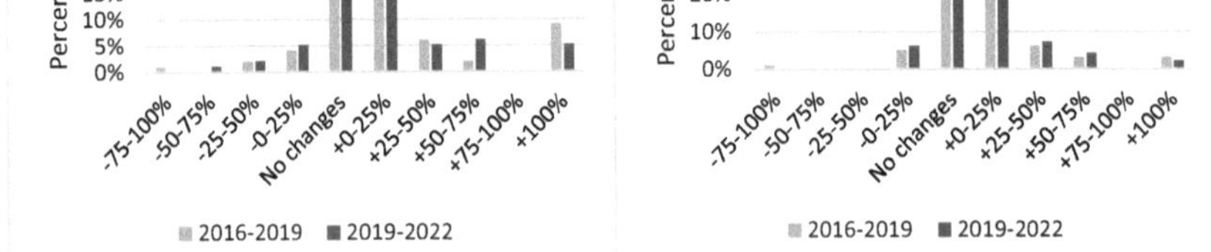

Figure 11.5 Changes in the number of risk segments for clients of insurance companies in 2016–2019 and the forecast for 2019–2022

Source: EIOPA (2019)

the insurance market. Firstcarquote, an insurance product developed by the British insurance company Admiral, was to estimate the amount of the insurance premium based on information published by the driver on Facebook (Accenture, 2018). The social network service prevented the app provider from using the data in 2017.

11.4 Threats

The use of Big Data creates great opportunities for insurers to improve the functioning of all segments of the insurance value chain. However, all the positives of Big Data come at a price. Over time, concerns about this technology have been voiced by regulators as well as consumer groups and business representatives.

The privacy and data protection notices refer to the appropriate use of personal data. Concerns in the field of privacy relate primarily to the consequences of the use by insurers of the personal data of individuals or groups of people. In fact, the collection and storage of sensitive data and the ability to analyze both individual and collective behavior, given the ability of computer systems to process billions of information in real time, pose a potential threat to everyone's privacy.

Thanks to Big Data, insurance companies can distinguish a greater number of risk segments into which they classify clients. This trend is nothing new in itself but is additionally reinforced by Big Data technology. With the development of medicine, through the use of information stored in the genetic code, it has become possible to more accurately predict the lifetime and the probability of disease in the insured (IAIS, 2020). In this way, the danger of creating extreme risk segments has arisen, which the insurance company will not want to insure or on which it will impose a very high insurance premium. The use of genetic data is of interest to regulators around the world. In Germany, genetic testing can only be used under certain criteria and in specific products – life insurance, disability insurance and long-term care insurance. In Switzerland, the use of genetic testing in socially important insurance is completely prohibited (IAIS, 2020). Some countries have been implementing solutions to prevent discrimination and insure high-risk customers since 2013. In Austria, Belgium, Spain, Luxemburg, Romania and the Netherlands, there are insurance systems financed by insurance companies that offer motor insurance to consumers who have been refused insurance cover by at least two insurance companies or have offered very high insurance premiums for their services (see Figure 11.6) (EIOPA, 2019).

Greater differentiation of the amount of the premium means its greater spread around the average value. Research on the standard deviation of the premium shows that this trend mainly applies to motor insurance, which adopts Big Data solutions faster (see Figures 11.3 and 11.5).

In the case of moral hazard, insurance institutions have to compensate for the difficulties in observing the subjective characteristics of the behavior of

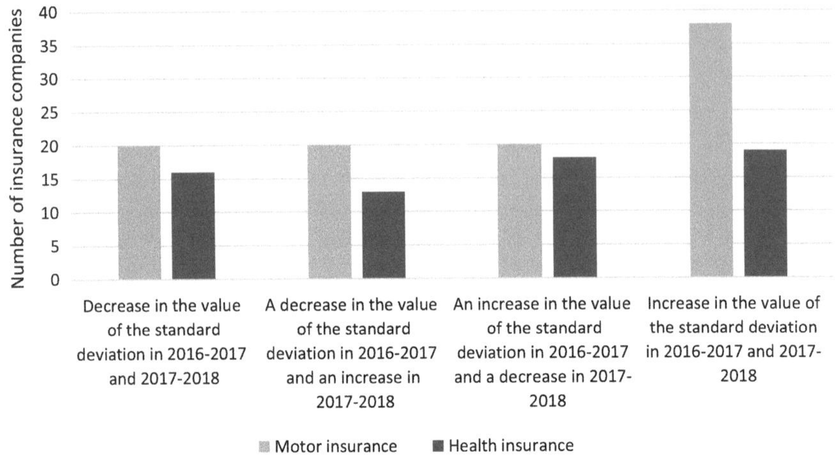

Figure 11.6 Change in the standard deviation of the value of the insurance premium in 2016–2018 for motor and health insurance

Source: EIOPA (2019)

individuals. In addition to traditional remedial measures, based on forms of partial damage coverage, the premium adjustment after the occurrence of damage over time is used.

Big Data is obtained mainly through mobile devices, as well as from interaction and message exchange via social networks from an often unaware user. As more and more data is obtained in the nature of personal data, concerns about the risk of new forms of privacy breach that may arise from the use of this data are perfectly understandable. There is a clear need to draw the attention of regulators to the potential contrast between Big Data and privacy. Regulatory measures have become necessary to properly use Big Data in terms of respecting individual privacy, potential discrimination and restricting competition. In response to the threats related to Big Data, the European Data Protection Supervisor in 2015 issued an opinion "Meeting the Challenges of Big Data: A Call for Transparency, User Control, Data Protection by Design and Accountability", in which he outlined four most important elements, based on for which the responsible and sustainable development of big data should be pursued in the future (EDPS, 2015):

- Organizations need to be more transparent about how they process personal data.
- Organizations need to give users more control over how their data is used.
- Organizations need to design user-friendly data protection solutions in products and services.
- Organizations must become more responsible for their activities.

The Regulation of the European Parliament and of the Council on the protection of individuals with regard to the processing of personal data should be considered a step in the right direction. However, this act did not completely solve the Big Data problem, as the Regulation focuses only on data that is personal data (Regulation, 2016). The basic principles of personal data protection remain largely inconsistent with the features of Big Data analytics (cf. further IAIS, 2020). It should be noted, however, that if an institution performs pseudonymization, i.e. processes personal data in a way that makes it impossible to identify the data subject, without access to key information stored elsewhere, it is practically not subject to the requirements of the Regulation. Similar consequences are brought about by the process of anonymization related to pseudoanimization, i.e. irreversible processing of personal data in a way that makes it impossible to identify a given person.

The progressive individualization and adaptation of the insurance offer to specific clients create new challenges for supervisors in the insurance sector. The question is how the development of insurance products should be monitored or regulated, since the terms of the insurance policy are not identical for each client (IAIS, 2020).

In 2019, the European Commission published guidelines on the ethics of using trustworthy Artificial Intelligence (AI). EIOPA has established a consultative group of experts to focus on digital ethics in insurance. Also in 2019, the Organization for Economic Co-operation and Development (OECD) adopted a Recommendation on AI addressed to decision-makers in relation to Big Data and AI (cf. further IAIS, 2020).

Concerns about Big Data inevitably must lead to difficult and complex trade-offs between all stakeholders – consumers, businesses, policymakers and regulators. As stated by The International Association of Insurance Supervisors, the use of customer data raises legitimate privacy, data protection and data ownership controversies (cf. further IAIS, 2020). There is also the question of how Big Data will affect the competitiveness of the insurance market and whether smaller insurance institutions will be able to exist in it. The future structure of the insurance industry will depend heavily on who has access to the data. It is questionable whether competition policy alone will be enough to ensure a truly competitive market in the long term.

Digital technologies favor the emergence of oligopolistic or even monopolistic market positions. Global technology companies have a very large share of their market segment and thus have unique access to customers and their data. Dominant positions can be abused to extend the monopoly to the insurance market or to extract value from an already existing market, as evidenced by the growing number of antitrust cases recorded in recent years.

Insurers should assess the consequences of using personal data on a case-by-case basis. The challenge for policymakers and regulators is to establish a flexible legal framework that will help stakeholders find the right balance. Research shows that insurance customers want to be more involved in managing their data. According to Accenture, 87% of surveyed consumers expressed a willingness to monitor and control their personal information shared online (Accenture, 2018). Insufficient privacy protection will harm the interests of consumers and, consequently, undermine their trust in financial institutions. On the other hand, too strict regulations will make it difficult for all parties to benefit from Big Data.

11.5 Conditions and directions of development

Big Data will undoubtedly constitute an important part of the financial and insurance industry in the future. Enterprises will have to adapt to the reality of Big Data, but they will also obtain a tool that offers them significant opportunities for further development. Information plays an increasingly important role in the functioning of economic entities, according to some it has become a new factor of production (cf. further Płoszajski, 2013). Considering the importance of information, concerns regarding Big Data and technological progress, the most important determinants of Big Data development in the coming years should primarily include:

- Increase in the amount of generated data. This trend does not apply only to insurance institutions or capital markets.
- The average annual increase in the number of transactions from 2014–2019 was equal to 12.5%, while from 2018 to 2019 - 14.1%. In connection with the Covid-19 pandemic, we should expect even greater growth in the number of transactions in the coming years.
- Increased interest and control by regulators. Industry regulators now require a detailed and clearer picture of both the financial health and the activities of financial and insurance institutions. The reporting obligations of these institutions are slowly changing their shape. Synthetic reports are replaced by the requirement to provide the relevant authorities with the "raw" data on which these reports are based. Therefore, financial institutions need to ensure that they can analyze their "raw" financial data with the same level of detail as regulators.
- Evolution of business models. Turning to Big Data in the face of increasing competition may in the future be the only way for financial institutions to maintain market share.
- Customer orientation. In 2018, the importance of customer relations was emphasized by 97% of insurers (Accenture, 2018).
- Evolution of information sources. On a global scale, the data in 2018 was of key importance in making decisions at the operational and strategic level for 80% of insurers (Accenture, 2018). The same percentage of respondents emphasized the importance of the credibility of the obtained data and the correctness of the methods of their analysis. It can be assumed that the pandemic will additionally increase their importance

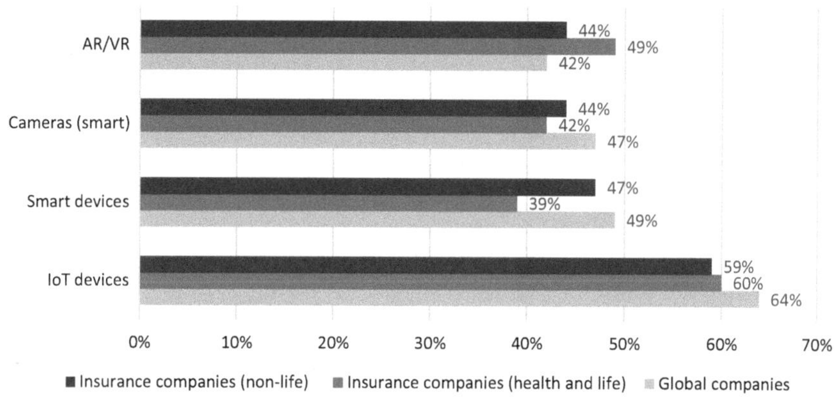

Figure 11.7 The most important technological solutions in the field of data acquisition by insurers
Source: Own study based on Accenture (2018)

for insurance companies. Insurers are looking for new data sources that could replace data generated internally and obtained from contractors. The insurance sector sees the greatest potential in this area in collecting data from the so-called IoT (Internet of Things) devices and smart devices (see Figure 11.7).

- Development of intellectual capital. Some organizations have identified the opportunities offered by Big Data, however, they lack the human capital with the appropriate level of skills to bridge the gap between this data and the potential opportunities. There is a noticeable lack of qualified personnel in the field of large data analysis and IT (cf. further Accenture, 2018).
- Development of IT infrastructure and organizational culture. Based on data from 2018, it can be concluded that over 80% of insurers see the need to develop infrastructure in order to maintain their position on the market (cf. further Accenture, 2018).
- Approach to privacy and data security. In the territory of the European Union, many issues related to data protection and privacy have been defined, which each institution must take into account when conducting Big Data analyses. The fifth article of the EU regulation clearly states that the processing of personal data must be adequate, relevant and not excessive (Regulation, 2016). Thus, natural persons may, in certain circumstances, request a given institution to delete or refrain from processing their personal data. In addition to the increase in costs related to handling customer requests, deletion of data may lead to a distortion of the entire data set, especially as certain social groups will be more aware of their rights than others, and thus also more active in this matter.

11.6 Conclusion

The approach to business based on the use of Big Data brings with it significant potential benefits for insurance institutions. It increases the efficiency of the entire insurance sector, reduces risk, creates additional options for consumers to choose and increases insurance coverage. It is obvious that in order to be successful and competitive in the constantly evolving insurance market, insurance institutions must use Big Data. In the future, it should be expected that information collected with the use of new technologies will play an increasingly important role in the activities of insurers.

However, the benefits of Big Data come at a price. The increased use of personal data requires far-reaching compromises between consumers, businesses, policymakers and regulators. It is extremely important to regulate this area of activity of insurance companies. Data collection must not affect the privacy of individuals. Risk classification based on Big Data should improve market efficiency, not restrict competition. And the use of personal life data to adjust premiums and insurance policies should not be an instrument of discrimination and segregation of customers.

Bibliography

Accenture, 2018. *Cyfryzacja sektora ubezpieczeń w Polsce (Digitization of the insurance sector in Poland).* https://piu.org.pl/wp-content/uploads/2018/11/ACC_PIU_Raport-Cyfryzacja-Ubezpieczen-w-Polsce.pdf [Accessed 21 March 2021].

European Data Protection Supervisor (EDPS), 2015. *Meeting the challenges of big data, a call for transparency, user control, data protection by design and accountability.* https://edps.europa.eu/data-protection/our-work/publications/opinions/meeting-challenges-big-data_en [Accessed 21 Febuary 2021].

European Insurance and Occupational Pensions Authority (EIOPA), 2019. *Big Data analytics in motor and health insurance: A thematic review.* https://www.eiopa.europa.eu/content/eiopa-reviews-use-big-data-analytics-motor-and-health-insurance_en [Accessed 21 March 2021].

European Insurance and Occupational Pensions Authority (EIOPA), 2020. *The Consumer Trends Report.* https://www.eiopa.europa.eu/content/consumer-trends-report-2020 [Accessed 17 March 2021].

Kitchin, R., McArdle, G., 2016. *What makes Big Data, Big Data? Exploring the ontological characteristics of 26 datasets.* https://doi.org/10.1177%2F205395171663 1130 [Accessed 21 August 2022].

Kostyunina, T., 2018. Classification of operational risks in construction companies on the basis of big data. *MATEC Web Conf.* 193.

Kuryłowicz, Ł., 2017. Usage-Based Insurance: the concept and study of available analyses. *Wiadomości Ubezpieczeniowe*, 2016, nr 4, s. 127–142.

National Institute of Standards and Technology (NIST), 2015. *NIST Big Data Interoperability Framework: Volume 1, Definitions.* https://bigdatawg.nist.gov/_uploadfiles/NIST.SP.1500-1.pdf [Accessed 29 August 2022].

Organisation for Economic Co-operation and Development (OECD), 2017. *Big Data: Bringing Competition Policy to the Digital Era. Executive Summary.* https://one.

oecd.org/document/DAF/COMP/M(2016)2/ANN4/FINAL/en/pdf [Accessed 11 Febuary 2021].

Organisation for Economic Co-operation and Development (OECD), 2017a. *Technology and innovation in the insurance sector.* https://www.oecd.org/pensions/Technology-and-innovation-in-the-insurance-sector.pdf [Accessed 11 Febuary 2021].

Płoszajski, P., 2013. *Big Data: nowe źródło przewag i wzrostu firm (Big Data: a new source of company advantages and growth).* http://www.e-mentor.edu.pl/artykul/index/numer/50/id/1016 [Accessed 21 March 2021].

Rozporządzenie Parlamentu Europejskiego i Rady (UE) 2016/679 z dnia 27 kwietnia 2016 r. w sprawie ochrony osób fizycznych w związku z przetwarzaniem danych osobowych i w sprawie swobodnego przepływu takich danych oraz uchylenia dyrektywy 95/46/WE (Regulation (EU) 2016/679 of the European Parliament and of the Council of 27 April 2016 on the protection of natural persons with regard to the processing of personal data and on the free movement of such data, and repealing Directive 95/46/EC).

The International Association of Insurance Supervisors (IAIS), 2018. *Issues Paper on the Increasing Use of Digital Technology in Insurance and its Potential Impact on Consumer Outcomes.* https://www.iaisweb.org/page/supervisory-material/issues-paper s// file/89244/issues-paper-on-use-of-big-data-analytics-in-insurance [Accessed 28 May 2021].

The International Association of Insurance Supervisors (IAIS), 2020. *Issues Paper on Use of Big Data Analytics in Insurance.* https://www.iaisweb.org/page/supervisory-material/issues-papers//file/89244/issues-paper-on-use-of-big-data-analytics-in-insurance [Accessed 28 May 2021].

Wikipedia, 2022. *Big Data.* https://en.wikipedia.org/wiki/Big_data [Accessed 12 December 2022].

Zillner, S., Rusitschka, S., Munne, R., Lippell, H., Lobillo, F., et al., 2014. *Big Data Public Private Forum. Final version of Sector's Roadmap.* https://www.big-project.eu/sites/default/files/BIG_D2_4_2_FINAL_v0_851.pdf [Accessed 26 Febuary 2021].

Part IV

Digitalization of capital markets

12 Smart contracts and artificial intelligence

Magdalena Dziedzic

12.1 Introduction

The development of new technologies influence the digitalization of many areas of the economy. They create the foundations of economic growth, constituting the added value on which all sectors of the economy are already based, in particular, they have a significant impact on the financial services market. Artificial intelligence (AI) in finance has been a research area of great interest for many decades. Here, finance refers to broad areas comprising capital markets, trading, banking, insurance, loans, investment, asset/wealth management, risk management, marketing, compliance and regulation, payment, contracting, auditing, accounting, financial infrastructure, blockchain, financial operations, financial services, financial security, and financial ethics (Cao, 2021, p. 1). Smart contracts and other technologies based on AI are changing the world even more profoundly than other technological innovations, and the impact of AI systems on the surrounding socio-economic realities seems to be the most significant, but at the same time poses certain threats. In the case of the financial market, AI systems are increasingly used as they lead to the emergence of new business models, applications, products, or processes, modifying the way financial services are provided as part of the operations of financial institutions.

In recent years, the financial institutions functioning in the capital markets have started to approach the digital revolution with some level of urgency. The deployment of new technologies is expected to increasingly drive competitive advantages for financial businesses thanks to first, improvement of the companies' efficiency through cost-cutting and productivity enhancement, thus leading to better profitability (e.g. enhanced decision-making processes, automated execution, gains from improvements in risk management and regulatory compliance, back-office, and other process optimization); and, second, enhancement of the quality of financial services and products offered to consumers (e.g. new product offering, high customization of products and services) (OECD, 2021, p. 7). As a result, financial consumers can take competitive advantage of such improved quality of products, lower costs, and a broader range of options and personalization of products.

DOI: 10.4324/9781003310082-18

Lately, the solutions based on AI and smart contracts have been applied in increasingly broader areas of finance, e.g. trading, banking, insurance, risk, regulation, and marketing, being applied in smart digital currencies, lending, payment, asset and wealth management, risk and regulation management, and accounting and auditing (Cao, 2021, p. 1). Smart contracts and AI systems are increasingly inseparable from the reality that surrounds us, which, according to many, results in the need to create a legal framework for their functioning. Solutions whose operations are based on AI are so specific that it is not easy to use existing and commonly known legal institutions in relation to them. Although in some circumstances AI systems should be treated as a more advanced type of software, an increasing number of these systems are characterized by a kind of autonomy. As a result, in the functioning of the above-mentioned systems, it is difficult to define the moment when the effect of a particular AI system is no longer within the intended and intellectual cause-and-effect relationship between the system itself and the person or persons who created it.

This paper offers a comprehensive and dense roadmap of AI systems and smart contracts applied to the capital markets. It presents a survey of the recent technical advances, challenges and opportunities offered by new technologies of this kind. The theoretical and practical aspects of AI applications are first outlined, followed by a comprehensive overview of smart contracts as a "new contract law". We then structure and categorize AI solutions in financial business, in particular in capital markets along with some representative examples. We also compare smart contracts and blockchain technology on capital markets and give a categorization of smart contract applications along with some representative examples. This paper comprises the available literature, scientific articles, professional literature, reports, and legal acts regarding the use of artificial intelligence systems and smart contracts by financial markets, it bases on the literature and legal acts on AI systems available until 2021.

12.2 The concept of AI

AI is most often described as the ability of a machine to copy or imitate human intelligence through the use of software implemented in it. For the purposes of the academic discussion on the application of this new technology, another definition is also cited, according to which

> artificial intelligence should be understood as a system that enables the implementation of tasks requiring a learning process and taking into account new circumstances when solving a given problem and which may to varying degrees - depending on the configuration - act autonomously and interact with the environment.
>
> (Zalewski, 2020, p. 3)

To assess the deployment of artificial intelligence systems in finance they are (AI systems) often defined as "*machine-based systems with varying levels of autonomy that can, for a given set of human-defined objectives, make predictions, recommendations or decisions*" (OECD, 2021, p. 7). AI models are increasingly applying huge amounts of alternative data sources and data analytics referred to as "big data". Such data feed machine learning (ML) models, which use such data to learn and improve predictability and performance automatically through experience and data, not being previously programmed to do so by humans.

For a computer scientist, the concept of AI is used to describe computer systems that analyse large amounts of data with the intention of categorizing them and finding repeatability in them, in order to make a specific decision based on this information. Such a system has the ability to learn based on the analysed data, and moreover, it can continue to learn in the course of actions taken. The ability to learn in the framework of AI takes place through the so-called machine learning, which includes a set of data processing techniques. These data may consist of a previously developed set, or they may be compiled in real time (IEC White Paper, 2018, p. 35). Machine learning aims to reduce the complexity of sets and discover patterns that are needed later to explain certain events, predict them, or take some action. Such a system is capable of interpreting data in order to improve its mode of operation. Machine learning capability allows a computer program to take action without developing programming code in the form of an "if-then" command.

When analyzing the concept of AI, it is worth paying attention to its additional aspect, which is its degree of autonomy or the dimension of functioning. This means that the learning ability of an AI system may result in providing data and information, which can then be used in accordance with the wishes of the system's creator. The first model of the system may based on the analysis of a certain number of elements in the set, for example, indicate the most advantageous transaction price at a given moment. In a more advanced dimension (the second model), the system may recommend specific actions to be taken, and the recommendation may be confirmed, rejected, or modified by the user. The most intelligent form of such a system (the third model) takes a specific action itself, which can then be possibly cancelled, and the role of the operator of such a system comes down to its supervision and, if necessary, intervention. The third model of the AI system can be modified in such a way that the operator accepts certain (in principle, the most important) actions of the system, or he/she takes actions fully independently, taking into account specific variables, analyzing them and then performing specific operations without the need to obtaining human consent (Zalewski, 2020, pp. 10–12). As indicated above, AI systems retain a different degree of autonomy, which translates into a different degree of interacting with the environment, being limited only to the digital dimension or involving the physical environment as well.

12.3 Smart contracts as "a new contract law"

While smart contracts were conceptualized by Nick Szabo in a series of papers in the 1990s, implementing them on distributed ledgers took place with the advent and maturing of the Bitcoin blockchain after 2009. A comprehensive definition of smart contracts was given in the opening paragraph of a 1994 paper, and said, as follows

> a smart contract is a computerized transaction protocol that executes the terms of a contract. The general objectives of smart contract design are to satisfy common contractual conditions (such as payment terms, liens, confidentiality, and even enforcement), minimize exceptions both malicious and accidental, and minimize the need for trusted intermediaries. Related economic goals include lowering fraud loss, arbitration and enforcement costs, and other transaction costs.
>
> (Szabo, 1994, p. 4)

Smart contracts are specified in digital form and comprise contractual elements that are in the form of an algorithm. They prevent agreements from tampering via cryptographic or other security features and one of the essential features they are self-executing (Szabo, 1997, p. 45). The digital form of a smart contract means they consist of lines of code as well as the software that prescribes its conditions, and contractual clauses are embedded therein.

A computer protocol in the form of an algorithm is a set of rules according to which data in relation to a smart contract is to be processed. Hence, it is possible to perform rules-based operations, such as the release of payment. It is a common misconception that there is only one model of a smart contract, in fact, there are a few of them, which means that such promises may be of contractual or non-contractual nature. First, the contract may be expressed in a code entirely. Second, the contract may be in code but be accompanied by a separate natural language version. Third, there may be a "split", which means the contract has a natural language version but a part of its performance has been encoded. Fourth, it is a natural language contract but a payment mechanism has been encoded (Chamber of Digital Commerce, 2016, p. 9).

At the heart of a smart contract lies the idea of automated performance. Being typically embedded in blockchain technology, smart contracts are regarded as irrevocable. When started, the result for which the contract has been programmed to operate cannot generally be stopped. Smart contract logic is locked within a "block" which is a software-generated container where sit together the messages referring to a particular contract (Rogers, Jones-Fenleigh, Sanitt, 2017, p. 22). Those messages might be treated as input or output of the smart contract programming logic.

Smart contracts are often stored on the blockchain and the relationship can be established automatically. According to one of the definitions, an intelligent contract is a compiled program source code saved on a blockchain, which ensures the self-execution and autonomy of the provisions resulting from and indicated in the code, under the conditions specified therein (Hazard, Haapio, 2017, p. 301). It should be emphasized that the algorithm of the self-executing contract, apart from the classic writing it on the blockchain, can be introduced via any other programming language. The Maltese Virtual Financial Assets (VFA) Act draws attention to this, according to which smart contracts should not be connected only with distributed ledger technologies (DLT), blockchain, bitcoin, or Ethereum.

There are many definitions of a smart contract, and even mentioning a few of them would significantly exceed the scope of this paper but it is worth paying attention to the most representative of them. According to one of the definitions presented by Goldenfine and Leiter (2018, p. 144), automated transactions have become very common in many areas, additionally, they are a way of value exchange, and some of their functionalities may be implemented without human assistance as their operator. Smart contracts, or more precisely the programming code that creates them, enable many activities, not only the most popular ones like payment transfer. Taking advantage of the technical possibilities, the system operators try to build into the contracts certain legal rules, which means that all the system shall contain its own regulatory modules relating to specific actions or behaviours, pointing to specific criteria that are important both from a technical and legal point of view. That has been coined "legal engineering", in other words, the process of creating legal regulations in technical architecture by constructing readable transactional module libraries in accordance with the classical understanding of the contract, thus allowing for final law enforcement.

Another definition was proposed by Sherborne (2017, p. 4), who defines smart contracts as automatically implemented contracts connected with a computer protocol, expressed in code, which automatically perform previously programmed functions in response to predefined conditions. He claims that as a result of the integration of block technology, smart contracts are able to automate and ensure the implementation of many different obligations without being forced to refer to some central authority, a legal system, or a law enforcement mechanism unfamiliar to the parties. Smart contracts, by minimizing the risk related to the participation of people in the process of their implementation, reduce possible human errors, and, what is more, they guarantee greater predictability or transparency.

In terms of Polish literature, there are more and more publications on smart contracts, their definitions, and analyses covering the possible effects of such a contracting model against the background of the applicable legal system. According to one of them, smart contracts may constitute a new technology of contract law (Pecyna, Behan, 2020, p. 187). Undoubtedly, the use of such contracts might result in the emergence of many technological risks related thereto, in principle, to the violation of contracts concluded thanks to them. Another definition says that a smart contract is "a complex programming code, a copy of which is saved in the blockchain register, and which presents the rules for the implementation of transactions between the parties" (Piech, 2018, p. 47). Moreover, the same author claims that a smart contract is a digital representation of rules or processes within an institution that contain instructions on how to proceed and how to make a transaction. According to another definition, a smart contract is "a legal bond that can function independently in the digital space, without having to refer to the real world" (Czarnecki, 2016, p. 7). The legal relationship is concluded via electronic means, without the need to refer to any paper documents or traditional signatures, what is more, it is to be changed in the same way. The implementation of the obligation relationship or its elements does not have to be associated with any action in the real world – it is subject to automatism and rules encoded in a given contract. The conclusion of such a contract, its modification, and its performance are independent of the will of a third party, including the court. What is more, a smart contract can be something more than a contract, as it may be used in a voting system or a public register.

It may seem controversial whether a smart contract falls within the concept of a contract in the classic meaning of civil law since for contract conclusion it is necessary to submit unanimous declarations of the will of the parties with the intention to establish a binding contractual relationship. Hence, the purpose of a smart contract would be the implementation of the transaction on the basis of which the property rights to digital goods expressed on the blockchain are transferred. Although it is true that the execution of a smart contract occurs automatically, at an earlier stage it is necessary for the parties who initiate such a contract to express their will. According to one of the views, the moment of submitting the declaration of will is the moment when the parties make a decision to use a smart contract as a kind of "agent" in order to conclude a specific contract and be bound by certain consequences (Pecyna, Behan, 2020, p. 205). The conclusion of the contract and its performance takes place through the use of a smart contract, and the element of trust between the parties, common in the obligation relationship, refers to the computer algorithm (Saveleyev, 2017, p. 15). It is assumed that the smart contract may be concluded and performed only in electronic form. The provisions of such an agreement are created by a computer code or program, which is protected under the provisions of intellectual property law. The language of the smart contract is expressed in the form of the formula "if… then…" [if… than…], which indicates its conditionality.

In the conclusion to the hereabove mentioned considerations, it should be emphasized that the use of the word "contract" may seem in some contexts incorrect since it indicates that we are dealing here with a contract in every case, and in fact, we are not. In practice, it may often happen that smart contracts are not contracts in the legal sense (Sherborne, 2017, p. 5; Szostak, 2018, p. 121). The same authors continue that due to their functions, smart contracts should be divided into two categories: (1) in the first sense, these are actually contracts concluded only electronically, through their acceptance by the parties or by downloading specific software, hence, such a contract is subject to automatic execution; (2) in the second sense, it is a recording tool (generally in the blockchain), which actually, in a traditional way, presents a previously concluded contract (for example concluded traditionally in paper), often constituting a framework or conditional contract, the execution of which is automatically implemented by a computer program (Szostak, 2018, p. 121). In this sense, a smart contract will not be the contract itself, but a form of contract conclusion (as a tool that identifies it and activates its implementation).

12.4 The use of AI in the financial sector

AI solutions have been increasingly deployed in finance, in areas such as risk assessment, risk management, fraud detection, financial advisory services, algorithmic trading, asset management, personalized banking, credit underwriting, and last but not least preventing cyber attacks. The deployment of such techniques is enabled by the abundance of available data and analytics as well as increasing computer capacity (e.g. cloud computing), which thanks to analysis performed by ML models are able to identify signals and detect underlying relationships in a way that is far beyond human abilities. Taking into consideration the present interconnectedness between asset classes and geographies, AI models allow for predictive capacity that is fast outdoing the power of even traditional algos in finance and trading (OECD, 2021, p. 24). Machine learning models (ML), as a subfield of AI, use big data to learn and improve predictability and performance automatically, without being programmed to do so by anyone.

AI solutions, especially deep learning, are most often used by financial institutions that use them to automate specific processes. These solutions have been adopted primarily for the preparation of stock market forecasts, when assessing credit risk, as well as in the process of asset valuation (Janusz, 2020, p. 43). Of course, the opportunities AI presents to the financial sector extend far beyond the current application. These perspectives may include complete automation of the planning and implementation processes of personalized and targeted campaigns or marketing strategies for specific financial products. AI allows increasing the security of operations while maintaining a similar level of flexibility of financial services and the usability of Internet tools. This application also includes the development of comprehensive demographic analyses or analysis of the behaviour of clients of financial institutions and the emotions they experience, based on the observation of their behaviour in social networks (Janusz, 2020, p. 43).

In highly digitalized financial markets, the application of AI and ML in asset management may increase the efficiency and accuracy of operational flows, improve performance and reinforce risk management (Deloitte, 2019, p. 3). Natural Language Generation (NLG), a subset of AI, may be exploited by financial advisors to "humanise" and simplify data analysis and reporting to clients (Gould, 2016, p. 2). ML mechanisms are able to monitor plenty of risk factors on a regular basis and test portfolio performance under plenty of market scenarios. As for operational benefits, AI applications help to decrease back-office costs of investment managers and replace manually intensive reconciliation with automated ones (OECD, 2021, p. 22).

In relation to different AI models, feeding ML systems with big data may offer asset managers recommendations (thanks to the gained insights into the investment processes) that impact decision-making concerning portfolio allocation and stock selection. Big data may allow asset managers to deploy AI for the implementation of new investment strategies, from fundamental analysis to systematic trading and quantitative analysis as well. AI makes it possible for asset managers to digest huge amounts of data from multiple sources and introduce appropriate adjustments in their strategies in a very short timeframe according to changing market conditions.

In terms of algorithmic trading, AI solutions may serve both in trading to provide trading strategy recommendations and to power automated trading models that make predictions, provide competitive pricing, manage liquidity, optimize, select the proper course of action and execute trades (OECD, 2021, p. 24). AI-based trading systems are able to identify and execute trades totally by themselves, without any human intervention, using AI techniques such as evolutionary computation, deep learning, and probabilistic logic (Metz, 2016, p. 2). Another AI technique, such as algo wheel, can support the creation of strategies for any upcoming trade in a systematic fashion by enabling an "if/then" process to be introduced (Bloomberg, 2019, p. 2). AI-enabled models in trading are also able to assist traders in their risk management and in the management of the flow of their orders, since they can track the risk exposure and adjust or exit the position in relation to the expectations of the investor, in an automated mechanism.

Banks and FinTech lenders are increasingly applying AI-enabled systems and big data to assess the creditworthiness of prospective borrowers and make underwriting decisions. In terms of credit scoring, ML techniques are applied to predict borrowers' defaults with much higher forecasting accuracy in comparison to standard statistical models (e.g. logic regression), which allows the lenders to better the management of their lending portfolio.

Although AI/ML-enabled systems offer vast potential for speed and efficiency of creditworthiness procedures, they also pose a threat of discriminatory or unfair lending, since the use of poor quality (inadequate, incomplete, or poorly labelled) data may result in questionable output, in spite of a well-trained underlying algorithm. Moreover, AI/ML-based models raise serious issues in terms of their transparency bearing in mind their lack of explainability, which may lead to difficulty in comprehending the performed credit-risk analysis. As a consequence, the lenders may not be able to explain the basis for denials of credit extensions, and the potential borrowers have limited ability to identify and contest unfair credit decisions or do not know what actions to undertake to improve their credit rating.

Financial markets authorities are increasingly researching potential benefits from the application of AI insights into "Suptech" tools, i.e. in FinTech-based applications used by authorities for regulatory, supervisory, and oversight purposes (FSB, 2020, p. 8). At the same time, regulated institutions are introducing FinTech solutions for regulatory and compliance requirements and reporting ('RegTech'). Financial institutions are developing AI solutions for internal controls and risk management, as well. What is more, a combination of AI technologies with behavioural sciences enables large financial institutions to prevent misconduct and detect fraud (Scott, 2020, p. 2). The growth in RegTech and SupTech solutions is caused by the increased availability of data, improvement of AI models, the potential for benefits in the efficiency and effectiveness of regulatory processes, possibility for enhanced insights into risk and compliance developments (FSB, 2020, p. 7).

12.4 The integration of blockchain-based technology (smart contracts) in financial products

Blockchain technology is referred to as safe and automatic transfer of value, and in simple terms, it can be defined as the Internet of values (Szpringer, 2019, p. 73). The functioning of the register, such as blockchain, comes down to the fact that specific events are recorded in chronological order based on a cryptographically encrypted block, which then appears together in the form of a chain. The integrity of the entire database is ensured thanks to a unique digital signature confirming a specific event.

The adoption of DLT, such as blockchain, has been very beneficial in recent years, in particular, in finance. The huge increase of blockchain-based applications is the consequence of the speed, efficiency, and transparency such technologies offer, which is strengthened by their automation and disintermediation (OECD, 2020, p. 33). Widespread use and benefits of blockchain-based technologies may especially be observed for financial operators in securities markets, in areas such as issuance and post-trade/clearing and settlement, in payments (digital currencies and stablecoins), and in the tokenization of assets.

The most important impact of the use of AI models in blockchain-based systems may result from their application in smart contracts. Smart contracts existed long before the advent of AI-enabled models and are based on software code. Even today, a great deal of them do not necessarily have a connection to AI. Nevertheless, AI applications may be very beneficial in enhancing smart contract capabilities, especially when it comes to risk management and the identification of mistakes in the code of a smart contract (OECD, 2021, p. 33). AI techniques such as natural language processing (NLP) can be of use while analyzing the patterns of a smart contract execution, detecting fraudulent behaviours, and increasing the security of the system. In theory, the application of AI in smart contracts could further improve their automation capacity by enhancing their autonomy and enabling the embedded code to be dynamically adjusted in line with market conditions.

It is argued that AI-based smart contracts can form the ground for the establishment of self-regulated chains. In the future, AI solutions might be integrated for forecasting and automating in "self-learned" smart contracts, like systems using reinforcement learning AI techniques (Almasoud et al., 2020, p. 2). Hence, AI could be beneficial for extracting and processing information from real-time systems and feeding such information into smart contracts.

There are four categories of capital market participants for whom blockchain technology and smart contract technology present measurable benefits: issuers, fund managers, investors, and regulators. For issuers, their benefit is easier, cheaper, and faster access to capital through programmable digital assets and securities. Such securities can be issued very quickly and the rights and obligations to them are code-based and automated. The main advantage of digital resources is the possibility of fractionating them, which means that they can be divided into cheaper and transferable units. This results in a greater flow of investors and greater diversity in specific markets. This opens up new opportunities for smaller issuers to remove barriers to the issuance of assets or securities, and the entire lifecycle of a specific asset can be automated, from investor services to dividend events. For fund managers, the benefit comes down to the faster and more transparent settlement of settlements, as blockchain creates the possibility of peer-to-peer trading of any assets in a verifiable ledger, which reduces the risk of default. Rapid processing allows funds and their managers to invest less capital and therefore better invest the capital they have. Fund operation, accounting, and administration are also simplified, and fees so far paid to third parties performing specific services for the fund (e.g. for accounting, administration, or storage) can be significantly reduced or even excluded thanks to the automation of the indicated services.

Blockchain technology and smart contracts will enable the emergence of many new financial products and instruments in the securities market, thereby creating new asset classes for capital investment. The ability to issue digital assets along with the fractionalization of existing ones will most likely translate into more potential investors. At the same time, lowering the cost of issuing new securities and increasing the speed of issuance allow new instruments to be better suited to the needs of new investors. The programmable nature of digital assets and financial instruments is one of the factors reducing potential risks for investors, especially those related to the lack of liquidity. The possibility of establishing a direct relationship between the investor and the capital seeker, which is created by blockchain technology and smart contracts, results in lower costs of a single transaction, higher potential liquidity of assets, closer adjustment of the product to the investor's needs, its time horizon or the level of acceptable risk. On a macro level, this means higher capital market efficiency, greater liquidity of capital, and a lower cost of capital. Additionally, a transparent, distributed and verifiable blockchain ledger allows the investor to view the quality of the offered instrument at any time, increasing the level of due diligence of the parties. This technology is also potentially able to prevent certain types of risk, through, among others, the immutability of the blockchain, which in practice means that the data of a specific transaction cannot be changed after its execution.

Blockchain technology and smart contracts can find many applications in securities markets. First of all, attention should be paid to the possibility of creating a digital representation of both traditional securities and completely new digital assets, which are introduced to the market in the form of tokens. Also, conventional assets covered by various securities can be digitalized and a token created in this way will represent them. Blockchain technology allows for new efficient mechanisms to bring digital securities to market, e.g. in the form of centralized or decentralized exchanges, matching algorithms, or bilateral negotiations. In addition, investors can benefit greatly from collateral management, which in its current form is inefficient due to limited ability to react to existing market conditions, for example, an investor has limited ability to optimize his margins. Collateral management with blockchain becomes more efficient by digitizing the collateral held in a single registry. In addition, smart contracts allow collateral to be managed more accurately through the ability to issue margin calls and rule calls for specific relationships, bilateral or indirect.

Another important application of smart contracts in the securities market can be found in the settlement, which is the process of making updates and organizing the movement of money and securities, i.e., the exchange of assets and financial instruments. Smart contracts can be programmed to associate payments with transfers made outside the chain of cash payments, cryptocurrencies, or stablecoins. The algorithm can combine various models that take into account risk acceptance and market liquidity needs, including atomic settlement, deferred settlement, and net deferred settlement.

Smart contracts along with the digitization of blockchain networks can act as a digital transfer agent whose primary function in the securities market is to handle customer settlements for money transfers and orders, i.e., it is responsible for maintaining the ownership register, which is an accounting record of all events regarding the participants' participation, for example, personal and contact information, information about all transactions: acquisition date, number and purchase price, etc. The transfer agent assists registered shareholders and manages transfers, issues, or redemptions of shares. A smart contract would maintain the chain of custody of assets and coded payment instructions for the asset lifecycle. Investors could thus receive payment or have access to review materials without additional tasks for the agent, and the digital agent could record net subscriptions and liquidations of redemptions initiated by the investor. In addition, a smart contract could identify share classes and automatically distribute dividends. The digital agent could also perform a number of other tasks if it were programmed properly.

12.6 Conclusions

The implications of new technologies, including AI, blockchain and smart contracts cause a number of discussions in legal and economic circles. Hence, the risk and benefits resulting from AI-based systems and smart contracts' use are to be identified and assessed, while ensuring that its application is consistent with safeguarding financial stability. The deployment of these technologies is particularly beneficial to the financial market, which, in order to fulfil its role of supporting the economy, needs to undergo reforms and be technically and legally adjusted to the current technological revolution. There are many positive consequences of using the above-mentioned technologies in the financial market, such as the elimination of intermediation, a significant reduction in transaction costs, the elimination of agencies, and depersonalized trust. At the same time, emerging risks from the use of AI techniques and smart contracts are to be identified and mitigated in order to promote responsible AI.

Bibliography

Almasoud, A.S., Eljazzar, M.M., Hussain, F.: Toward a self-learned smart contracts. In: *2018 IEEE 15th International Conference on e-Business Engineering (ICEBE)*, Xi'an, pp. 269–273, 2018.

Bloomberg, "*What's an Algo Wheel'? And Why Should You Care?*, Bloomberg Professional Services, 2019.

Cao L., *AI in Finance: Challenges, Techniques and Opportunities*. 1, 1, 2021.

Chamber of Digital Commerce, *Smart Contracts: 12 Use Cases for Business and Beyond*, 2016. https://www.perkinscoie.com/images/content/1/6/v2/164979/Smart-Contracts-12-Use-Cases-for-Business-Beyond.pdf

Czarnecki J., *Czym są inteligentne kontrakty i DAO?*, w J. Czarnecki (red.) *Blockchain, inteligentne kontrakty i DAO*, Warszawa, 2016.

Deloitte, Artificial *Intelligence, The Next Frontier for Investment Management Firms*, 2019. https://www2.deloitte.com/content/dam/Deloitte/dk/Documents/financial-services/artificial-intelligence-investment-mgmt.pdf

FSB, *The Use of* Supervisory *and Regulatory Technology by Authorities and Regulated Institutions: Market Developments and Financial Stability Implications*, 2020. https://www.fsb.org/wp-content/uploads/P091020.pdf

Goldenfine J., Leiter A., *Legal Engineering on the Blockchain: Smart Contracts as Legal Conduct*, Social Science Research Network, 2018.

Gould M., *Why the Finance Industry Id Ripe for AI Disruption*, Techonomy, 2016.

Hazard J., Haapio J., *Wise Contracts: Smart Contracts that Work for People and Machines*, Social Science Research Network, 2017.

IEC White Paper, *Artificial Intelligence across Industries XI*, 2018.

Janusz W., *Oczywiste i mniej oczywiste zastosowania sztucznej inteligencji w sektorze finansowym*, [w:] *Raport:Sztuczna inteligencja w bankowości*, 2020.

Metz C., *The Rise of the Artificially Intelligent Hedge Fund*, Wired, 2016.

OECD, *Artificial Intelligence, Machine Learning and Big Data in Finance: Opportunities, Challenges, and Implications for Policy Makers*, 2021.

Pecyna M., Behan A., *Smart Contracts – Nowa Technologia Prawa Umów*, Transformacje Prawa Prywatnego, 2020.

Piech K., *Leksykon pojęć na temat technologii blockchain i kryptowalut*, 2018.

Rogers J., Jones-Fenleigh H., Sanitt A., *Arbitrating Smart Contract disputes, International Arbitration Report*, Northon Rose Fulbright, October 2017.

Saveleyev A., *Contract Law 2.0: "Smart" Contracts as the Beginning of the End of Classic Contract Law*, Information and Communications Technology Law, 2017.

Scott S., *It's not Enough for Banks to Admit Misconduct. They've Got to Prevent It*, American Banker, 2020.

Sherborne A., *Blockchain, Smart Contracts and Lawyers*, 2017. International Bar Association 2017, https://theblockchaintest.com/uploads/resources/International%20Bar%20Association%20-%20Blockchain%20smart%20contracts%20and%20lawyers%20-%202017%20-%20Dec.pdf

Szabo N., *Smart Contracts*, 1994. http://www.fon.hum.uva.nl/rob/Courses/InformationInSpeech/CDROM/Literature/LOTwinterschool2006/szabo.best.vwh.net/smart.contracts.html

Szabo N., *Formalizing and Securing Relationship on Public Networks*, Volume 2, Number 9, 1997.

Szostak D., *Blockchain a Prawo*, Warszawa, 2018.

Szostak D., *Sztuczna inteligencja a kody. Czy rozwiązaniem dla uregulowania sztucznej inteligencji jest smart contract i blockchain?*, [w:] *Prawo sztucznej inteligencji* (red.) L. Lai, M. Świerczyński, Warszawa, 2020.

Szpringer W., *Blockchain jako innowacja systemowa*, Warszawa, 2019.

Zalewski T., *Definicja sztucznej inteligencji* [w:] *Prawo sztucznej inteligencji* (red.) L. Lai, M. Świerczyński, Warszawa, 2020.

13 Development of cryptoassets and their wider impact

Katarzyna Ciupa

13.1 Introduction

Capital markets are constantly changing, with new technologies often considered as their main drivers. It results from the fact that new technologies create opportunities both to change existing solutions as well as to define new concepts able to challenge the established status quo. In recent years, blockchain technology has started being considered as one of the key technologies with the strongest potential to change the world order. The reason behind that is its broad spectrum of application possibilities across multiple sectors and its possibility to enable the creation and operation cryptoassets. Cryptoassets, with cryptocurrency called bitcoin described in a paper entitled "Bitcoin: a peer-to-peer cash system" (Nakamoto, 2008) being their first representative, are examples of broad representatives of value generated (created), exchanged, and reported in a decentralized and distributed blockchain ledger (Ciupa, 2019, 2020). They lack a universal and well-accepted definition because of, on the one hand, their continuous development and emergence of new proposals, and, on the other hand, their global nature, requiring coordinated efforts to harmonize and structure the proposed approaches. For example, according to Markets in CryptoAssets Regulation, which was introduced in 2020 "'crypto-asset' means a digital representation of value or rights which may be transferred and stored electronically, using distributed ledger technology or similar technology" (European Commission, 2020). In turn, the Financial Stability Board defines cryptocurrency as "a type of private asset whose perceived or intrinsic value is based primarily on cryptography and a distributed ledger or similar technology" (Financial Stability Board, 2019). Due to the growing interest in cryptoassets among both individual and institutional players, cryptoassets have begun to be considered even as an entirely new asset class (Brave New Coin, 2018; Hu et al., 2018), which, interestingly, could often lead to more confusion rather than offer more clarity. Conscious of the growing number of challenges related to the emergence and development of cryptoassets, the aim of this chapter is to discuss the development of the cryptoasset market, with a main focus on the emerging trends, ongoing changes and possible prospects for further development. The

DOI: 10.4324/9781003310082-19

structure of this chapter is as follows: first, a brief introduction to the world of cryptoassets including their role and place within the blockchain system is provided. Next, the types of cryptoassets are characterized including the overview of changes occurring within the cryptoassets' market. Finally, this chapter ends with a concise summary including key takeaways.

13.2 Blockchain technology and its role in the development of cryptoassets

The concept of a decentralized and distributed ledger, also referred to as a database or registry, was first introduced in a paper published in 2008. This document, titled "Bitcoin: a peer to peer cash system," describes the concepts of an independent and non-centrally governed monetary system (Nakamoto, 2008; Nowakowski, 2017), which, despite the lack of central coordination, is able to be self-governed and thus to deliver its promise. The concept appeared shortly after the collapse of Lehman Brothers, one of the world's largest financial institutions, which is often seen as the official start of the Great Financial Crisis (Koehn, 2009; Konopczak et al., 2010). The timing of the publication was not accidental as the concept presented in the paper is considered a manifesto against the central and often highly manipulated solutions which led to the outbreak of the second biggest financial crisis in the history of mankind.

The concept described in the paper proposes a full decentralization, dispersion, independence from central entities, transparency and pseudo-anonymity. It also offers the solution to the problem of copying, which until its publication was an inherent risk to the digital world (Catalini & Gans, 2018; Davidson et al., 2016; Pilkington, 2016). Because of its features and structure, the concept aims to be considered a self-contained system enabled by a skillful combination of advanced cryptographic technologies and peer-to-peer networks. It introduces a concept of value representatives and is managed and governed by central and predefined tailored rules and principles that comprise the logic of the solution (Antonopoulos, 2018; Nowakowski, 2013). The element that is fundamental to this concept is decentralized and distributed ledger, often called blockchain, despite the fact that the term "blockchain" is not used even once in the cited paper. Blockchain, considered a decentralized and distributed structure and infrastructure, however, is only one (i) out of three key elements of the newly proposed system. The other two are (ii) records, i.e. examples of value representatives, and (iii) centralized logic, i.e. a set of rules, principles and procedures defining how the system should work. Once the system is described as a combination of these three critical elements, it automatically suggests that all three elements are necessary for its proper functioning, which play a key role in the proposed concept. Such definition and understanding of the system, as a result, also implies that cryptoassets, being the main subject of this chapter, are a fundamental element of the system and thus play a crucial role in this concept as well.

The first term that was used to refer to the records generated and stored in the decentralized and distributed ledger, which in this chapter are described as examples of value representatives, was the term "cryptocurrency". Their very first representative, the so-called bitcoin, did not represent or backed anything and was also not associated with any particular object or solution. Its value resulted from both the value given to it by the users of the system and supply and demand forces. Additionally, the author of the cited paper in which bitcoin was described, used the term "cash" in the subtitle. It all resulted in the fact that the very first name that was given to or associated with the concept of digital value representative was cryptocurrency.

As time passed, new proposals, more or less similar to the original concept, have been defined. It caused the term "cryptocurrency" to become both insufficient and often inappropriate, especially with regard to these proposals that differed significantly from the first example.

This led to the introduction of a new term, namely "token", which started being used with regard to all different examples of value representatives (Conley, 2017; Pilkington, 2016).

This term was supplemented with adjectives and nouns, depending on the specific proposition of each newly introduced structure, which made it possible to distinguish among different types of tokens. With the number of new concepts and thus new terms constantly growing, especially during the 2016–2018 time period (often called the "ICO bubble" due to the rapid increase and even more rapid fall of crypto-financed businesses), it became extremely challenging to navigate through such an environment. As a result, the taxonomy of tokens (or more precisely, cryptotokens) was required. One of the first players that comes up with possible categorization was the Swiss Capital Markets Regulator, FINMA, which identified four types of cryptotokens (FINMA used the term "token" in their publication, thus the term "token" is being used to describe the FINMA's approach): (i) payment token, (ii) utility token, (iii) asset token, (iv) hybrid token (FINMA, 2018). Figure 13.1 presents the summary of the token types and their definitions provided by FINMA.

Due to the list of cryptocurrencies constantly growing along with the capitalization of the whole crypto market, all cryptotokens but especially cryptocurrencies, have started being considered as an increasingly important element of the financial market. This led to the introduction of yet another term, namely "cryptoassets" which despite still being used for all crypto-concepts, was also referring to another term "assets", widely spread and used across financial markets (Brave New Coin, 2018; Hu et al., 2018). As a result, cryptoassets have started being referred to not only as an increasingly important element of the financial market but also as an entirely new asset class which stood out from traditional financial assets. While it was hard to disagree with the former, the latter observation turned out not to be always correct. This was due to the fact that while cryptocurrencies were definitely a new technological solution, they were not always a completely new concept.

Type	Payment Tokens	Utility Tokens	Asset Tokens	Hybrid Tokens
Definition	Payment tokens (synonymous with cryptocurrencies) are tokens which are intended to be used, now or in the future, as a means of payment for acquiring goods or services or as a means of money or value transfer. Cryptocurrencies give rise to no claims on their issuer.	Utility tokens are tokens which are intended to provide access digitally to an application or service by means of a blockchain-based infrastructure.	Asset tokens represent assets such as a debt or equity claim on the issuer. Asset tokens promise, for example, a share in future company earnings or future capital flows. In terms of their economic function, therefore, these tokens are analogous to equities, bonds or derivatives. Tokens which enable physical assets to be traded on the blockchain also fall into this category.	Tokens in which the requirements are cumulative; (…) i.e. the tokens are deemed to be both securities and means of payment.

Figure 13.1 Token types by FINMA
Source: Based on Guidelines for enquiries regarding the regulatory framework for initial coin offerings (ICOs)

In case when cryptotokens, despite being newly generated in the blockchain, were the examples of value representatives of common financial instruments, the basic concept behind the cryptotoken was still a traditional financial instrument, only this time represented in a new blockchain-powered way. Nevertheless, there have been also such cryptotokens, which were introduced and represented the new proposition, fully justifying the usage of the term "cryptoassets" as a new category. In the further part of this chapter, the terms "cryptotoken" and "cryptoasset" are used interchangeably.

Before proceeding to a detailed discussion on the market of cryptoassets, it is worth explaining why the records placed in a decentralized and distributed database are referred to as value representatives. Such an approach to one out of three key elements of the blockchain system is dictated by the fact that each such record on the blockchain, namely cryptotoken, represents a specific but widely understood value. As there is a wide range of different values, there is a long catalog of cryptotokens, which, however, as was already mentioned above, could be grouped into three or four main categories, as suggested by FINMA. Payment cryptotokens, often called cryptocurrencies, are examples of value representatives of universal value carriers, and thus could be considered as an alternative to traditional fiat currencies (money). It results from the fact that cryptocurrencies, like fiat currencies, do not have an intrinsic value derived from the value of the material used for their production or any other object, but their value results from both the trust in the issuer of such currency and the supply/demand forces. Therefore, cryptocurrencies, in theory, could be used analogously to fiat currencies. However, in practical sense cryptocurrencies lack the status of legal tender and are not recognized by or guaranteed by central banks (with a few exceptions such as El Salvador which in mid-2021 announced that bitcoin would be treated as a legal tender) and therefore their acceptance as a means of payment is limited (Browne, 2022). Utility cryptotokens, on the other hand, are examples of value representatives of the value of specific products or services, because such utility cryptotokens are required for the usage of the product or service with which they are interlinked. The third category, namely asset cryptotokens, are examples of value representatives of the value of broadly defined assets, and thus the value of such asset cryptotoken is determined by the value of the underlying (represented) asset. The fourth category of cryptotokens, called hybrid cryptotoken, is, as the name suggests, used with regard to such cryptotokens which, due to their mixed nature and features, cannot be categorized as one of the categories listed above.

One additional point which should be emphasized is the fact that contrary to cryptocurrencies which together with the other two key elements of the blockchain system, make such a system or solution complete, the other types of cryptotokens do not allow for that. It results from the fact that other types of cryptotokens are only value representatives of objects or solutions which exist externally to the three-element blockchain system. One can use such cryptotokens in order to track the value of the underlying object or use the application where such cryptotoken is required. However, one still needs an underlying object or solution in order to take consumable advantage of it. Also ensuring that the cryptotoken represents the true value of the interlinked object or solution and that such object or solution exists are only a few of many challenges that are accompanying the usage of cryptotokens and their development.

The final category of cryptotokens identified by FINMA is a hybrid cryptotoken which applies to all constructs which do not fall under one of three previously described categories.

13.3 Development of the cryptotokens' market

Development of the cryptotokens' market consists of overview and analysis of changes that have occurred in relation to different categories of cryptotokens, including newly defined versions of already existing cryptotokens, as well as cryptotokens which have aimed to represent a completely new proposition. As suggested in the previous subsection, there is no universally accepted taxonomy which categorizes all cryptotokens unambiguously and precisely, and the taxonomy proposed by FINMA is only a good starting point. The reason behind the lack of universally accepted categorization is the fact that cryptoassets' market is still dynamically evolving and many new proposals are being defined on an ongoing basis, forcing continuous assessments and updates (Bartolucci & Kirilenko, 2020; Hu et al., 2018; Momtaz, 2018). Despite the lack of a single standard and universally accepted classification, it is possible to identify the changes and trends that have occurred with respect to types and categories of cryptotokens suggested by FINMA.

The first example of a cryptotoken is, as already mentioned, bitcoin, referred to as a cryptocurrency or as an example of a value representative of a universal value carrier. It represents the native cryptocurrency and is often perceived as a classic and original cryptocurrency, due to its characteristics and universal usage. The innovativeness of bitcoin and its uniqueness, provide an incentive to define new examples of cryptotokens, starting with other cryptocurrencies, which in their essence were analogous to bitcoin, however often differ significantly in terms of their features and built.

Cryptocurrencies such as litecoin,[1] bitcoin cash,[2] monero[3] and zcash[4] can be considered analogous examples of cryptocurrencies, which differ from bitcoin, for example, in the speed of transactions or the ability to ensure full anonymity. A characteristic feature of cryptocurrencies is a fixed supply limit. In the case of bitcoin, the limit is 21 million, while for litecoin it is 84 million (supply limits for selected cryptocurrencies are presented in Figure 13.2). Setting a supply limit is an important differentiator for cryptocurrencies from the commonly used fiat currencies, the number of which can be, in practice, freely modified. Such a fixed supply limit is supposed to be perceived as an incentive to own cryptocurrencies as a kind of protection mechanism against rising inflation often present among fiat currencies. The rigid limit, however, also poses a challenge because, among other things, it encourages price speculation proved by the dynamic and significant changes in the price of cryptocurrencies. Dynamic and significant price changes, in turn, make it difficult to use cryptocurrencies as a means of payment and as a means of settlement, which further encourages their usage for speculative purposes.

Name	Short name	Supply Limit
Bitcoin	BTC	21 millions
Ripple	XRP	100 billions
Bitcoin Cash	BCH	21 millions
Litecoin	LTC	84 millions
Stellar	XLM	100 billions
Cardano	ADA	45 billions

Figure 13.2 Cryptocurrency supply limit – overview
Source: Based on Cryptocurrencies and blockchain. Legal context and implications for financial crime, money laundering and tax evasion

In response to the observed challenge of extreme price volatility among classic cryptocurrencies, the concept of stablecoin was proposed. As the name suggests, stablecoin aims to maintain a stable price by linking cryptocurrency either to (i) fiat currencies (e.g., the U.S. dollar) or other examples of assets, or to (ii) other cryptocurrencies, or (iii) through hybrid mechanism, or (iv) in yet another way that allowed for stability (Blockdata, 2018; Bullmann et al., 2019). As it turns out, stable cryptocurrencies, however, are not free from problems either. They were for example accused of not having the right amount of collateral, a controversy that involved the tether cryptocurrency (Chohan, 2019). Other examples of stablecoin cryptocurrencies are MakerDao,[5] NuBits[6] or Paxos.[7]

In addition to classic cryptocurrencies and stablecoins, the concept of a central bank digital currency (CBDC), which is also referred to as a central bank digital currency (Alonso et al., 2021; Dabrowski & Janikowski, 2018; European Central Bank, 2012) has been defined and since then has been gaining in popularity. As of June 2022, the CBDC is not only being researched, but several countries also decided to launch their own CBDC incl. The Bahamas or Nigeria and others are undergoing pilot projects to test this concept (China, South Africa, Sweden)[8] (Alonso et al., 2021; Kosse & Mattei, 2022). It is worth noting that the concept includes very different solutions, which while all assume the issuance of cryptocurrency (digital currency) by the central bank, they differ significantly in terms of details of the issuance and operating rules, with some proposing only a new technological solution, and others planning a new monetary system, operating on different monetary principles.

In addition to cryptocurrencies, the continuous development of blockchain technology and the creativity of people willing to experiment with it, led to the development of new categories of cryptotokens, starting with utility cryptotokens (Benoliel, 2017; Camacho, 2018; Mougayar, 2018). They emerged with the invention of the Ethereum blockchain which is also famous for the introduction of the concept of self-executing programs, commonly referred to as smart contracts (Bartoletti & Pompianu, 2017; Kostro, 2019). In order to use the Ethereum blockchain, however, one has to have its native cryptotoken, called ether. It is because every act that is aimed to be performed on the Ethereum blockchain, requires the payment of the so-called "gas fee", which can only be done in ether. Ethereum thus linked the usage with the requirement of having enough ether, and thus defined the new category of cryptotokens. Their association with a specific solution, and thus lack of universal applicability, typical for classic cryptocurrencies, have led to them being given the very new name of utility cryptotokens. The concept of utility cryptocurrency, since its first introduction, has gained significance and has been met with great interest which is confirmed by a long catalog of solutions using utility cryptotokens. This catalog includes, for example, such initiatives as Filecoin,[9] which is a decentralized data warehouse, Golem[10] defined as a solution that allows the exchange and trading of computing power between interested parties or Steemit,[11] which assumes a mechanism for rewarding creators for posting content in the network. It is worth noting that the concept of utility cryptotoken was only introduced by the Ethereum blockchain and initiatives aimed at using utility cryptotokens are not forced to rely on the Ethereum blockchain. It is possible to design and build other blockchains with their own utility cryptotokens, and there are many examples of ventures that have decided to do so, such as Waves,[12] Cardano[13] , or Solana[14] just to name a few.

Unlocking the possibility of linking the cryptotoken with the dedicated solution has also caused the concept to start gaining in popularity as a sort of funding or fundraising mechanism. This mechanism, commonly referred to asInitial Coin Offering (ICO) (although the correct name according to the author of the chapter should be Initial Cryptotoken Offering due to different types of cryptotokens being applied across different ICOs, not limited to cryptocurrencies), was firstly presented in 2012, however, it received much attention in the period of 2016–2018 (Ante et al., 2018; Arnold et al., 2019; Blockdata, 2018; Fisch, 2018; Hacker & Thomale, 2017; Momtaz, 2019). The idea behind ICO is to link the payment (usually in fiat money) with the possibility to use the newly built solution in the future. The financing donor (often referred to as the investor) in exchange for its payment, also receives the cryptotoken which can often be traded and exchanged on cryptocurrency platforms, the so-called cryptoexchanges. ICO thus brought liquidity into early-stage financing and due to its open nature, allowed everybody to participate in this new financing mechanism. This led to the huge popularity of ICO among both financing donors and financing recipients, who have often invested and received very significant amounts of funds through it.

This is confirmed, for example, by the EOS (https://eos.io/) initiative, which raised funding in excess of $4 billion. In 2018, the market value of the funding raised through ICO exceeded $21 billion (Momtaz, 2019; Smith & Crown, 2019; Suberg, 2018). Mechanisms, however, proved to be abused by many businesses. Over the course of 2017 alone, more than 80% of the initiatives that raised funding through ICO turned out to be fraudulent and were never implemented (Alexandre, 2018). This led to the gradually diminishing interest with ICOs being used mostly in private and limited communities.

It is worth noting that the ICO mechanism, while initially assuming the issuance of utility cryptocurrency, was not limited to this category of cryptotokens. With their popularity gradually increasing and the link to financial aspects, they turned out to be used to issue cryptotokens that by their characteristics and principles of operation often resemble financial instruments. Financing donors, aware that many initiatives are only at the beginning of the implementation of the presented concepts, and thus are burdened with a high risk of inability to deliver or even complete uncertainty, wanted to be rewarded for the risk or uncertainty they were willing to take. As a result, cryptotokens, in addition to being linked to the usage of newly built solutions and the exchanging/trading possibility, also turned out to offer, for example, an appropriate share in the profit generated by the financed solution. In order to distinguish the new opportunity from the initial ICOs, they began to be referred to as Security Token Offering (STO) (Aitken, 2019; Sinha, 2019). The use of this STO mechanism, however, despite the great similarity to the solutions present in the traditional financial market, often took place in isolation from the existing regulations. The use of new technology solutions to implement well-known concepts in the financial markets however does not exempt such solutions from compliance with existing regulations. As a result, the regulatory regime should apply. Such a regime however should also be appropriately updated to reflect the changing environment and existing regulations need to be adapted to new technological possibilities. It has been noted by many supervisory bodies around the world, which either individually or jointly have been working on defining the regulatory landscape applicable to blockchain-based solutions.

Cryptotokens thus increasingly often turned out to become a blockchain representation of broadly understood objects or assets[15], which often exist outside the blockchain ecosystem. These objects turned out to be physical objects such as precious stones, evidenced by the Everledger project,[16] which creates blockchain-based value representatives of the value of physical diamonds. Other examples are initiatives Goldchain[17] and Aurus[18] which offer blockchain-based value representatives of the value of precious metals such as gold. In addition to stones or precious metals, there have been multiple attempts to create blockchain-based value representatives of the value of real estate or medical drugs (an initiative carried out, for example, by Merck and IBM) as well as many other physically occurring objects (Groenfeldt, 2017; IBM, 2016, 2017, 2019; Lemp, 2018; Miller, 2019).

Apart from physically existing objects and financial instruments, examples of representatives of digitally existing objects also began to appear. The use of blockchain allowed for the generation of their unique value representatives, commonly referred to as non-fungible tokens (NFT), thanks to which the management of digital objects and the optimal distribution of the value generated by these objects aimed to be improved. One spectacular (in terms of value) example was the NFT token representing Jack Dorsey's (CEO of Twitter and Square) first tweet which went on sale for $48 million and was sold at auction for $290 million (Shalvey, 2021).

Additionally, more and more financial incumbents also started understanding and thus experimenting with the new opportunities, also favoring or even demanding a clear regulatory regime (Chang et al., 2020; Tapscott & Tapscott, 2017). Such financial industry players have seen the huge potential of blockchain with regard to multiple, often long and administrative-heavy processes. They have started considering blockchain as a technology able to improve existing infrastructure or create new solutions which can considerably improve and speed up the execution, handling and reporting of various types of transactions. The result of these endeavors often has been also, as already mentioned, the creation of blockchain representatives of already existing or newly issued financial instruments.

The application of blockchain in relation to financial industry processes was not only limited to existing players. It has been also undertaken by many other, independent and new entities, which sought to eliminate existing inefficiencies. It is worth noting that taking actions to use blockchain and cryptotokens could be seen as a kind of natural response of the financial market to new opportunities because a substantial number of financial instruments are primarily in a digital form. Handling, processing and transacting of such digital forms however due to their digital nature, is prone to the risk of being copied and thus requires the participation of multiple entities governing the usage of digital forms of financial instruments. It is that digital form and the observed challenges associated with it that caused cryptotokens to become digital representations of different classes of already existing assets. Since when it has become possible to represent these assets in a way that was not vulnerable to the risk of copying, it is not surprising why such an opportunity has attracted interest.

Being aware of how the cryptoassets market has developed due to the emerging types and their popularity, it is worth referring to the value of the cryptoassets market and how this value has changed over time.

Based on statistics presented on Coinmarketcap,[19] a portal dedicated to the cryptocurrency market, the first values relating to the value of the cryptoassets market go back to the end of April 2013, when the value reached around $1.7 billion. The value of the market has gradually increased, with the greatest growth occurring during the period of popularity of the ICO mechanism, when in January 2018 the market was worth more than $743.7 billion. The period between 2016 and 2018 (in particular, the end of 2017 and the beginning of 2018) was described by many observers as a speculative bubble, which may be supported, also by the fact that less than a year later, the value of the market reached "only" $113.3 billion. Subsequently, again, the cryptoassets market was subject to slight changes, however, as a result of the COVID-19 pandemic, after initial declines, it reached a value significantly exceeding the previously observed levels. Indeed, on May 13, 2021, the value of the cryptocurrency market reached $2.42 trillion. However, already on May 20, 2021 this value fell to the level of 1.66 trillion dollars, thus losing almost a trillion dollars in the course of a week.

Taking the bitcoin example, it can be easily observed and proved how highly volatile is the cryptoasset market. The dynamic changes are evidenced by the price of bitcoin, which within only 24 hours could fall by about 25% (March 2020), as well as grow from a level of about 10,000 to over 60,000 dollars in six months (October 2020–March 2021).

The market capitalization of bitcoin at the time of preparing this part of the chapter (May–June 2022) was also subject to dynamic changes due to the worsening economic conditions and the fear of economic recession. From a level of about 48,000 in March 2022 fell to the level of about 19,000 dollars[20] (as of June 18, 2022, it is exactly 19,193.24 dollars[21]). Prices of other cryptocurrencies are also subject to significant fluctuations, nevertheless, due to significantly lower prices than the price of bitcoin, their market valuation is also at lower levels (for example, the price of ether is $1,000.77, litecoin $45.18, bitcoin cash $117.02[22]). It is also worth mentioning the stablecoin tether, which is not subject to price fluctuations (as its price remains stable i.e. 1 tether = 1 dollar), however, is famous for both its daily trading volume being (usually) the highest among the cryptocurrencies and the problem of not being fully collateralized. As of June 18, 2022, for example, tether's daily trading volume is over $50 billion which is almost twice as large as bitcoin's trading volume, which is being over $33 billion.

These statistics overall confirm the aforementioned considerable volatility of the cryptoassets market, referring to the values themselves, but also to the speed of changes. Additionally, the dynamic and significant price changes, accompanied by the constant development of the cryptoassets market itself, make it highly challenging to predict its future prospects. Moreover, the observed price volatility among almost all cryptotokens, including the changes in the price of bitcoin, has been another important argument in favor of regulation for cryptoassets (Gibraltar Finance. HM Government of Gibraltar, 2018; Hughes, 2017; Obie & Rasmussen, 2018; The Law Library of Congress, 2018). However, due to the global nature of cryptoassets and thus their market having no geographical boundaries by design, a global regulatory approach is required. This, in turn, implies the need for joint work across multiple jurisdictions and regulatory regimes, which will likely take time. In the meantime, various local approaches would be defined, which, however, may only have brought additional complexity into the already highly complex cryptoassets market. One key challenge which is often observed relates to the definitions themselves. As there is no universally accepted definition of cryptotoken, many more or less similar definitions have been defined. Unfortunately often different players try to take advantage of such vulnerability and prove that their constructs do not fall into defined categories.

What is however required is common sense so that one is not bounded by definitions but can reasonably identify what is and what is not a blockchain-based cryptotoken.

13.4 Summary

The market for cryptoassets is one of the most dynamically changing markets. Its development has, so far, been carried out in an unregulated manner, determined, on the one hand by new technological opportunities, and on the other by the growing interest of players.

Since the first example of a cryptotoken, namely cryptocurrency bitcoin, was introduced, there have been many very different examples of cryptotokens, which can be grouped into three or four key categories. These types are payment include cryptotokens, utility cryptotokens, asset cryptotokens and hybrid cryptotokens. Due to the increasing interest in cryptotokens among multiple players, more and more physical and digital objects have been given their blockchain-based value representations.

The dynamic price changes of the cryptotoken market, which within a week could decrease by almost a trillion dollars, prove how important is to provide both structure and regulation into this segment of the global economy. Due to the global nature of the cryptotoken market, only the globally accepted and harmonized approach could be successful. These however require a significant amount of time and effort to be defined. In the meantime local approaches to cryptomarket will dominate, bringing only more challenges in an already highly challenging environment.

Notes

1 https://litecoin.org/.
2 https://bitcoincash.org/.
3 https://www.getmonero.org/.
4 https://z.cash/.
5 https://makerdao.com/en/.
6 https://nubits.com/.
7 https://paxos.com/.
8 https://www.atlanticcouncil.org/cbdctracker/.
9 https://filecoin.io/.
10 https://www.golem.network/.
11 https://steemit.com/.
12 https://waves.tech/.
13 https://cardano.org/.
14 https://solana.com/.
15 The term object or asset in this chapter is used to describe all possible physical or digital examples of anything that can be (or more accurately, whose value can be) presented on a blockchain.
16 https://everledger.io/.
17 https://goldchaincrypto.io/.
18 https://aurus.io/.

19 https://coinmarketcap.com/.
20 Dollar used in the paper are meant to be the American dollars.
21 https://coinmarketcap.com/, 14:45.
22 https://coinmarketcap.com/, 14:50.

Bibliography

Aitken, R. (2019, March 8). *After "Crypto's Winter", ICOs Growing Less but Maturing with Shift to STOs.* Forbes. https://www.forbes.com/sites/rogeraitken/2019/03/08/after-cryptos-winter-icos-growing-less-but-maturing-with-shift-to-stos/

Alexandre, A. (2018). *New Study Says 80 Percent of ICOs Conducted in 2017 Were Scams.* Cointelegraph. https://cointelegraph.com/news/new-study-says-80-percent-of-icos-conducted-in-2017-were-scams

Alonso, S. L. N., Jorge-Vazquez, J., & ReierForradellas, R. F. (2021). Central Banks Digital Currency: Detection of Optimal Countries for the Implementation of a CBDC and the Implication for Payment Industry. *Journal of Open Publication,* 7(21). https://www.econstor.eu/bitstream/10419/241657/1/1752630688.pdf

Ante, L., Sandner, P., & Fiedler, I. (2018). Blockchain-Based ICOs: Pure Hype or the Dawn of a New Era of Startup Financing? *Journal of Risk and Financial Management, 11*(4), 80. https://doi.org/10.3390/jrfm11040080

Antonopoulos, A. (2018). *Bitcoin dla zaawansowanych. Programowanie z użyciem otwartego łańcucha bloków.* Helion.

Arnold, L., Brennecke, M., Camus, P., Fridgen, G., Guggenberger, T., Radszuwill, S., Rieger, A., Schweizer, A., & Urbach, N. (2019). Blockchain and Initial Coin Offerings: Blockchain's Implications for Crowdfunding. In H. Treiblmaier & R. Beck (Eds.), *Business Transformation through Blockchain: Volume I* (pp. 233–272). Springer International Publishing. https://doi.org/10.1007/978-3-319-98911-2_8

Bartoletti, M., &Pompianu, L. (2017). *An empirical analysis of smart contracts: Platforms, applications, and design patterns.*

Bartolucci, S., & Kirilenko, A. (2020). A model of the optimal selection of crypto assets. *Royal Society Open Science.* https://royalsocietypublishing.org/doi/full/10.1098/rsos.191863

Benoliel, M. (2017, August 8). *Understanding the Difference between Coins, Utility Tokens and Tokenized Securities.* Medium. https://medium.com/startup-grind/understanding-the-difference-between-coins-utility-tokens-and-tokenized-securities-a6522655fb91

Blockdata. (2018). *Stablecoins—An Overview of the Current State of Stablecoins* (pp. 1–31). Blockdata. https://download.blockdata.tech/blockdata-stablecoin-report-blockchain-technology.pdf

Brave New Coin. (2018). *General Taxonomy for Cryptographic Assets.* https://bravenewcoin.com/enterprise-solutions/taxonomy

Browne, R. (2022, April 28). *Central African Republic Becomes Second Country to Adopt Bitcoin as Legal Tender.* CNBC. https://www.cnbc.com/2022/04/28/central-african-republic-adopts-bitcoin-as-legal-tender.html

Bullmann, D., Klemm, J., & Pinna, A. (2019). *Occasional Paper Series in Search for Stability in Crypto-Assets: Are Stablecoins the Solution?* (No. 230; pp. 1–55). European Central Bank. https://www.ecb.europa.eu/pub/pdf/scpops/ecb.op230~d57946be3b.en.pdf

Camacho, J. (2018, December 11). *Utility Tokens: A General Understanding.* Medium. https://medium.com/coinmonks/utility-tokens-a-general-understanding-f6a5f9699cc0

Catalini, C., & Gans, J. S. (2018). *Initial Coin Offerings and the Value of Crypto Tokens* (Working Paper No. 24418). National Bureau of Economic Research. https://doi.org/10.3386/w24418

Chang, Y., Iakovou, E., & Shi, W. (2020). Blockchain in Global Supply Chains and Cross Border Trade: A Critical Synthesis of the State-of-the-Art, Challenges and Opportunities. *International Journal of Production Research, 58*(7), 2082–2099. https://doi.org/10.1080/00207543.2019.1651946

Chohan, U. W. (2019). *Are Stable Coins Stable?* (SSRN Scholarly Paper ID 3326823; pp. 1–10). Social Science Research Network. https://papers.ssrn.com/abstract=3326823

Ciupa, K. (2019). Blockchain – zdecentralizowany system o scentralizowanej logice. *Bank i Kredyt, 50*(3), 295–328.

Ciupa, K. (2020). *Blockchain. Wartość w Trzech Wymiarach*. Difin SA.

Conley, J. P. (2017). *Blockchain and the Economics of Crypto-tokens and Initial Coin Offerings*. http://www.accessecon.com/Pubs/VUECON/VUECON-17-00008.pdf

Dabrowski, M., & Janikowski, L. (2018). *Virtual Currencies and Central Banks Monetary Policy: Challenges Ahead*. 33.

Davidson, S., De Filippi, P., & Potts, J. (2016). *Economics of Blockchain*. 23.

European Central Bank. (2012). *Virtual Currency Schemes*. European Central Bank. https://www.ecb.europa.eu/pub/pdf/other/virtualcurrencyschemes201210en.pdf

European Commission. (2020). *Markets in Crypto-Assets Regulation*. European Commission. https://eur-lex.europa.eu/resource.html?uri=cellar:f69f89bb-fe54-11ea-b44f-01aa75ed71a1.0001.02/DOC_1&format=PDF

Financial Stability Board. (2019). *Crypto-assets: Work Underway, Regulatory Approaches and Potential Gaps* (pp. 1–15). Financial Stability Board. https://www.fsb.org/wp-content/uploads/P310519.pdf

FINMA, E. F. (2018, February 16). *FINMA publiziert Wegleitung zu ICOs*. Eidgenössische Finanzmarktaufsicht FINMA. https://www.finma.ch/de/news/2018/02/20180216-mm-ico-wegleitung/

Fisch, C. (2018). *Initial Coin Offerings (ICOs) to Finance New Ventures: An Exploratory Study* (SSRN Scholarly Paper ID 3147521). Social Science Research Network. https://papers.ssrn.com/abstract=3147521

Gibraltar Finance. HM Government of Giblartar. (2018). *Token Regulation* (p. 9).

Groenfeldt, T. (2017, March 25). *IBM And Maersk Apply Blockchain to Container Shipping*. Forbes. https://www.forbes.com/sites/tomgroenfeldt/2017/03/05/ibm-and-maersk-apply-blockchain-to-container-shipping/

Hacker, P., & Thomale, C. (2017). *Crypto-Securities Regulation: ICOs, Token Sales and Cryptocurrencies under EU Financial Law* (SSRN Scholarly Paper ID 3075820). Social Science Research Network. https://papers.ssrn.com/abstract=3075820

Hu, A., Parlour, C. A., & Rajan, U. (2018). *Cryptocurrencies: Stylized Facts on a New Investible Instrument* (SSRN Scholarly Paper ID 3182113). Social Science Research Network. https://papers.ssrn.com/abstract=3182113

Hughes, S. D. (2017). Cryptocurrency Regulations and Enforcement in the U.S. *W. St. U. L. Rev., 45*, 1.

IBM. (2016, June 30). *IBM + Credit MutuelArkea Complete Blockchain Project* [CTB10]. www-03.ibm.com/press/us/en/pressrelease/50087.wss

IBM. (2017, August 22). *IBM Announces Major Blockchain Collaboration with Dole, Driscoll's, Golden State Foods, Kroger, McCormick and Company, McLane Company, Nestlé, Tyson Foods, Unilever and Walmart to Address Food Safety Worldwide*. https://www.

newswire.ca/news-releases/ibm-announces-major-blockchain-collaboration-with-dole-driscolls-golden-state-foods-kroger-mccormick-and-company-mclane-company-nestle-tyson-foods-unilever-and-walmart-to-address-food-safety-worldwide-641378083.html

IBM. (2019, August 9). *Maersk and IBM Introduce TradeLens Blockchain Shipping Solution—August 9, 2018*. IBM News Room. https://newsroom.ibm.com/2018-08-09-Maersk-and-IBM-Introduce-TradeLens-Blockchain-Shipping-Solution

Koehn, N. (2009, September 16). Lehman in Context: A Historical Perspective. *Harvard Business Review*, June 2009. https://hbr.org/2009/09/lehman-and-the-opportunity-for

Konopczak, M., Sieradzki, R., & Wiernicki, M. (2010). Kryzys na światowych rynkach finansowych – wpływ na rynek finansowy w Polsce oraz implikacje dla sektora realnego. *Bank iKredyt*, *41*(6), 45–70.

Kosse, A., & Mattei, I. (2022). Gaining momentum – Results of the 2021 BIS survey on central bank digital currencies. *BIS, Monetary and Economic Department*, *125*, 1–23.

Kostro, P. (2019, May). Blockchain czynikontraktyinteligentnymi. *MIT Sloan ManagementReviewPolska*. https://mitsmr.pl/blockchain-czyni-kontrakty-inteligentnymi/

Lemp, L. (2018, May 23). *Everledger's Pioneering Blockchain Work for Diamonds*. THINK Blog. https://www.ibm.com/blogs/think/2018/05/everledger/

Miller, R. (2019, May 28). IBM-Maersk Blockchain Shipping Consortium Expands to Include Other Major Shipping Companies. *TechCrunch*. http://social.techcrunch.com/2019/05/28/ibm-maersk-blockchain-shipping-consortium-expands-to-include-other-major-shipping-companies/

Momtaz, P. P. (2018). *Initial Coin Offerings* (SSRN Scholarly Paper ID 3166709; pp. 1–42). Social Science Research Network. https://papers.ssrn.com/abstract=3166709

Momtaz, P. P. (2019). Token Sales and Initial Coin Offerings: Introduction. *The Journal of Alternative Investments*, *21*(4), 7–12. https://doi.org/10.3905/jai.2019.21.4.007

Mougayar, W. (2018, August 6). *Tokenomics—A Business Guide to Token Usage, Utility and Value*. Medium. https://medium.com/@wmougayar/tokenomics-a-business-guide-to-token-usage-utility-and-value-b19242053416

Nakamoto, S. (2008). *Bitcoin: A Peer-to-Peer Electronic Cash System*. https://bitcoin.org/bitcoin.pdf

Nowakowski, W. (2013). Kryptograficzne aspekty technologii wirtualnej waluty BitCoin. *Elektronika*, 58–62.

Nowakowski, W. (2017). *Geneza i Rozwój Kryptowalut oraz technologii blockchain*. Instytut Maszyn Matematycznych. https://wojciechmnowakowski.files.wordpress.com/2017/12/plikgenezakryptowalut.pdf

Obie, S. J., & Rasmussen, M. W. (2018, July 17). How Regulation Could Help Cryptocurrencies Grow. *Harvard Business Review*, July 2018. https://hbr.org/2018/07/how-regulation-could-help-cryptocurrencies-grow

Pilkington, M. (2016). *Blockchain Technology: Principles and Applications*. University of Burgundy.

Shalvey, K. (2021, March 24). *Twitter CEO Jack Dorsey's First Tweet Sold for $2.9 Million on Sunday. The Buyer Said It's the Mona Lisa of Tweets*. www.businessinsider.com. https://www.businessinsider.com/twitter-ceo-jack-dorsey-sell-first-tweet-nft-sunday-2021-3?IR=T#:~:text=Twitter%20CEO%20Jack%20Dorsey's%20first, the%20Mona%20Lisa%20of%20tweets.&text=An%20NFT%20version%20of%20Twitter, Mona%20Lisa%2C%20said%20the%20buyer

Sinha, S. (2019, September 1). *IEOs, ICOs, STOs and Now IDOs—How to Raise Funds for Crypto in 2019?* CoinDesk. https://cointelegraph.com/news/ieos-icos-stos-and-now-idos-how-to-raise-funds-for-crypto-in-2019

Smith & Crown. (2019). *EOS.* Smithandcrown.com. sci.smithandcrown.com/projects/eos

Suberg, W. (2018, June 1). *EOS About to Secure a Record $4 Bln in Year-Long ICO.* Cointelegraph. https://cointelegraph.com/news/eos-about-to-secure-a-record-4-bln-in-year-long-ico

Tapscott, D., & Tapscott, A. (2017, March 22). Blockchain Could Help Artists Profit More from Their Creative Works. *Harvard Business Review*, March 2017. https://hbr.org/2017/03/blockchain-could-help-artists-profit-more-from-their-creative-works

The Law Library of Congress. (2018, June). *Regulation of Cryptocurrency around the World.* https://www.loc.gov/law/help/cryptocurrency/cryptocurrency-world-survey.pdf

14 Digitalization of reporting standards on the capital markets

Arkadiusz Szymanek and Tomasz Wiśniewski

14.1. Introduction

Technological changes that deepen the digitization of financial markets also include the reporting area. In the capital markets, in recent years, we have observed an increase in the scope of information obligations that must be met by listed entities with the simultaneous development of information processing technologies, resulting in the need to introduce uniform standards for defining various data so that there is a possibility of their structured collection and automatic processing.

Reporting processes occurring in the capital market are characterized by different principles of information flow. Natural standardization processes are insufficient. Despite the less and less use of paper forms, the digitalization of reporting leads to a large diversity and difficulties in obtaining consistency and comparability of the submitted reports. Due to the great variety of entities in the capital market, reporting includes text formats, spreadsheets, documents in PDF format, and files in XML and XSD structures. At the same time, it should be emphasized that the electronic formats of the files sent by no means enforce standards in terms of content and do not ensure the required data quality. Precise numerical information is necessary for the financial statements of listed companies, investment funds, brokerage houses, or in reports for banks and as tax documents. One such solution that allows you to achieve both goals is the eXtensible Business Reporting Language (XBRL).

XBRL is an international, electronic and interactive concept for standardizing the description of the business and economic data. Its purpose is to organize and systematize the organization of data in reports sent by participants of the economic environment. Standardization allows for the automatic transmission and verification of data and, consequently, enables the implementation of advanced analytical methods. XBRL is a free standard maintained by over 600 organizations and companies affiliated with XBRL International Consortium.

DOI: 10.4324/9781003310082-20

14.2 EFES with XBRL – the standard for issuers in the EU

In connection with the announcement of the European Securities and Markets Authority (ESMA), with effect from 2020, all annual consolidated financial statements of issuers of securities admitted to trading on a regulated market in the European Union, prepared in accordance with International Financial Reporting Standards (IFRS), require preparation in a uniform European reporting format using XBRL tags. The basis is the Regulation of the European Union Commission 2019/815 on the uniform electronic reporting format as European Single Electronic Format (ESEF).

In the consolidated financial statements prepared in the uniform ESEF reporting format for reporting periods beginning in 2020 or later, it is necessary to present only basic information (statement of comprehensive income, statement of financial position, statement of changes in equity, statement of cash flows, in consolidated financial statements prepared in accordance with IFRS).

Starting from January 1, 2022, reporting in the uniform ESEF format will also include notes to the consolidated financial statements, but the marking of additional information will be performed in a block format. However, it should not be ruled out that the need for detailed marking of the amounts included in the explanatory notes will be the next stage in the implementation of XBRL reporting.

Listed companies (generally issuers) taking into account the taxonomy according to the guidelines, ESMA should consider, among others:

- The need to apply the extensions to own annual financial statements and determine which items in the existing financial statements will require the application of the extensions. What are the requirements for a potential extension?
- Clarification of whether all the necessary financial data can be provided via existing systems or whether the accounting IT systems need extensions.
- Should the process of preparing the annual financial statements, including roles, competencies and responsibilities, be optimized?
- What other areas should be included? Should the format of financial data provided by subsidiaries be changed in the future?

The implementation of the standard is a challenging issue from the perspective of entities and supervisory body. In the case of Poland, Financial Supervision Authority (KNF) released the functionality of sending test versions of ESEF reports from January 11, 2021, in the production environment of the Electronic Information Transmission System. The regulator combined the higher number of risks related to implementation with issuers of securities from the regulated market, who prepare and publish consolidated annual reports containing consolidated financial statements prepared in accordance with IFRS. While writing the article, the process of reporting financial statements of listed companies for 2020 was just beginning.

14.3 XBRL history

In 1998, Charles Hoffman, a tax advisor examined XML for electronic reporting of financial information and he communicated to Wayne Harding, chairman of the AICPA (Association of International Certified Professional Accountants) High Tech working group. AICPA Committee Organization Committee decided to finance the project of creating a prototype set of financial statements in XML format. In 1999 prototype was presented to AICPA, which requested that a business plan be prepared to investigate the business case for XML-based financial statements.

In 1999 the AICPA Board of Directors decided to fund the XFRML effort and joined the project as members of their Steering Committee. The committee included AICPA, Arthur Andersen, Deloitte & Touche, Ernst & Young, KPMG, Microsoft Corporation, PricewaterhouseCoopers and many others. AICPA and ten organizations began experimenting with creating financial statements in this standard, which allowed for testing the concept of creating and sending financial statements based on XML. In 2000 the organization was officially renamed to the XBRL Steering Committee and published the first specification for US companies as "XBRL for Financial Statements". In the following years, the system developed and broke through to regulators of capital, banking and fiscal markets in various countries.

14.4 The concept of standardization

The basic idea of XBRL is to allow the conceptual extension and physical separation of the data area (event reporting) from the organization of a multi-level metadata system. In the past, business organizations generated financial information and made it available to users in low-structured, static, paper-based or electronic documents. Comparing data and aggregating financial information from different companies required re-entering the data into a spreadsheet or other program for further work in specialized programs. Such programs require formatted data, usually in the form of flat files. XBRL, on the other hand, allows companies to work with financial data interactively, reuse and update it. This applies to all economic organizations that make financial information available to various public organizations and a wide range of analysts and stock market investors.

Rather than treating financial information as a block of text – like a standard web page or printed document – XBRL uses an identification identifier for every single piece of data. It is readable by a variety of computer programs. For example, a company's net profit has its own unique tag. Computers can "intelligently" treat XBRL data because they can recognize information in an XBRL document, mark it, analyze it, store it, exchange it with other computers and present it to users automatically in various ways.

Metadata is used to convey the conceptual meaning of reporting data items in a standardized manner. The XBRL data model is an extension of the basic data types functioning in XML, which is the basis for XBRL. It is also possible to enter additional datasets so that XBRL becomes synonymous with real-time business reporting. This opens the possibility for the standard to be widely used in businesses related to Internet activities and for companies specializing in reporting for suppliers and report users.

An XBRL document is an XML document that conforms to the XBRL format and typically contains the information required in a single periodic financial report, report or statement. Each data item in an XBRL document is tagged with an identification tag defined in the XBRL taxonomy. So, every piece of information in an XBRL document has a definitive definition of what it is, what it means, and what rules it follows.

XBRL uses the same mechanism given that it is XML-based, but extends it along with an extensive metadata infrastructure to carry a wider range of diverse information about the data. This applies to information about:

- Relationships (hierarchical and non-hierarchical)
- Presentation formats
- Calculations & Rules
- Semantic definitions

The XBRL community is creating an increasing number of shared, free taxonomies, each containing thousands of data elements, covering multiple accounting standards in multiple languages. XBRL taxonomies have so far been developed for:

- GL (Global Ledger), content modeling of accounting books, sub-books and other types of transaction logs;
- US GAAP (Generally Accepted Accounting Principles), which covers US financial statements, notes and disclosures, and management opinions and analysis;
- IFRS, which is the core of IFRS disclosures, which are then expanded on a country-by-country basis to meet local statutory requirements;
- COREP (Common Reporting), covering the requirements of 25 European countries for reporting by banking supervision authorities under Basel II;
- GAAP national taxonomies in Japan, Germany, South Korea and Sweden.

An interesting direction is a work on the development of taxonomies for various economic sectors, the so-called industry taxonomy. On the other hand, geographically, XBRL has received support in Asia and the Pacific, and is also gaining recognition in Europe.

14.5 The benefits and disadvantages of the reporting ecosystem

From the perspective of comparability, XBRL has two main directions: the first involves a level of standardization that improves the comparison of financial and non-financial data between corporations and/or subsidiaries. The second direction focuses on company-level taxonomies that reduce the comparability of financial and non-financial data (Alles & Piechocki, 2012). Therefore, standard taxonomies have the advantage of using common terminology and similar concepts for element mapping (Plumlee & Plumlee, 2008). Additionally, XBRL enables the interpretation of data from different taxonomies (Debreceny et al., 2009), as it represents a data standard with an identical structure.

In the case of transparency, according to Mihaela (2013), XBRL increases transparency by allowing access to the detailed information provided by organizations, including easy access and the ability to process information, even if it is reported in multiple languages or is dependent on different regulations. XBRL enables a consistent representation of aggregated data provided by multiple branches/subsidiaries as every underlying business transaction can be tracked (Valentinetti & Rea, 2013).

Since the information in the XBRL standard is standardized, it can be exchanged between various applications and systems, which allows to increase the complexity of various processes (Piechocki, 2007b). On the other hand, the frequency of errors decreases as mapping or reconciling information due to incompatible applications is not a problem. XBRL improves the accuracy of corporate disclosures presented (Debreceny & Gray, 2001).

Based on the literature, it is necessary to point out the positive impact of XBRL, which is the improvement of audit processes related to the transfer and efficient performance of audit procedures on standardized financial data (Robert, 2003). According to Grasegger and Weins (2012), continuous audit improves the overall quality of the audit and XBRL opens the possibility of conducting the continuous, ongoing audit.

Authors of publications on XBRL agree that the standard increases access to relevant financial information (Debreceny & Gray, 2001; Troshani & Rao, 2007; Alles & Piechocki, 2012). This improves the performance of search, reporting and analysis functions. The fact that less time is spent on data mapping, analysis and decision-making has a positive effect on the added value in the area of analysis.

Aksoy and others (2021) researched reporting on the Turkish capital market. The XBRL mandate could be much more burdensome to smaller firms in Turkey. This may stem from the fact that larger firms may tend to use the in-house approach for XBRL and can afford more advanced financial reporting systems with automated coding algorithms attached to streamline their XBRL filings, whereas smaller firms are more likely to use the outsourcing approach due to the difference in the level of resources available for XBRL preparation.

It is often found in the literature that XBRL enables end-of-reporting process improvement, as the electronic generation, processing, and electronic communication of financial information via XBRL encounter reduced cycle times (Valentinetti & Rea, 2012; Enachi, 2013). Therefore, many authors conclude that XBRL enables faster reporting (Gomaa et al., 2011). Consequently, it would be conducive to quick decision-making.

The researchers conclude that XBRL may indirectly reduce information asymmetry in financial markets (Efendi et al., 2011a). Investors benefit from greater transparency and the power of information providers is limited. It can be stated throughout the academic literature that corporations submitting documents to XBRL support investor aspirations, while the availability of XBRL filing benefits investors (Jones & Willis, 2003). The overall efficiency of the financial market improves.

The success of XBRL development largely depends on the availability and development of the software as otherwise, the entire process is very error-prone and impossible to manage without a reliable software application. However, software vendors providing solutions are still at an early stage of development (Piechocki, 2007a). The current state of available software is still poor compared to other standardized reporting tools (Miloš & Zuzana, 2006). The literature cites several reasons for the limited offer of XBRL tools: investor demand is low due to the high complexity of XBRL, incomplete know-how and XBRL-enabled software that is available as free shareware (Boyer-Wright, 2010). In addition, existing solutions are standalone XBRL applications that do not offer integrated solutions for the entire financial statement process. It can be assumed that IT tycoons such as SAP (Cohen, 2009), Peoplesoft, and IBM, by following the development of the data mat, will more easily identify missing products in their offer and supplement the portfolio of products or business partners in the form of smaller application suppliers. Examples include SAP, which acquired Cundus XBRL Solutions in 2010 (SAP, 2010) and IBM, which acquired Clarity XBRL Solutions in 2010,

Most of the current financial reporting requirements have emerged in isolation from the independent needs of various external and internal organizations. The consequence is an increase in direct or indirect costs for all organizations involved in financial reporting. The most common challenges include:

- Data collection – resources and versioning of collected information
- Data Quality – information accuracy and quality assurance management costs
- Redundancy – multiple reports or multiple report versions of a given report
- Inconsistency – contradictory/ambiguous terminology or different aggregation rules
- Information consistency – inconsistent rules or formats used for different reports and/or sent in different reporting periods

These challenges are manifested in costs for all participants of the reporting ecosystem. These are not just one-off, often volatile, costs, and are scattered throughout the reporting ecosystem and over the lifetime of the reporting ecosystem.

In 2006 in the Netherlands the General Reporting Feasibility Study delivered the first set of functionalities required for financial purposes XBRL reporting, the Dutch taxonomy is a structured list of reporting definitions, guidelines, references, rules and relationships in accordance with the relevant laws and regulations. The assumption is that public agencies are freed from unnecessary tasks related to compliance and monitoring of enterprises, and that they are motivated to improve reporting procedures. However, the implementation of the new architecture has proven to be a complex process in which many organizations are involved and must take into account the functioning of heterogeneous technologies and a changing regulatory environment (legislation). Despite several years of the project's implementation, the benefits have not been fully realized and some reporting needs in business relationships, government agencies still remain with the days of paper forms. The launch of the Dutch SBR (Standard Business Reporting) system required deeper changes to the reporting method and consideration of how the company maintains and uses its own financial, accounting and payroll information to meet reporting requirements imposed by various government agencies. The implementation process lasted three years before the necessary conditions for starting SBR production were met. The transformation processes of the Dutch reporting ecosystem have not been completed. One obstacle to further transformation was the lack of regulatory support that would pressure the use of XBRL in other areas of financial reporting (Figure 14.1).

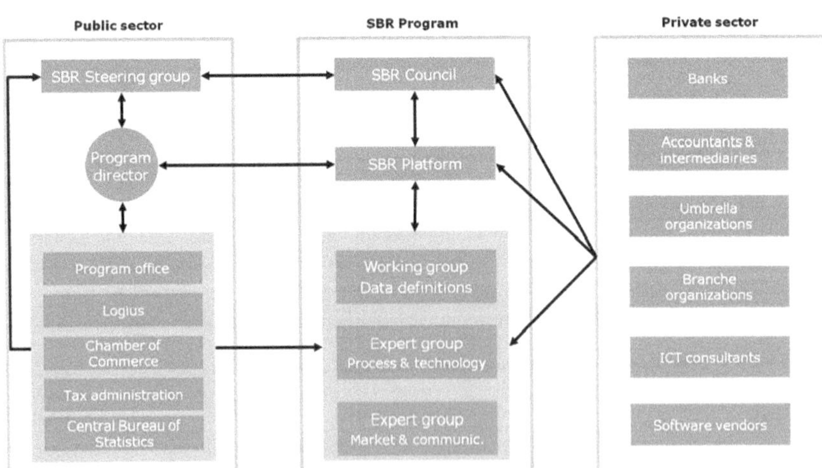

Figure 14.1 Schematic of the concept of the SBR program in the Netherlands
Source: Logius

In 2007, Australia began the implementation of "standard business reporting" as part of the Standard Business Reporting project. The first phase of work on the implementation of XBRL was related to communication standards between government agencies and companies, as well as cooperation between various government agencies. The benefits of implementing the project resulted in lower costs for enterprises by up to 25%, i.e. over a billion dollars a year (Standard Business Reporting, 2012). The project of deepening the digitization of business reporting is being implemented gradually and is becoming a global approach to the implementation of XBRL at the state administration level. Similar projects are already underway in many countries such as New Zealand and Singapore.

14.6 Regulatory activities for reporting in the EU

In 2004, the European Commission officially called on its members to use the XBRL taxonomy. It also began to support the harmonization of the standard and cooperation to promote the standard. CEBS (the Committee of European Banking Supervisors) also recommended the adoption of the XBRL standard. As a result, at the end of 2005, the Committee of European Banking Supervisors incorporated the XBRL standard into the financial reporting framework. The main aim of this project is to enable comparability of financial statements and simplify reporting of cross-border credit institutions in an integrated European financial market. The process of describing taxonomies to be applied at national level by regulators and supervision has begun. The taxonomies covered the areas of COREP (Basel II) and FINREP (Financial reporting – IFRS). In the first period, the digitization of financial reporting in the EU was carried out on a voluntary basis, but there was also pressure from national regulators to base the digitization on XBRL for technical matters. Therefore, in some EU countries, it started to be used earlier in financial reporting than in other European countries.

The results of local, fragmented implementations encouraged wider use of the XBRL taxonomy and obtain global benefits (CEBS, 2015). XBRL enabled the achievement of a uniform format for the exchange of financial and business information, which allowed to reduce the human labor intensity in the reporting ecosystem on financial markets. This process will reduce human involvement and significantly simplify analytical work for supervisors and other financial market participants. The initial phase was completed at the end of 2007, presenting the most important findings, conclusions and recommendations for the organization of the rest of the project (Annual Report, CEBS, 2017). Convergence was largely achieved, especially in FINREP reports by commercial banks. The effects were weaker in the COREP reports.

In the second phase of the project, CEBS recommended the adoption of XBRL for financial reporting purposes, albeit still on a voluntary basis, where the project was reviewed with a view to making more progress in the convergence of bank financial reporting. The main role of CEBS was to provide assistance to members and to adapt the standard to specific reporting needs. XBRL can be used to standardize data transmission both among enterprises and financial institutions. COREP is intended for credit institutions and investment firms to report their solvency ratios under the Capital Requirements Directives (CRD) 2006/48 and 2006/49. A second, called FINREP (Financial Reporting), has been designed for credit institutions that apply International Accounting Standards (IAS)/International Financial Reporting Standards (IFRS) to their published statements (Table 14.1).

Table 14.1 Example of XBRL implementation

Entity	*Description*
The Danish Enterprise Authority (DBA)	Collects XBRL financial reports from approximately 240,000 private companies operating in Denmark. Such a broad and structured database allows for the introduction of innovative applications of machine learning techniques to predict possible corporate bankruptcies and other dynamic phenomena in various economic sectors. The purpose of DBA is to provide early warning to entrepreneurs whose companies show signs of bankruptcy.
The National Securities and Exchange Commission (NSSMC)	Financial reports prepared in Inline XBRL will be filed with the NSSMC, and the data will also be passed on to other government agencies. Reported data will also be made publicly available to improve transparency in the financial market. The aim of the Ukrainian project was to develop a business reporting standardization mechanism (SBR "one-time report") and ultimately reduce administrative burdens and costs by simplifying the number of data definitions and introducing a single communication portal for sending financial and business reports later to various interested state institutions.
The Deutsche Bundesbank	The project assumed the use of the ability to generate XBRL financial statements for tax purposes. Moreover, commercial banks have access to the digital database of reports. They use XBRL reports to perform credit risk assessments and determine creditworthiness.
ING Bank	In 2015, ING started to offer discounted fees on loan and credit applications to its SME clients if they provided XBRL financial statements via the Dutch SBR platform. When information is delivered in digital format, banks are better informed about their clients' financial profiles. In 2017, ING introduced a requirement for its clients and potential clients to use a digital standard or to pay extra for the traditional paper-based application.

Source: own elaboration based on www.xbrl.org

It was assumed that the digitization process based on the XBRL taxonomy will introduce clearly defined substantive concepts and implement strong data validation rules. Transparent data organization structures will improve the quality and comparability of data for wider use. The authors of the project hoped to expand digital reporting implementations and disseminate XBRL also to other sectors besides banks.

As an interesting fact, the World Bank published its annual report on sustainable development in the XBRL format to promote digital agency. This allowed users to get a clearer picture of the social, environmental and economic aspects of its business. The World Bank already regularly uses XBRL to prepare financial reports and analytical documents exchanged with the European Bank for Reconstruction and Development (EBRD).

The European Banking Authority produces a remarkable range of aggregated data from its EU-wide banking records. For analysts from banking supervisors, the level of detail is unique, allowing them to select an area of interest and analyze geographic data, business lines, risk areas and institutional groups, as well as refine these results for individual institutions. For example, if an analyst is interested in non-performing loans in the south of Europe, it takes just a few clicks to get this information.

14.7 Implementation of digital reporting in local markets

The demonstrated properties of the XBRL standard constitute the basis for its widespread use on the capital market. According to XBRL International data, at the end of 2020, reporting according to this standard was valid in 54 markets around the world. Table 14.2 summarizes the countries, organizers and taxonomy models.

Japan's Financial Services Agency FSA has made XBRL reporting compulsory in order to make it easier for investors to appraise companies and conduct benchmark analyses. The Japanese regulator relatively early, as already in 2008, ordered enterprises to submit annual financial reports to the EDINET system in the XBRL format. Although the regulator assumes that the introduction of digital reporting according to the XBRL taxonomy will increase the transparency and quality of financial statements, on the other hand, there are skeptical opinions related to the high costs of implementing and learning the flow of information in the new model, inadequate to reduce the asymmetry of available information between professional and non-professional investors on the capital market. The obligation to implement the XBRL taxonomy previously in smaller capital markets was easier to implement due to the size of the market. In Japan, thousands of listed companies have been forced to use the XBRL format in a short period of time.

The American state of Florida consists of over 400 separate municipalities, including 282 cities. In line with US accounting standards, these municipalities prepare comprehensive annual financial statements (CAFR), but

Table 14.2 Capital markets reported in XBRL

Date of introduction	*Country*	*Regulations*
2005	Spain	Financial Markets Supervision
2006	Japan	XBRL Disclosure
2007	South Korea	An electronic disclosure system
2008	China, Israel, Japan	Financial Markets Supervision
2009	United States	Securities and Exchange Commission
2010	Australia, Taiwan	Reporting by listed companies on Taiwan Stock Exchange and SIC Australia
2011	Peru	The Superintendency of the Securities Market
2013	Saudi Arabia	Board Decision to implement XBRL
2014	United Arab Emirates	Emirates Securities and Commodities Authority
2015	Malaysia	Securities Commission
2016	Kuwait, Mexico, Turkey	Capital Markets Authority
2018	India	SEBI (Listing Obligations and Disclosure Requirement) (Amendment) Regulations, 2018
2020	European Union	European Single Electronic Format - ESEF
2021	European Union	European Single Electronic Format - ESEF

Source: own elaboration based on www.xbrl.org

their reports are in analog format. Given the importance of municipal bond markets in the long-term financing of local and state infrastructure, Florida is moving toward digital financial reporting and government performance. The state will require the joint design and implementation of XBRL-based reporting from its municipalities. The CAFR will be in digital form and all municipalities' financial statements for the fiscal years ending September 1, 2022, or later will be submitted in XBRL format.

14.8 XBRL in corporate governance and other non-financial reports

The issue of corporate governance has been one of the main topics of discussion in the capital market for many years, especially among international corporations. It includes the need to comply with many rules and regulations in the absence of a heterogeneous "corporate governance system" (Weimer & Pape, 1999; Leuz et al., 2003; Tylecote & Visintin, 2007), and the existence of compiled rules taken from various national solutions (Cadbury, 1993) and specific industry standards (Mach et al., 2006; Bebchuk & Spamann, 2010).

Therefore, measures are taken to integrate business disclosure rules, including the use of XBRL (Chen & Sun, 2009; Debreceny et al., 2010; Alles & Piechocki,

2012). Can XBRL help reduce the complexity of corporate governance reporting (Alles & Piechocki, 2012)? There are many articles in the scientific literature showing that XBRL can increase transparency and improve corporate governance in financial reporting (Abdullah et al., 2009; Roohani et al., 2010; Alles & Piechocki, 2012; Müller-Wickop et al., 2013). An additional research question should also be raised as to whether the use of XBRL for non-financial corporate governance reporting can contribute to increased transparency.

Corporate Governance Reporting (CGR) has become very complex for multinationals as it requires compliance with various statutory regulations and rules. It requires dealing with heterogeneous "CG systems" on an ongoing basis (Tylecote & Visintin, 2007; Weimer & Pape, 1999) and additionally compiling codes (Cadbury, 1993) and industry standards (Mach et al., 2006; Bebchuk & Spamann, 2010). XBRL was developed in accordance with the recognized standard of interactive corporate reporting (Chen, 2009; Matherne & Coffin, 2001; Debreceny et al., 2010; Felden, 2011; Alles & Piechocki 2012). The use of XBRL for Corporate Governance (CG) non-financial reporting can also be attributed to increased transparency.

Disclosure of CG information can be standardized for financial institutions, despite the increasing complexity and differences resulting from national CG regulations. However, due to the benchmarking and benchmarking process, corporations are constantly looking for best-in-class concepts that are the most efficient and provide a competitive advantage. This market impact can be traced in research (La Porta et al., 2000). Based on the results of the study, it can be concluded that only a few international financial institutions deviate from the CGR. In addition, companies, even if they do not have Anglo-Saxon CG experience, adhere to international CG principles.

GRI has developed a taxonomy covering sustainability reporting. Sustainability reporting consists of "the practice of measuring, disclosing and accountable to internal and external stakeholders for the organization's performance in order to achieve the goal of sustainable development" (Global Reporting Initiative, 2011). "Sustainability reporting" is a general term that includes reporting on economic, environmental and social impacts (Kolk, 2004).

This taxonomy was developed by the Global Reporting Initiative (GRI), a global non-profit organization that created a sustainability reporting framework that has been widely used and used around the world since the 1990s (Hedberg & von Malmborg, 2003; Kolk, 2004). The taxonomy contains quantitative and qualitative data and is available on the organization's website (Global Reporting Initiative, 2013).

14.9 Conclusions

XBRL is increasingly being adopted around the world as the standard for business and financial information exchange and reporting for more than 15 years. This study provides important initial evidence documenting the benefits of XBRL to the capital markets around the world.

The findings of this study suggest that firms that file using XBRL experience a reduction in information asymmetry and, for those smaller firms where the information environment may be poor, XBRL plays an important role in attracting an analyst following. These results are robust after controls for endogeneity and self-selection bias.

Additionally, globalization led to an intricate set of interactive relationships between individuals, organizations and states and to an unprecedented correlation of massive global systems causing systemic risk to increase exponential. Unprecedented global interaction possibilities have made communication more complex than ever before in history as the whole has different properties than the sum of its increasingly diversified parts.

Future research may empirically try to consolidate how behavioral economics can improve markets. Stakeholder-specific facets of behavioral sciences and the different scientific disciplines' approach toward digitalized economics could be outlined in the search for governance recommendations to regulate markets efficiently. Delineating the potential of behavioral economics to guide the introduction of digitalization into contemporary society portrays economics as a real-world relevant means to minimize societal downfalls and imbue trust in the digitalized world economy.

In these future research endeavors, scientists and practitioners are advised to also take a critical approach to the economic analysis of the corporation. By drawing from the historical foundations of political economy, a critical stance on behavioral sciences' use for guiding corporate concerns could also be adopted as a heterodox spin. Behavioral Economics insights should be used for improving economic analyses to foster the accuracy and efficiency of corporate sustainability reporting. The analysis could thereby also take a heterodox economics stance in order to search for interdisciplinary improvement recommendations for the use of economics in the corporate world. Investigations should feature a broad variety of research methods and tools to conduct independent projects in a truly multi-methodological approach. Overall, all these endeavors will help gain invaluable information about the interaction of economic markets with the real-world economy with direct implications for corporate decision-makers, governance experts and financial practitioners.

Bibliography

Abdullah, A., Khadaroo, I. and Shaikh, J. (2009), Institutionalisation of XBRL in the USA and UK, *International Journal of Managerial and Financial Accounting*, Vol. 1, No. 3, pp. 292–304.

Aksoy, M., Yilmaz, M.K., Topcu, N. and Uysal, Ö. (2021), The impact of ownership structure, board attributes and XBRL mandate on timeliness of financial reporting: Evidence from Turkey, *Journal of Applied Accounting Research*, Vol. 22, No. 4, pp. 706–731. https://doi.org/10.1108/JAAR-07-2020-0127

Alles, M. and Piechocki, M. (2012), Will XBRL improve corporate governance? A framework for enhancing governance decision making using interactive data, *International Journal of Accounting Information Systems*, Vol. 13, No. 2, pp. 91–108.

Bebchuk, L.A. and Spamann, H. (2010), Regulating bankers' pay, *Georgetown Law Journal,* Vol. 98, No. 2, pp. 247–287.

Boyer-Wright, K., Summers, G. and Kottemann, J. (2010), XBRL: Is it time? (extensible business reporting language), *Issues in Informing Science & Information Technology,* Vol. 7, No. 509–516.

Bulyga, R.P. and Safonova, I.V. (2020), XBRL as a digital reporting format for economic entities: International experience and Russian practice abstract, *Accounting. Analysis. Auditing,* pp. 6–17. (In Russ.) https://doi.org/10.26794/2408-9303-2020-7-3-6-17

Cadbury, S.A. (1993), Thoughts on corporate governance, *Corporate Governance: An International Review,* Vol. 1, No. 1, pp. 5–10.

Chen, G., Kim, J.-B., Lim, J.-E. and Zhou, J. (2018), XBRL adoption and bank loan contracting: early evidence, *Journal of Information System,* Vol. 32, pp. 47–69.

Chen, H.M. and Sun, W.C. (2009), Application and neediness of extensible business reporting language, *2009 International Forum on Information Technology and Applications, Vol 2, Proceedings,* Vol. 1, No. 1, pp. 409–412.

CEBS (2015/2017), https://www.eba.europa.eu/cebs-archive (accessed 29/1/2022).

Cohen, E.E. (2009), XBRL's Global Ledger Framework: Exploring the standardised missing link to ERP integration, *International Journal of Disclosure and Governance,* Vol. 6, No. 3, pp. 188–206.

Debreceny, R. and Gray, G.L. (2001), The production and use of semantically rich accounting reports on the Internet: XML and XBRL, *International Journal of Accounting Information Systems,* Vol. 2, No. 1, pp. 47–74.

Debreceny, R., Farewell, S., Piechocki, M., Felden, C. and Gräning, A. (2010), Does it add up? Early evidence on the data quality of XBRL filings to the SEC, *Journal of Accounting and Public Policy,* Vol. 29, No. 3, pp. 296–306.

Debreceny, R., Felden, C., Ochocki, B., Piechocki, M. and Piechocki, M. (2009), Multidimensionality in XBRL. *XBRL for Interactive Data.* Springer, Berlin: Heidelberg.

Efendi, J., Park, J.D. and Subramaniam, C. (2016), Does XBRL reporting format provide incremental information? A study using XBRL disclosures during the Voluntary Filing Program, *ABACUS, A Journal of Accounting, Finance and Business Studies,* Vol. 52, pp. 259–285.

Enachi, M. (2013), XBRL and financial reporting transparency, *BRAND. Broad Research in Accounting, Negotiation, and Distribution,* Vol. 4, No. 1, pp. 10–19.

Felden, C. (2011), Characteristics of XBRL adoption in Germany, *Journal of Management Control,* Vol. 22, No. 2, pp. 161–186.

Garner, D., Henderson, D., Sheetz, S.D. and Trinkle, B.S. (2013), The different levels of XBRL adoption, *Management Accounting Quarterly,* Vol. 14, pp. 1–14.

GlobalReporting Initiative. (2011), *Sustainable Reporting Guidelines"* www. globalreporting.org (accessed 12/01/2022).

GlobalReporting Initiative. (2013), *GRI-Taxonomy 2013,* www. globalreporting.org (accessed 12/01/2022).

Gomaa, M.I., Markelevich, A. and Shaw, L. (2011), Introducing XBRL through a financial statement analysis project, *Journal of Accounting Education,* Vol. 29, No. 2–3, pp. 153–173.

Grasegger, P. and Weins, S. (2012), Continuous auditing, *Zeitschrift Interne Revision-ZIR,* Vol. 47, No. 5, p. 231.

Hao, L., Fang, J. and Zhang, J.H. (2014), Does voluntary adoption of XBRL reduce cost of equity capital?, *International Journal of Accounting & Information Management,* Vol. 22, pp. 86–102.

Harding, W. and Zarowin, S. (2000), Finally, business talks the same language, *Journal of Accountancy*, Vol. August, pp. 24–30.

Hedberg, C.J. and von Malmborg, F. (2003), The global reporting initiative and corporate sustainability reporting in Swedish companies, *Corporate Social Responsibility and Environmental Management,* Vol. 10, No. 3, pp. 153–164.

Jones, A. and Willis, M. (2003), The challenge of XBRL: Business reporting for the investor, *Balance Sheet,* Vol. 11, No. 3, pp. 29–37.

Khedmati, M., Navissi, F., Sualihu, M. and Tofik-Abu, Z. (2020), The role of agency costs in the voluntary adoption of XBRL-based financial reporting; Emerald Insight at: https://www.emerald.com/insight/1743-9132.htm

Kolk, A. (2004), A decade of sustainability reporting: Developments and significance, *International Journal of Environment and Sustainable Development,* Vol. 3, No. 1, pp. 51–64.

LaPorta, R., Lopez-De-Silanes, F., Shleifer, A. and Vishny, R. (2000), Investor protection and corporate governance, *Journal of Financial Economics,* Vol. 58, No. 1–2, pp. 3–27.

Leuz, C., Nanda, D. and Wysocki, P.D. (2003), "Earnings management and investor protection: an international comparison, *Journal of Financial Economics,* Vol. 69, No. 3, pp. 505–527.

Liu, C., Luo, X. and Wang, F.L. (2017), An empirical investigation on the impact of XBRL adoption on information asymmetry: Evidence from Europe, *Decision Support Systems,* Vol. 93, pp. 42–50.

Mach, A., Schnyder, G., David, T. and Luepold, M. (2006), Transformations of self-regulation and new public regulations in Swiss corporate governance (1985–2002), *Swiss Political Science Review,* Vol. 12, No. 1, pp. 1–32.

Matherne, L. and Coffin, Z. (2001) XBRL: A technology standard to reduce time, cut costs, an enable better analysis for tax preparers, *Tax Executive,* Vol. 53, No. 1, pp. 67–68.

Mihaela, E. (2013), XBRL and financial reporting transparency, *BRAND: Broad Research in Accounting, Negotiation, and Distribution,* Vol. 4, No. 1, pp. 10–19.

Miloš, T. and Zuzana, J. (2006) International financial reporting and information technologies – is XBRL the Panacea?, *International Scientific Journal of Management Information Systems,* Vol. 1, No. 1, pp. 80–83.

Müller-Wickop, N., Schultz, M. and Nüttgens, M. (2013), *XBRL: Impacts, Issues and Future Research Directions, Enterprise Applications and Services in the Finance Industry,* New York: Springer.

Piechocki, M. (2007a), Conception of XBRL use in the financial reporting supply chain, *Tagungsband zum Doctoral Consortium der WI 2007,* Vol. 133, No. 1, pp. 43–58.

Piechocki, M. (2007b), *XBRL financial reporting supply chain architecture.* Freiberg <Sachsen>: TU Bergakademie Freiberg.

Plumlee, R.D. and Plumlee, M.A. (2008), Assurance on XBRL for financial reporting, *Accounting Horizons,* Vol. 22, No. 3, pp. 353–368.

Robert, P. (2003), XBRL awareness in auditing: a sleeping giant?, *Managerial Auditing Journal,* Vol. 18, No. 9, pp. 732–736.

Roohani, S., Xianming, Z., Capozzoli, E.A. and Lamberton, B. (2010). Analysis of XBRL literature: A decade of progress and puzzle, *The International Journal of Digital Accounting Research,* Vol. 10, No. 16, pp. 6.

SAP. (2010), *Annual Report,* online: www. sap.de (accessed 15/1/2022).

Shan, Y.G., Troshani, I. and Richardson, G. (2015), An empirical comparison of the effect of XBRL on audit fees in the US and Japan, *Journal of Contemporary Accounting and Economics*, Vol. 11, pp. 89–103.

StandardBusiness Reporting. (2012), https://treasury.gov.au/consultation/use-of-standard-business-reporting-for-financial-reports (accessed 25/1/2022).

Stantial, J. (2007), ROI on XBRL, *Journal of the American College of Cardiology*, Vol. 203, pp. 32–35.

Troshani, I. and Rao, S. (2007), Drivers and inhibitors to XBRL adoption: A qualitative approach to build a theory in under-researched areas, *International Journal of E-Business Research (IJEBR),* Vol. 3, No. 4, pp. 98–111.

Tylecote, A. and Visintin, F. (2007), A new taxonomy of national systems of corporate governance. In: Mjoset, L. and Clausen, T. H. (eds.) *Capitalisms Compared.* Oxford: Elsevier, pp. 71–122.

Valentinetti, D. and Rea, M.A. (2012), IFRS Taxonomy and financial reporting practices: The case of Italian listed companies, *International Journal of Accounting Information Systems,* Vol. 13, No. 2, pp. 163–180.

Valentinetti, D. and Rea, M.A. (2013), XBRL for Financial Reporting: Evidence on Italian GAAP versus IFRS, *Accounting Perspectives,* Vol. 12, No. 3, pp. 237–259.

Weimer, J. and Pape, J. (1999), A taxonomy of systems of corporate governance, *Corporate Governance: An International Review,* Vol. 7, No. 2, pp. 152–166.

Yoon, H., Zo, H. and Ciganek, A.P. (2011), Does XBRL adoption reduce information asymmetry?, Journal of Business Research, Vol. 64, pp. 157–163.

XBRL.org (2002), XBRL: understanding the XML standard for business reporting and finance. White Paper; available at: www.xbrl.org/Business/General/SoftwareAG-CaseForXBRL.pdf.

15 The growing role of non-financial reporting in the age of digital finance

Lidia Sobczak

15.1 Introduction

Businesses nowadays are moving away from the idea of maximizing shareholder value. This shift is in favor of building a long-term position by attending to the interests of not only owners/shareholders but also employees, customers, suppliers, the local community, and society at large. This is reflected in openly communicating information that is relevant to stakeholders. In addition to financial information, non-financial information is being increasingly disclosed. Depending on the needs, it can be communicated via different channels. It can be systematic or arise in response to an emerging need. It can be in the form of a report or an onę-off message. It can be oral or written.

Reporting can be viewed broadly as informing about achievements, intentions, or business conditions in any form. It can also be viewed narrowly as submitting systematic reports on achievements, intentions, and business conditions. The narrow approach was opted for in this chapter. Non-financial information can also be viewed broadly as all descriptive, numerical and indicative information disclosed outside financial statements and the auditor's (chartered accountant's) opinion and report. It can also be viewed narrowly as information that holds the company to social responsibility. The broad approach was used in the case under analysis.

The digitization of finance has had a significant impact on the nature of business entities operating in financial markets. Apart from fintechs and bigtechs, there are traditional financial service providers who have successfully incorporated digital technologies into their model (Gołąb, Monkiewicz, 2021, pp. 51–52). Their overall (ethical) responsibility toward stakeholders and society has long been discussed. For such companies, credibility and image are essential, with particular efforts to this end being taken by publicly traded companies as they are more exposed and have a greater number of stakeholders.

Market reporting is changing, too. Non-financial information is increasingly present in the information disclosed by companies. Are these changes

DOI: 10.4324/9781003310082-21

reflected in the reporting of publicly listed companies? The purpose of this chapter is to answer this question. To this end, a literature review and a case study of a publicly traded digital-finance institution were conducted.

15.2 The theoretical background of non-financial reporting

The growing role of non-financial information in companies' communication with different groups of stakeholders is aptly explained by the stakeholder theory.

The term "stakeholders" was first launched into social discourse by the Stanford Research Institute in 1963. It originally referred to groups without whose support the organization would cease to exist. However, thanks to R. E. Freeman, it was soon worked into the management theory for good. Freeman (1984, p. 46) defined a stakeholder as a group or entity that can either influence or be influenced by an organization pursuing its own goals. By using the term "stakeholder", Freeman drew the attention of managers to market participants who were neither employees nor shareholders but who nonetheless had a tangible impact on the fate of the undertaking (Rotengruber, 2017). According to his concept, stakeholders should be identified.

Correct identification of stakeholders requires admitting the following benchmarks (Donaldson, Preston, 1995):

1 stakeholders in a company are individuals or groups with legitimate interests in the procedural and/or substantive aspects of that company's activity;
2 stakeholders are identified on the basis of their corporate interests, regardless of whether the company shows relevant functional interest in them;
3 the interests of all stakeholders have intrinsic value, meaning that each stakeholder group is not only noteworthy on its own but also for its ability to support the interests of another group, e.g. stockholders.

By adopting these notions, we can identify and classify stakeholders in multiple ways. The simplest and most direct distinction is between internal and external stakeholders. The internal ones are usually employees and management, while the external ones are customers, competitors, suppliers, etc. We can talk about stakeholders in the narrow and wide sense. In the narrow sense, stakeholders are those who are most influenced by the organization's policy. This group typically includes shareholders, employees, management, suppliers, and performance-driven clients. In the wide sense, stakeholders are those who are weakly influenced by the organization's policy. Typically this group includes government, clients less dependent on company performance, social environment, and other peripheral groups. There are also primary and secondary stakeholders. The primary stakeholders are those without whom the organization could not function, whereas the secondary stakeholders are those who are not essential to its functioning. We can also talk about active and passive stakeholders, i.e. those who want to participate in the activities of the organization (without having to be part of the organization's formal structure) and those who do not. Stakeholders are also categorized as voluntary and involuntary. The first group is made up of those who, willingly and by choice, engage in the activities of the organization. The second group consists of those who cannot withdraw from their relationship with the organization and are stuck with it despite their will. There are also legitimate and illegitimate stakeholders, i.e. those who have legitimacy and those who have not. A distinction is made between recognized and unrecognized stakeholders, i.e. those whose interests and points of view are taken into account in devising business strategy and those whose are not. Finally, there are direct and indirect stakeholders, i.e. those who are aware of the expectations toward the organization and can express them, and those who are not aware and cannot express them on their own (ACCA, 2016, pp. 21–22). Regardless of the method of classification, stakeholders should be perceived not only as existing but also as submitting justified demands to the company (ACCA, 2016, p. 20).

Businesses should take into consideration the needs of the various groups interacting with them. There are two reasons for this: instrumental and normative. This means that a business should meet the demands of stakeholders wishing to maximize profits as well as pursue other goals. It also means that it has a moral duty to consider stakeholders' concerns and opinions while working to maintain social cohesion, morality, and overall good financial health (Donaldson, Preston, 1995). It is precisely the meeting of the needs of a wide range of stakeholders that a company's success in achieving economic and social goals depends on (Pirsch, Gupta, Grau, 2007).

Stakeholder theory identifies two approaches to stakeholder expectations. The company following a positive approach may handle all legitimate claims and expectations sustainably and seek effective methods to manage them. It comes down to identifying the most influential stakeholders and prioritizing actions that meet their needs. Under a normative approach, the company runs its businesses taking into account the claims and expectations of all stakeholders, regardless of their significance. In practice, however, the expectations of less influential stakeholders are not taken into account by the management board (Mućko, Niemiec, Skoczylas, 2021).

Satisfying the needs of stakeholders includes, among other factors, meeting their information needs (Da Silva, Aibar-Guzmán, 2010). Since priority is given to activities that meet the needs of the most influential stakeholders, it is under their pressure that greater or less significant disclosures in terms of achievements, intentions, and business conditions take place (Farneti, Casonato, Montecalvo, de Villiers, 2019).

15.3 Non-financial information

Non-financial information is transmitted primarily to meet the information needs of a wide range of stakeholders (Walińska, Bek-Gaik, Gad, 2016, p. 158). The term "non-financial information" has not yet been universally defined (Haller, Link, Groß, 2017). It has long been used in various contexts, referring to different kinds of disclosures and messages, often relying on non-traditional communication channels (Erkens, Paugam, Stolowy, 2015). The message can be descriptive (a narrative), numerical (expressed in natural or monetary units) or relative (key indicators) (Bauer, Hońko, Orzeszko, Szadziewska, 2020, p. 193).

Perrini (2006) describes non-financial information as information that helps stakeholders better understand the company's performance, business strategy, and development prospects. He includes in this set information on quality and risk management, corporate governance, strategic direction, and social and environmental performance. Orens and Lybaert (2007) indicate that such information is disclosed outside financial statements. Erkens, Paugman and Stolowy (2015), for their part, define it as information provided to stakeholders in a way other than traditional financial results and disclosed outside financial statements. Murphy and Hogan (2016), as cited in *The Financial Times*, define non-financial information as one that is not expressed in money and is reflected in annual and quarterly reports, as well as beyond them. Haller, Link, and Groß (2017) argue that non-financial information includes all quantitative and qualitative data on policy, business operations, and performance without being directly linked to the record-keeping system. For Manes-Rossi, Tiron-Tudor, Nicolò, and Zanellato (2018), meanwhile, it concerns information related to the organization's policy, its environmental and social footprint (e.g. the use of resources and energy, greenhouse gas emissions, pollution, biodiversity, climate change, waste disposal, employees' health and safety, gender equality, education) and is key to improving accountability and transparency toward stakeholders. Torre et al. (2018) approach this term in a similar fashion. According to them, the term refers to disclosures in relation to society and the environment. The plurality of approaches to defining non-financial information was noted by Tarquinio and Posadas (2020). They identified a total of six approaches to non-financial information that can be found in the literature. These are:

- information on corporate social responsibility (CSR), referring to the organization's policy, activities, and impact on the environment and society;
- information on overall business performance, not focusing on the social and environmental footprint;
- information on value creation disclosed outside of financial statements;
- non-accounting information, which is not expressed in financial terms;
- environmental, social, and corporate-governance information, or more broadly, sustainability information;

- information related to business strategy, outlining for stakeholders the mission, values, and strategic directions driving the organization.

As can be seen, non-financial information is multifaceted and diverse and can be considered both broadly and narrowly. In broad terms, the concept includes all information (descriptive or numerical, and not necessarily expressed in monetary terms) published (mandatorily or voluntarily) as part of the company's annual report, with the exception of financial statements and the auditor's own opinion and report (Bek-Gaik, Krasodomska, 2018). This means that non-financial information is additional information supplementing the information already present in financial statements (Bauer, Hońko, Orzeszko, Szadziewska, 2020, p. 194). The narrow approach to non-financial information has gained momentum along with the rooting of the concept of CSR, according to which businesses are expected to account for social and environmental matters in their operations and relationships with stakeholders (UNIDO, 2021). In the narrow sense, non-financial information is limited to matters related to (Sobczyk, 2017):

- sustainability,
- corporate social responsibility (CSR),
- environmental, social, and governance (ESG) indicators,
- ethics,
- human capital,
- environment, health, and safety (EHS).

15.4 Scope and reasons for non-financial disclosures

The scope of non-financial disclosures has changed over time. There is increasingly more information being disclosed. Bauer, Hońko, Orzeszko, and Szadziewska explored this problem (2020, pp. 195–198). They divide the timeline into four periods:

- until the late 1960s,
- from the late 1960s to the late 1970s,
- from the late 1970s until the end of the 2010s,
- from the start of the 2020s until today.

Each period was assigned the scope of disclosures against the background of changing social expectations, along with relevant guidelines and standards. The author's findings have been detailed below.

In the first period, non-financial information existed in the form of disclosures about the use of resources and social commitment. The reason for this was the growing public interest in the ethical and social aspects of corporate management and environmental degradation.

During the second period, information on fair business practices, social commitment, and the environment started being disclosed. This was prompted by the ongoing debate on the role of corporations in society and the negative impacts of their operations.

In the third period, non-financial disclosures already covered information relating to the environment, society, employees, corporate governance, risk, employee matters, company growth prospects, R&D, and non-financial key performance indicators. The background for this was:

- increasing environmental degradation,
- increasing social awareness of corporations' business models,
- adoption by the European Union of sustainability policy,
- increased interest in the concept of CSR,
- development of non-financial reporting guidelines by a number of organizations,
- the emergence of the first legal regulations for non-financial reporting in selected countries,
- Elkington's (triple bottom line – TBL) approach assuming the equivalence of the economic, environmental and social dimensions,
- growing mistrust in the information contained in financial reporting,
- and finally, the 2007 global financial crisis.

In the fourth period, financial disclosures include a description of the business model; a description of policies and their outcomes in relation to matters concerning society and employees, the environment, respect for human rights and anti-corruption practices; a description of due diligence procedures; a description of risks, key performance indicators (environmental, social, employment, respect for human rights, combating corruption and bribery). At the root of the extended scope of disclosed information were the fallout of the 2007 financial crisis, the debate on a new corporate reporting model, the commencement of works by the European Commission on developing Directive 2014/95/EU, and the gradual embrace of the concept of integrated reporting.

Along with the expansion of the scope of non-financial disclosures in the third period, non-mandatory reporting guidelines and standards emerged, such as OECD guidelines, GRI 1 & 2, AA1000 Standards, the UN Global Compact, SA8000 Standard, the EMAS system, ISO 14001 Standard, the Dow Jones Sustainability Index, the FTSE4Good Index, 2001/45/EC European Commission Recommendation of 30 May 2001 on the recognition, measurement, and disclosure of environmental information. The fourth Council Directive of 25 July 1978 on the annual accounts of certain types of companies also became effective. In the following period, two more directives entered into force: Directive 2013/34/EU of the European Parliament and of the Council on the annual financial statements, consolidated financial statements, and related reports of certain types of undertakings replacing Fourth Directive, Directive 2014/95/EU of the European Parliament and of the Council as regards disclosure of non-financial and diversity information.

In addition to this, new voluntary guidelines GRI 3 & 4, ISO 26000, and the International IR Framework emerged.

15.5 The role of non-financial disclosures in external reporting

Non-financial information can be transmitted via various channels. The way it flows depends on the stakeholders involved in the information flow. As regards investors, communication may be through teleconferences, meetings, stock and press releases, annual reports, etc. In the case of customers, communication may take place through customer interviews, websites and social networks, customer satisfaction surveys, complaints, etc. For employees, this may be via the Intranet, social forums, chats, meetings, irregularity reporting, employee satisfaction surveys, periodic interviews, etc. Communication with the local community may take place through meetings with students, employee volunteering, non-financial reports, etc. Lastly, reporting for the environment as a silent stakeholder is carried out through environmental rankings, environmental reports submitted to state authorities, the reporting of non-financial information, etc. (Bauer, Hońko, Orzeszko, Szadziewska, 2020, pp. 221–227).

Non-financial information already has a strong foothold in external reporting. The current reporting model hardly resembles a statement limited only to financial data. Instead, its content is a product of numerous modifications adopted in response to the criticism of the financial statements and the growing demand of stakeholders for extra insight into prospective and managerial information.

The reporting model is constantly being improved, and so is the model of financial statements. This process is accompanied by activities aimed at expanding disclosures to include information that would hold the company socially accountable. There are five stages in this improvement process (Figure 15.1).

In the first stage, the report was limited only to financial data in the form of a balance sheet and profit-and-loss account. In the second stage, the cash flow statement and the statement of change in equity first appeared, including additional notes. The gradual adoption of non-financial information, apart from that disclosed in additional notes, gave rise to annual reports. In the next stage, a large part of non-financial information was separated from the annual report and presented in a separate report – the management commentary (activity report). This was in response to the calls for greater transparency in terms of information concerning business operations. The current stage of corporate reporting (stage V) is marked by the intensive development of other reports, mainly non-financial (Walińska, Bek-Gaik, Gad, 2016, pp. 28–30).

All these changes have led to annual reports, business reports, and integrated reports being now the basic toolkit to communicate with the public. The annual report exhaustively describes the company's activities and

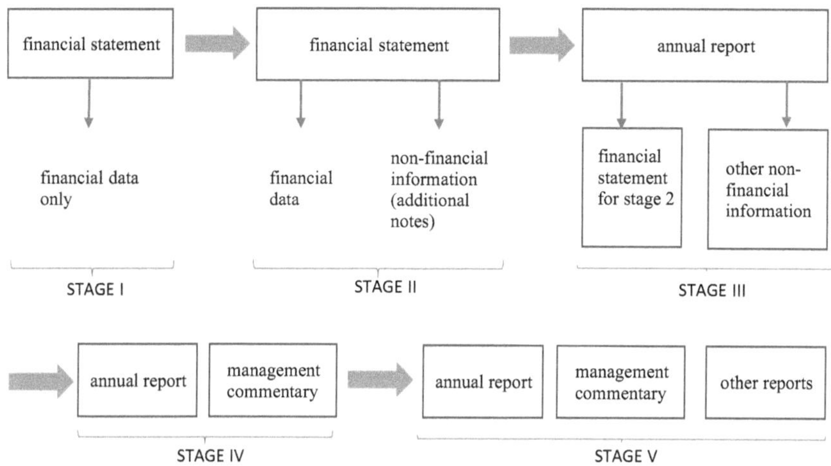

Figure 15.1 Business reporting development stages
Source: Walińska, Bek-Gaik and Gad (2016, p. 28)

contains information that facilitates decision-making. It consists of the financial statement,[1] supplementary information,[2] and supplementary reports.[3] Basic reports, along with notes, generally convey neutral information. Prospective information is presented outside financial statements (Walińska, Bek-Gaik, Gad, 2016, p. 148).

A business report can be defined in three ways. In the first approach, it is understood as a financial report (annual report), i.e. a report covering the financial statement and additional disclosures, including the management report. In the second approach, it is understood as a report separate from the financial statements, containing financial and non-financial information that facilitates decision-making on behalf of – and concerning – the organization. In the third approach, it is understood as a report separate from financial statements, containing only non-financial information (Walińska, Bek-Gaik, Gad, 2016, p. 153).

Integrated reporting is the method and tool used for communicating financial and non-financial information simultaneously. In principle, it is a concise message on the contribution to the organization's strategy, corporate governance, and external performance in creating value in the short, medium, and long term. It includes a financial report (here: financial statement and management commentary) and a relevant supplementary report (here: CSR report, sustainability report, corporate governance statements) (Walińska, Bek-Gaik, Gad, 2016, p. 155).

The stakeholder theory emphasizes communication with stakeholders. This communication can be one-way (unilateral) or two-way (bilateral). In the one-way model, the company provides information to stakeholders without expecting feedback. In the two-way model, the company provides information expecting feedback. In this second model, communication can be asymmetrical or symmetrical. Two-way asymmetrical communication occurs when it is controlled by the sender. In this case, the company presents information and obtains feedback only to the extent that is of interest to it. Two-way symmetrical communication, on the other hand, occurs when the company truly dialogues with stakeholders. Reporting non-financial information usually takes the form of one-way or two-way asymmetrical communication.

In the digital age, the most prevalent technological tool to distribute information is the Internet. For all kinds of organizations, it is an information space that is used by an ever-increasing number of people. In January 2022, there were as many as 4.95 billion Internet users worldwide used, 4% more than in the previous year. This means that 62.5% of the world's population uses the Internet (Kemp, 2022). The Internet is a space where large amounts of information can be grouped, integrated, and clearly communicated. Companies use this space for reporting in PDF, XLS, XHTML (eXtensible Hyper Text Markup Language)[4] (from 2020) file formats, previously also XML (Extensible Markup Language),[5] or via interactive files.

15.6 The growing role of non-financial reporting. A case study of a listed Polish financial institution

The importance of non-financial reporting is reflected in the constant evolution of its form and content. Efforts for the convergence of reporting standards are being undertaken by the: World Economic Forum, Global Reporting Initiative (GRI), Sustainability Accounting Standards Board (SASB), International Integrated Reporting Council (IIRC), Climate Disclosure Standards Board (CDSB), Carbon Disclosure Project (CDP), IFRS Foundation, and the European Union. The World Economic Forum has published a document on common metrics and consistent reporting. The GRI, SASB, IIRC, CDSB, and CDP are working together toward comprehensive corporate reporting. The IFRS is looking into the possibility of developing a global non-financial reporting framework. The European Union is updating its Non-Financial Reporting Directive and is considering developing non-financial reporting standards (KPMG, 2020, p. 8).

Changes in the approach to reporting non-financial information in a narrow sense on a global scale are noted by the international company KPMG. In it's *The time has come. Survey of Sustainability Reporting 2020* (KPMG, 2020), an increase in sustainability reporting is signaled. KPMG notes an increase in two groups of companies surveyed: the group of top 100 companies in terms of revenues from each of the 52 countries (N100) and the group of the top 250 world's largest companies in terms of revenue (G250). Sustainability reporting increases are significant. In 2020, 80% of the N100 and 96% of the G250 companies reported on sustainability. Compared to 1999 (the first publication of the G250 reporting rate), this means an increase of 56 p.p. in the N100 and of 61 p.p. in the G250 group. Strong increases were observed until 2011 in the G250 group. Since 2011, 90% or more of the G250 reported on sustainability. Systematic increases were observed since 1993 in the N100 group. The exception was the year 2002 (KPMG, 2020, p. 10).

In the same report, KPMG highlights the increased share of non-financial sustainability disclosures. The quality of disclosures has become so important to disclosing entities that in 2020 more than 50% of the N100 and more than 70% of the G250 outsourced data verification. Compared to 2005, this means an increase of 18 p.p. in the N100 and of 41 p.p. in the G250 group (KPMG, 2020, p. 23).

The growing role of non-financial information was also observed by Löw, Erichsen, Liang, and Postulka (2021). The authors analyzed the CSR disclosures of 70 listed and unlisted ECB-supervised banks and found the following:

- banks disclosed information on social responsibility in integrated, CSR and non-financial reports, or in GRI disclosures/explanations;
- back in 2017, most banks disclosed relevant information in integrated reports, while in the following years this trend was reversed;
- regardless of the year of analysis, most banks disclosed non-financial information in CSR or non-financial reports;
- the number of disclosures has increased after the entry into force of the Non-Financial Reporting Directive (2014/95/EU);
- listed banks disclosed more non-financial information;
- the number of disclosures relating to the code of conduct, the code of ethics, and integrity has increased; the largest increase was observed for the environment/biodiversity category.

Non-financial reporting is also playing an increasingly important role when it comes to traditional financial institutions that have successfully incorporated digital solutions into their model. This is the case of a publicly traded Polish financial institution.

PZU is the largest non-life and personal insurance company in Poland, holding a third of the market share by value of gross written premiums. PZU Group is the largest financial institution in Poland and Central-Eastern Europe. Since 2010, it has been listed on the Warsaw Stock Exchange. As the Group itself remarks, it is a large-scale organization aware of the growing expectations of various entities, including investors, clients, employees, partners, industry experts, and the social environment from which the Group's employees and clients originate. PZU carries out the management of relations with stakeholders and their impact on the business environment in a conscious and sustainable manner. To this end, it ongoingly updates its reporting methods, as has been detailed below.

So far, PZU SA has been rather successful in adopting this new reporting trend. It presents financial and non-financial information in the form of reports. The former is mainly disclosed in financial statements. It also appears derivatively in other reports. The key reports of PZU SA's current reporting model are the annual report, integrated report, and SFCR.[6] The annual report is a consolidated and standalone PZU report for a 12-month period. It is a set of consolidated and standalone financial statements, statutory auditor's reports, non-financial reports, management reports, and consolidated and standalone XHTML data(the relevant financial statements for 2020 are retrievable in XHTML, XML, or any other electronic format). The integrated report is a uniform report that combines information for a broad group of recipients from the reports constituting the annual report. The SFCR is a set of reports prepared for the Group, PZU SA, and PZU Życie, the auditor's reports for PZU SA and PZU Życie, and additional materials. It has common elements with the annual report and elements supplementing or detailing it.

PZU SA's current reporting model was adopted in response to changes in reporting supported by relevant regulatory requirements.

Annual reporting for its part has evolved, too. Consolidated and standalone statements have been content-modified several times. In its consolidated data, PZU has been publishing a financial report, a statutory auditor's report (opinion), a board report, and selected financial data, invariably since 2010. In the years 2010–2014, the European Embedded Value was additionally published. In 2010–1012, PZU published a letter from the president of the management board, which in 2013 was incorporated into the management activity report. In 2017, a non-financial report was included in the annual report. In 2019, two statements from the supervisory board, and board information were additionally included. Supplementary materials have also changed. Presentation and announcement of financial results have been published invariably. In the individual data for the years 2010–2016, PZU published a financial report, a statutory auditor's report (opinion), a board activity report, selected financial data, and a letter from the president of the management board. In 2017, selected financial data was withdrawn from the set and a non-financial report was introduced as an attachment to the management report. In 2018, the existing set was expanded to include an e-report, board information, two statements from the supervisory board, and an actuarial opinion. In 2019, a report in the electronic XML format was launched, while the e-report was abandoned. Significant changes to the main components of the annual report have also been made. Financial reporting does not cease to evolve. More and more information is being disclosed in board reports.

In the years 2010–2020, PZU Group's financial statements followed the same pattern, having been drafted in accordance with the International Financial Reporting Standards. They were composed of: a consolidated profit-and-loss account, a consolidated statement of comprehensive income, a consolidated statement of financial position, a consolidated statement of change in equity, a consolidated cash flow statement, as well as additional information and explanatory notes. The scope of disclosed additional information and explanatory notes is increasing, and so is the volume of the report.

While in 2010 it was 129 pages long, in 2020 the length was 207 pages. The standalone financial statements are prepared in accordance with Polish domestic accounting standards. They consist invariably of the following: introduction to the financial statements, balance sheet and off-balance-sheet items, a non-life and personal insurance technical account, a P&L account, a statement of change in equity, a cash flow statement, technical accounts – total direct activity, technical insurance account – active reinsurance in general, actuarial opinion, and additional information and explanations. The volume in question also increased from 150 pages in 2010 to 167 pages in 2020 (PZU, 2021a).

The management board's activity report has also seen its content change over the years. Until 2015, it was prepared separately for the operations of PZU Group and PZU SA. In 2016, the report on the activities of PZU was disclosed as consolidated and standalone data, and from 2017 joint reports on the activities of PZU Group and PZU SA have been released. PZU Group's activity report in 2010–2012 consisted of an introduction, year-specific financial results, year-specific activity, additional information, and statements from the management board. This changed in 2013. Until 2015, it was composed of letters from the president of the management board and the chairman of the supervisory board, an overview of PZU Group, external environment, activity, development strategy, organization, infrastructure and human resources, consolidated financial results, risk management, PZU's standing in the capital and debt market, CSR, corporate governance, management statements, and attachments. From 2017, CSR disclosures were excluded, while development strategies were disclosed in the sections PZU 2020- more than insurance and operating model – distribution, innovation. In the same year, the report on non-financial information was attached to the management report; in the following years, it was already a separate report. In 2018, the operating model was replaced with a business model. Essentially, PZU SA's activity report had a form similar to the Group's activity report. The difference concerned CSR disclosures, which only appeared in the Group's reports. Additionally, only once in 2013, the letters of the president of the management board and the chairman of the supervisory board were included in the report (PZU, 2021a).

Since 2010, PZU SA has been publishing non-financial reports. In 2017, they were part of the annual reports. The scope of non-financial information disclosed in these reports varied between 2010 and 2020. Until 2017, PZU SA published such reports voluntarily in a two-year system; since 2017, it does so annually. The first CSR report was developed based on GRI G3 (2006) guidelines with the use of a finance sector supplement. The report communicated to market participants information about the company's operations, capital market, and the insurer's liability, products, people, nature, and social environment. The second non-financial report was published for the years 2011–2012. It was prepared on the basis of GRI G3 guidelines with the use of a finance sector supplement. The report communicated to market participants information about the company, customer-service standards and business ethics in place, activities for the benefit of society, employee matters, and awareness of environmental impact. The third non-financial report, for the years 2015–2016, was drafted after GRI G4 guidelines. The report was divided into information about the company, business, and the world in ten key aspects. The key aspects were: the transparency of PZU's offering and accountable sales process, customer-service standards, product innovations responding to customer needs, compliance, adherence to the highest standards of external communication, approach to claims handling, combating corruption, communication channels with customers, customer data protection, PZU's commitment to industry-enhancing expert and research projects. In addition to these, the report disclosed information of less significance and described it in a less detailed manner. This included matters related to employee satisfaction and commitment, risk management, and environmental policy (PZU, 2021a).

In 2018, PZU Group and PZU SA published their first mandatory non-financial statement for 2017. It was prepared in accordance with the requirements of non-financial reporting contained in the Accounting Act and drawing on the PN-ISO 26000 standard, GRI guidelines, and the GRI G4 finance sector supplement. It communicated information divided into the following areas: management, social, employee, environmental, human rights, anti-corruption, non-financial risk management, and selected non-financial data. It was prepared in accordance with the Accounting Act, the Core version of GRI guidelines, and the IIRC guidance. The reporting spanned the following areas: management, anti-corruption, non-financial risk management, environment, social impact, employee matters, and human rights. Significant sub-areas were as follows: plans and strategy for the future, shaping ethical culture and corporate governance, company policy, due diligence procedures, communication transparency, management of individual risk groups, transparency and communication of decisions made by the Group, reducing the environmental footprint, communication initiatives related to aid support, legislative patronage, employee structure, initiatives to tackle workplace discrimination, contractual clauses regarding the observance of human rights, presentation of activities ensuring equal employment opportunities. The third mandatory report was prepared in accordance with the Accounting Act, GRI guidelines, the IIRC guidance, as well as the European Commission's guidelines for non-financial reporting detailing the reporting of climate-related deliverables and the recommendations of the Task Force on Climate-Related Financial Disclosures (TCFD). The key themes include management of individual risk groups, including ESG (Environmental, Social, Governance), business challenges in the area of digitization, R&D activities, developing technological innovations, developing innovative products, managing environmental issues within the offerings and assets, and investment (indirect impact). The fourth mandatory report, already 223 pages long, was published in 2021.

It was prepared in accordance with the Accounting Act, the GRI guidelines, the IIRC guidance, as well as the European Commission's guidelines for reporting non-financial information detailing the reporting of climate-related deliverables and the recommendations of the TCFD. Eighteen themes in four areas were identified as relevant. These areas are employee matters and human rights, social commitment, responsible management, and the environment (PZU, 2021a).

The ever-expanding volume of these non-financial reports reflects the growing role of non-financial information in PZU SA's reporting. In 2010, disclosures were 30 pages long, and in 2020, already 223 pages of reports were disclosed. The growth has been observed in all categories but is particularly evident in environmental and climate-related aspects. This is the result of new regulations and requirements, but also of concern for the environment and the public. The importance of information disclosed to this end is also evidenced by the fact that it is published on the website in a separate Sustainability section.

Since 2013, PZU SA has been releasing annual reports online on dedicated websites. The structure of these disclosures has not been homogenous. In 2013, the reports concerned the following areas: environment, activity, strategy, organization, financial results, risk management, PZU's standing in the capital market, social responsibility, and corporate governance. In 2014–2016, PZU SA reported on the following: PZU Group in 2014, activity, CSR, strategy, stock exchange and investors, corporate governance, risk management, and financial results (PZU, 2014, 2015, 2016, 2017). In 2017, a business model description and market reporting were launched, while the Social Responsibility section was scrapped (PZU, 2018). In 2018, the risk area was expanded by ethics (PZU, 2019). In 2019, report-specific information was added (PZU, 2020). Over time, the online report became more interactive and legible. In 2020, PZU SA published an online integrated report for the first time. It reported there on the areas reported so far, plus on capital and challenges (PZU, 2021b).

Meanwhile, PZU SA's SFCR has a rather short history. It has been published in a more precise form only since 2016. It invariably contains the description of operating activities and performance, management system, risk profile, valuation of assets and liabilities, and capital management. It has not been included in the annual report and functions as an independent supplementary annual report (PZU, 2021a).

PZU SA communicates its achievements and intentions to market participants on the PZU SA website, on the Annual Report page, as well as on social and streaming media. In doing so, it provides stakeholders with financial and non-financial information. The financial information is disclosed on the PZU SA website, on the Investor Relations page, and on the Annual Report page. PZU SA discloses non-financial information on its website, on its Annual Report page, and on social and streaming media. In what concerns the website, the disclosures are shared on the Investor Relations and Sustainability pages. As for the latter, PZU SA showcases its activity on Facebook, Twitter, LinkedIn, Instagram, and YouTube. In this chapter, the narrow approach to reporting was adopted, hence communicating information via social and streaming media was not considered.

On the Investor Relations page, information is presented in the form of reports traditionally grouped by publication date and type, thereby leaving a clear message to the recipient of a specific report. On the Sustainability page, information is presented in an interactive form. The interactive formula makes for more effective navigation. The 2013 annual report is presented online in an interactive form. The online report allows the user to browse it in a way that is most suitable to them. Integrated navigation is a tool that streamlines browsing through the report. It also appears in the 2019 annual report and the 2020 integrated report. It is a tool that allows the user to search for related content more effectively. PZU SA reports on the Investor Relations page are available in PDF, XML (2018 and 2019), and from 2020 also in XHTML file format.

Let us note that the only electronic file format officially recommended for non-financial reporting is XBRL (eXtensible Business Reporting Language). XBRL is used today worldwide by over 10 million companies in 60 countries to deliver high-quality structured data to over 100 regulators. Each of the European Banking Authorities (EBA), the European Insurance and Occupational Pensions Authority (EIOPA), the European Central Bank (ECB), and the European Securities and Markets Authority (ESMA) have endorsed the European Single Electronic Format (ESEF). SASB, CDP, and AECA support electronic formats not only to promote better data quality and NFI analysis but also to overcome the disparity between the reporting of important non-financial information and financial reporting (EFRAG, 2021).

15.7 Conclusion

In today's world, stakeholder value has become the focal point for companies. Businesses are expected to create long-term value while attending to the needs of shareholders, employees, customers, suppliers, local communities, and society at large. This means openly informing stakeholders about achievements, intentions, and business conditions. It also entails the need to communicate financial and non-financial information.

The reporting model is evolving. Reporting shows a growing share of non-financial information in both financial and non-financial statements. In the digital age, online reporting has become the norm, with reports being published on websites in PDF, XLS, XML (from 2018), XHTML (from 2020) formats, or as interactive files. Digitization has changed the place, form, and format of reporting.

The prevailing trend in market reporting is reflected in the reporting of PZU SA. It is highly likely that the same holds true for the reporting of other publicly traded digital-finance institutions.

Notes

1 Financial statements consist of basic components and notes. The basic components are: performance report (profit-and-loss account), financial position report (balance sheet), cash flow statement, statement of change in equity. The additional notes explain the numbers included in the basic components and the accounting benchmarks applied. Examples include accounting policy analysis for reported data.
2 Examples of supplements to financial statements include: activity report, letter of the president of the management board, reports of the supervisory board.
3 Examples of reports supplementing financial statements include: CSR/ESG report, sustainability report, information on the balance sheet model, information on intellectual capital.
4 If the financial report contains a consolidated financial statement prepared in accordance with IAS, issuers will then mark the statements using the Inline XBRL markup language.
5 XML is a platform-independent standard used to exchange structured data.
6 The Solvency and Financial Condition Report (SFCR) is an information requirement for insurers imposed by the Act of 11 September 2015 on insurance and reinsurance activity. The shape of the SFCR report is outlined mainly in Commission Delegated Regulation (EU) 2015/35 of 10 October 2014, supplementing Solvency II Directive (Delegated Regulation).

Bibliography

ACCA, 2016, *ACCA Approved. Study Text. Paper 1. Governance, Risk and Ethics. For exams in September 2016, December 2016, March 2017 and June 2017.* London: BPP Learning Media.

Bauer K., Hońko S., Orzeszko T., Szadziewska A., 2020, *Informacje finansowe i niefinansowe w ocenie działalności banku.* Katowice: Wydawnictwo IUS PUBLICUM.

Bek-Gaik B., Krasodomska J., 2018, Informacje niefinansowe jako obszar współczesnej sprawozdawczości przedsiębiorstw – definicja, źródła i proponowane kierunki badań, *Zesz. Nauk. UEK*, 2 (974), pp. 25–40.

Da Silva S. M., Aibar-Guzmán B., 2010, Determinants of environmental disclosure in the annual reports of large companies operating in Portugal, *Corporate Social Responsibility and Environmental Management*, 17 (4), pp. 185–204.

Donaldson T., Preston L. E., 1995, The stakeholder theory of the corporation: concepts, evidence, and implications, *The Academy of Management review*, 20 (1), pp. 65–91.

EFRAG, 2021,*Current non-financial reporting formats and practices*, https://www.efrag.org/Assets/Download?assetUrl=%2Fsites%2Fwebpublishing%2FSiteAssets%2FEFRAG%2520PTF-NFRS_A6_FINAL.pdf&AspxAutoDetectCookieSupport=1, [accesed on 12 October 2021].

Erkens M. H. R., Paugam L., Stolowy H., 2015, Non-financial information: state of the art and research perspectives based on a bibliometric study, *ACCRA*, 21 (3), pp. 15–92.

Farneti F., Casonato F., Montecalvo M., de Villiers C., 2019, The influence of integrated reporting and stakeholder information needs on the disclosure of social information in a state-owned enterprise, *Meditari Accountancy Research*, 27 (4), pp. 556–579.

Freeman R. E., 1984, *Strategic Management: A Stakeholder Approach*. Boston, MA: Pitman Publishing Inc.

Gołąb P., Monkiewicz J., 2021, Finance cyfrowe: ramy teoretyczne, in: Gąsiorkiewicz L., Monkiewicz J. (eds.), *Finanse cyfrowe: informatyzacja, cyfryzacja i danetyzacja*. Warszawa: OficynaWydawnicza PW.

Haller A., Link M, Groß T., 2017, The term 'non-financial information' – A semantic analysis of a key feature of current and future corporate reporting, *Accounting in Europe*, 14 (3), pp. 407–429.

Kemp S., 2022, *Digital 2022: global overview report*, https://datareportal.com/reports/digital-2022-global-overview-report [accesed on 5 May 2022].

KPMG, 2020, *The time has come. The KPMG Survey of Sustainability Reporting 2020*, https://assets.kpmg/content/dam/kpmg/be/pdf/2020/12/The_Time_Has_Come_KPMG_Survey_of_Sustainability_Reporting_2020.pdf [accesed on 30 October 2021].

Löw E., Erichsen G., Liang B, Postulka M. L., 2021, *Corporate Social Responsibility (CSR) and Environmental Social Governance (ESG) – Disclosure of European Banks*. EBI Working Paper Series no 83.

Manes-Rossi, F., Tiron-Tudor, A., Nicolò, G., Zanellato, G., 2018, Ensuring more sustainablereporting in Europe using non-financial disclosure – de facto and de jure evidence, *Sustainability*, 10 (4), pp. 1162–1182.

Mućko P., Niemiec A., Skoczylas W., 2021, Dobrowolny przymus? Uwarunkowania raportowania w zakresie zrównoważonego, *Zeszyty teoretyczne rachunkowości*, 45 (4), pp. 91–109.

Murphy L., Hogan R., 2016, Financial reporting of nonfinancial information: the role of the auditor, *The Journal of Corporate Accounting & Finance*, 28 (1), pp. 42–49.

Orens, R., Lybaert, N., 2007, Does the financial analysts' usage of non-financial information influence the analysts' forecast accuracy? Some evidence from the Belgian sell-side financial analyst, *The International Journal of Accounting*, 42 (3), pp. 237–271.

Perrini, F., 2006, The practitioner's perspective on non-financial reporting, *California Management Review*, 48 (2), pp. 73–103.

Pirsch, J., Gupta, S., Grau, S. L., 2007, A framework for understanding corporate social responsibility programs as a continuum: an exploratory study, *Journal of Business Ethics*, 70 (2), pp. 125–140.

PZU, 2014, *Raportroczny 2013*, http://raportroczny2013.pzu.pl/pl/ [accesed on 30 January 2022].

PZU, 2015, *Raportroczny 2014*, http://raportroczny2014.pzu.pl/ [accesed on 30 January 2022].

PZU, 2016, *Raportroczny 2015*, http://raportroczny2015.pzu.pl/ [accesed on 30 January 2022].

PZU, 2017, *Raportroczny 2016*, http://raportroczny2016.pzu.pl/ [accesed on 30 January 2022].

PZU, 2018, *Raportroczny 2017*, https://raportroczny2017.pzu.pl/ [accesed on 30 January 2022].

PZU, 2019, *Raportroczny2018*, https://raportroczny2018.pzu.pl/ [accesed on 30 January 2022].

PZU, 2020, *Raportroczny 2019*, https://raportroczny2019.pzu.pl/pl/pzu-raport-roczny-2019-home [accesed on 30 January 2022].

PZU, 2021a, *Raporty*, https://www.pzu.pl/relacje-inwestorskie/raporty [accesed on 30 January 2022].

PZU, 2021b, *Raportzintegrowany 2020*, https://raportroczny2020.pzu.pl/ [accesed on 30 January 2022].

Rotengruber P, 2017, R. Edward Freeman wobec koncepcji interesariusza. W obronie przekonań normatywnych uczestników życia gospodarczego, *Prakseologia*, 159, pp. 63–82.

Sobczyk M., 2017, Zakres pojęciowy terminu "informacja niefinansowa" jako źródło zróżnicowania ujawnień niefinansowych przedsiębiorstw, *Finanse, Rynki Finansowe, Ubezpieczenia*, 4 (88), pp. 395–401.

Tarquinio L., Posadas S. K., 2020, Exploring the term "non-financial information": an academics' view, *Meditari Accountancy Research*, 28 (5), pp. 727–749.

Torre M.L., Sabelfeld, S., Blomkvist M., Tarquinio, L., Dumay J., 2018, Harmonising non-financial reporting regulation in Europe: Practical forces and projections for future research, *Meditari Accountancy Research*, 26 (4), pp. 598–621.

UNIDO, 2022, *What is CSR*, https://www.unido.org/our-focus/advancing-economic-competitiveness/competitive-trade-capacities-and-corporate-responsibility/corporate-social-responsibility-market-integration/what-csr [accesed on 11 May 2022].

Walińska E., Bek-Gaik B., Gad J., 2016, *Sprawozdawczość finansowa i niefinansowa przedsiębiorstwa – w kierunku integracji*. Łódź: Wydawnictwo Uniwersytetu Łódzkiego.

Index

Note: **Bold** page numbers refer to tables; *italic* page numbers refer to figures and page numbers followed by "n" denote endnotes.

FSC
www.fsc.org
MIX
Papier | Fördert gute Waldnutzung
FSC® C083411

Kolibri 360 GmbH
Ferdinand-Jühlke-Straße 7
99095 Erfurt, Deutschland
produktsicherheit@kolibri360.de